SURVEYS BY TELEPHONE

A National Comparison with Personal Interviews

This is a volume of

Quantitative Studies in Social Relations

Consulting Editor: Peter H. Rossi, University of Massachusetts, Amherst, Massachusetts

SURVEYS BY TELEPHONE
A National Comparison with
Personal Interviews

Robert M. Groves

*Survey Research Center and
Department of Sociology
University of Michigan
Ann Arbor, Michigan*

Robert L. Kahn

*Survey Research Center and
Department of Psychology
University of Michigan
Ann Arbor, Michigan*

ACADEMIC PRESS
A Subsidiary of Harcourt Brace Jovanovich, Publishers
New York   London   Toronto   Sydney   San Francisco

ACADEMIC PRESS, INC.
111 Fifth Avenue, New York, New York 10003

United Kingdom Edition published by
ACADEMIC PRESS, INC. (LONDON) LTD.
24/28 Oval Road, London NW1   7DX

Library of Congress Cataloging in Publication Data

Groves, Robert M
   Surveys by telephone.

   (Quantitative studies in social relations)
   Bibliography: p.
   Includes index.
   1. Telephone surveys——Random digit dialing.
2. Interviewing. I. Kahn, Robert Louis, Date
joint author. II. Title.
HN29.G75   001.4'33   79–51703
ISBN 0–12–304650–5

PRINTED IN THE UNITED STATES OF AMERICA

79 80 81 82   9 8 7 6 5 4 3 2 1

Contents

Preface

This book describes an experimental evaluation of a major development in the history of survey methods: sampling and interviewing by telephone. The practical importance of random generation of sample telephone numbers and current work on telephone interviewing techniques is exceeded only by the introduction of areal probability sampling in the 1940s and the more recent use of computers for the analysis and storage of survey data. Innovations of such importance deserve serious evaluation, especially when considerations other than the reliability and validity of data may influence decisions to adopt them.

The attractions of telephone surveys are substantial: sampling random telephone numbers is relatively easy and inexpensive, and conducting interviews by telephone is quick and economical. Telephone lines go where interviewers may fear to tread, and reach behind doors that householders may fear to open. Locating interviewers in a headquarters office instead of a respondent's living room simplifies administration and makes possible the immediate entry of interview data into the computer; the telephone interviewer can work with a terminal keyboard and oscilloscope screen instead of pencil and paper. Opposing those advantages are the long-recognized biases of limited

telephone coverage of the household population; the less-known constraints of using the telephone system as a sampling frame; and the
largely unknown effects of the telephone medium itself on the quality
of interview data.

We became convinced several years ago that a thorough evaluation
of telephone surveys was needed, that the evaluation should include
an extensive comparison with areal sampling and personal interviews,
and that it should be conducted on a nationwide basis. The continuing
personal interview studies at the Survey Research Center form the
basis for this comparison. The research itself, including the full cost of
the telephone surveys, was supported by National Science Foundation Grant 76-07519.

Our objective in writing this book was to answer the questions that
confront every research worker planning to collect data from household populations. These questions involve matters of error and precision, costs and benefits, administration and organization. Interest in
all these issues has been growing as the costs of research rise, the
societal need for accurate information becomes more urgent, and the
methodological sophistication of research workers increases.

The increasing sophistication of research workers is expressed in
their concern with total survey error and its several components—
incomplete coverage of the target population by the sampling frame,
failure to obtain responses from some households that fall in the
sample, poor question design, limitations of memory, inadequate respondent motivation, and sampling error. Of this long list, only sampling error has been estimated and reported in the past, and even that
practice has not been routine.

In this book we compare the two major methods of survey research,
telephone and personal interviews, with respect to a whole array of
attributes—administrative arrangements, costs, and components of error. Our purpose in making this comparison is to facilitate the use of
our findings in many settings. This study is intended for application;
we wish to contribute directly to the improvement of survey practice
rather than to the extension of theory.

One of the several sets of readers we have in mind, colleagues using
survey methods in their daily work will find this book helpful. Our
comparisons of sampling designs, sampling and non-sampling errors,
response rates, administrative procedures, and research costs will provide answers that post hoc comparisons of unrelated surveys cannot.

Research workers who occasionally use survey methods may use
this book in a program of orientation to current survey methods. A
comparative study such as this will help them make decisions about

sampling methods, modes of interviewing, and administrative arrangements. Finally, we hope to interest students learning about survey methods. This monograph, in combination with more traditional texts on survey methods, may give such students a realistic picture of national surveys as currently conducted and of the choices to be made in designing such surveys.

A methodological treatise in any developing field must necessarily document a brief moment in a process of constant change. We believe that this moment is an important one in the study of human populations. We are just beginning formal examination of telephone methods of sampling and interviewing. Part of this book's value lies in contributing to and guiding that examination. We hope that questions left unanswered by this work will provide material for other research workers to explore, and that their exploration benefits from ours.

Some of the material in this monograph appeared earlier in journal articles. Permission to reprint was kindly provided by the *Journal of Marketing Research, Social Science Research,* the *American Statistical Association,* and *Public Opinion Quarterly.*

The Special Projects Program of the National Science Foundation and its director, Murray Aborn, have a long-term commitment to the improvement of survey methods through methodological research; we are deeply appreciative of their interest and support. Two additional sources of support deserve mention: the Survey Research Center, which provided supplementary funds for the preparation of the manuscript, and the Netherlands Institute for Advanced Study (N.I.A.S.). Some early analyses of our data were presented to the Netherlands Statistical Association, and it is a pleasure to acknowledge the unusual opportunity for scholarship and scholarly interaction that N.I.A.S. provides, the foresight and generosity of the Netherlands Government in funding such a facility, and the dedication of its staff—particularly of its director, H. A. J. F. Misset, and of its associate director, J. E. Glastra van Loon.

Several colleagues throughout the country provided useful comments on the text before publication. We thank Barbara Bailar, James A. Davis, William Klecka, William Nichols, Seymour Sudman, Albert Tuchfarber, and Joseph Waksberg. Charles Cannell, Irene Hess, Leslie Kish, Stanley Presser, Howard Schuman, and John Scott, colleagues at the Survey Research Center, have offered criticism and guidance in the design and analysis of this research.

Several people participated in the preparation of this manuscript. Robert Swearingen served as research assistant and provided helpful suggestions on the analytic plan. Steven G. Heeringa assisted in the comparison of sample designs presented in Appendix III. Barbara Thomas had major responsibility for the cost analysis in Chapter 7. Others provided clerical and editorial assistance, among them Heidi McMartin, Mary Wreford, Linda Wark, and Marjorie MacKenzie.

To all these colleagues, we express our appreciation.

Chapter 1

Measuring Populations in Person and on the Telephone

Although procedures for taking measurements on human populations have been used for centuries, data collection efforts received their greatest advance with the application of the statistical theory of survey sampling. In the United States in the first half of this century, the need to know about availability of products, the prevalence of specific attitudes, or the social and economic status of society, combined with the willingness of the populace to supply information about such topics, permitted the development of an entire set of techniques for selecting, locating, and measuring populations.

The heart of these procedures was the personal interview, in which selected individuals were visited by field interviewers and asked to provide answers to the questions posed by the interviewers. For most national surveys of the adult population, these interviews took place in the homes of the respondents. The use of personal interviews necessitated the construction of certain organizational structures for designing and administering national surveys. For example, since interviewers visited the homes of sample individuals, sample designs were clustered into primary areas in order to limit the costs of hiring, training, and interviewer travel. Probability sampling methods that selected geographical areas as quasi-permanent sampling units were developed, and permanent staffs of field interviewers working in their home areas were recruited. With such dispersed staffs of interviewers, it was necessary to devise special methods of hiring, training, communication, and coordination in order to keep the process moving efficiently. For example, in designs using 70–100 primary areas, 15–20 supervisors often share the responsibility for such tasks. Each of these persons is assigned to a subset of the primary areas and travels among them visiting interviewers to administer remedial instruction, conducting verification interviews with respondents of local interviewers, and aiding the local interviewers with special problems they might be having.

A higher level of coordination is generally located in the central office of the organization where a staff supervises the production of the questionnaire, various forms of documentation, and instructional materials describing the field procedures. This staff is responsible for coordinating the printing of these materials, sorting them into packets to be mailed to individual interviewers, answering questions from field interviewers about the study, keeping records on the progress of the interviewing, and forwarding materials to the coding and data processing staffs.

Much of the organization and procedure we have just described results directly from the decision to use personal interviews for data collection. Since this was the mode of collection most frequently used throughout the formative years of survey research, many researchers regard it as the only way in which survey research *can* be conducted. Furthermore, since methodological investigations on research design and measurement have been conducted mostly with personal interviews, procedures found to be good practices have been limited to those possible within a personal survey mode. The uses of survey research have often been limited to those well suited to the personal interview survey, and things not possible within that mode have generally been left unexplored. We have learned what can be done with personal interview surveys, but we have failed to learn whether or not better techniques might be implemented in other modes of data collection.

Dependence on a single methodology creates few constraints on the researcher when the method functions well. However, personal interview surveys in the United States face two problems of growing magnitude: increased cost of data collection and lower response rates, especially in large metropolitan areas. Salaries both in the field and in the central office have kept pace with those in other settings. Travel costs for visiting sample households follow prices of gasoline that have increased over 100% in recent years. In 1978 some household interview surveys are incurring total costs of over $100 per interview for sampling and data collection alone, and the numbers continue to rise. These cost inflations naturally generate the desire to investigate other and less expensive ways to collect needed information.

The higher costs of data collection are related to another problem, the difficulty of obtaining interviews from sample persons. Today, far more than earlier in this century, more than one adult in a family holds a full-time job. The stereotype of the housewife and working husband is less and less true, and more household members are at home for only a few hours every day. As a result, the number of calls required to find someone home at a sample address is increasing. Once a household member *is* located, in some areas there is greater reluctance than previously to consent to an interview. The greater the required number of calls, the more likely it is that the interview request will be met with some reluctance. In the central cities of large metropolitan areas the final proportion of respondents that are located *and* consent to an interview is declining to a rate sometimes close to 50%.

There are a variety of hypotheses about the causes of this decline. One of the more difficult to test is the assertion that the population has been overstudied, is fatigued, or finds little reason to cooperate. Flowing from the view that in the early years of survey research respondents felt that good citizenship demanded cooperation, this argument observes that people are now more sophisticated about the limitations on the use of survey data for improvements in their conditions of life. They have learned two things: (*a*) that surveys usually do not ask the questions that are of greatest importance to them; and (*b*) that the data typically are not utilized by policymakers who have control over activities that affect the respondents' lives.

A counterargument rejects the notion that the public has been overstudied and argues that uses of the methodology have changed since its beginnings. The first studies by the U.S. Department of Agriculture asked farmers about their expected crop yields and the impact of government farm policies on their lives. The unambiguous applicability of those findings and the appeal to self-interest inherent in the request for interview are not matched by many present uses of the survey method. In addition to gathering specific facts about populations, surveys are often used to measure personal attitudes toward events or objects that cannot easily be affected by social policies. Often the intended use of the data is not public policymaking, but a test of theories of human thought and behavior.

When the appeal to self-interest is removed (and indeed, replaced by potential threats to the privacy of the respondent) and when clear applicability of the findings to social policy is absent, the motivation of the respondent to cooperate is diminished. This conclusion is supported by the sensitivity of survey response rates to the topic being studied and the agency doing the work. The continued high response rates of the Census Bureau's unemployment survey (Current Population Survey, or CPS) is ample evidence of this, as is the general higher response rates to government agencies (where policymakers may be perceived to be closer to the data) than to academic and commercial survey organizations.[1]

A third hypothesis about lower cooperation rates focuses on the urban environment, where the greatest decline in response has occurred. The increase in personal and property crime in large urban areas has altered the lifestyle of their residents. Locked central entrances to apartment buildings and the greater concern of residents about opening their doors to strangers prevent interviewers from entering many multiunit dwellings, which are a growing segment of all housing units in the country. Even in single family dwellings, however, there may be increasing reticence to admit strangers to the home. And such fear is probably greater in areas with higher crime rates. The response rate is further reduced by the similar fears about personal safety held by the interviewers who administer the survey. Some interviewers will refuse to enter areas perceived to be dangerous. When sample households lie in those areas, they often become nonrespondent for that reason alone.

Each of the arguments presented has different implications for the conduct of methodological studies on survey research. The assertion of population fatigue from surveys may require some reduction in the number of surveys to rejuvenate the populace. The fact of varying response rates by topic and agency prompts greater attention to the types of questions that are asked, and their appropriateness to the survey purpose and auspices. The observations about the fear of crime reducing cooperation prompts a review of data collection methodologies that reduce the effect of that fear on cooperation.

One method of survey data collection addresses both crises in personal interview methods—higher costs and lower response rates. Telephone surveys have been found both to be cheaper than personal

---

[1] Some of the higher response rate may be explained by the use of any responsible household member by the Census Bureau and specifically selected respondents by other organizations.

interview methods and to achieve higher response rates. However, we shall see that the transition from personal interview methods to telephone methods requires a total reorganization for collecting data.

1.1 COMPONENTS OF TELEPHONE SURVEY METHODOLOGY

We noted earlier that the need to visit each respondent personally in face-to-face surveys led to the use of area probability methods, a clustering together of the selected respondents in order to reduce travel costs. With travel eliminated in telephone surveys, we are freed from the need to cluster the design and can sample telephone numbers individually throughout the population without increasing the cost of the research. Since clustered samples generally produce estimates with lower precision than those in which elements are selected independently, the ability to do independent selection is a clear advantage for telephone surveys. The greater precision is matched with reduction in the amount of materials required for the sample and with greater ease of drawing the sample. The materials required for each stage of personal interview samples include census counts of persons within sampling units, data on the characteristics of those units, updates of the distribution of population within the units, and maps to construct the correspondence between census counts and areal units. The only necessary item for telephone samples is some list of the set of telephone numbers covering the area defining the population of inference.

Two approaches to selection methods have been used for telephone samples in the past: use of listed telephone numbers and random selection of digits to form sample telephone numbers. There are many variations and combinations of the two approaches. In general, the larger the dependency on lists of numbers, the larger the threat that some residential numbers (the unlisted group) will be excluded from the sampling frame. Conversely, the fewer the restrictions on the random generation of telephone numbers, the larger the proportion of sample numbers generated that are not working household numbers.

If samples are drawn from listed telephone numbers exclusively, then all unlisted numbers will be ineligible for selection. Conversely, if the sample is drawn by using random ten-digit numbers (three-digit area code, three-digit prefix, four-digit suffix), all telephone households become eligible for selection, but only a small percentage of the sample numbers so generated are working household numbers. In any sample so drawn the vast majority of numbers would be unassigned to any use and some would be nonresidential numbers.

There have been attempts to measure the undercoverage resulting from sampling only listed numbers and to describe households with unlisted numbers (Brunner & Brunner, 1977; Glasser & Metzger, 1975). Such descriptions are useful to those planning telephone surveys, but there is great heterogeneity in the unlisted rates across areas (especially urban–rural categories) and in the density of working numbers within area codes and exchanges. Research workers planning local studies can often obtain information about the local telephone system that will permit intelligent use of the telephone directory as a sampling frame, or appropriate reduction in the banks of numbers that are included as candidates for random selection of sample numbers. For national samples, however, the magnitude of the task expands quickly.

Regardless of what method is used for selecting sample numbers, researchers must be aware of the noncoverage by telephone surveys of households without telephones. This population is shrinking, but now is 8–10% of all households and is much larger among the poor and rural populations. The bias in statistics linked to absence of nonphone households depends on the nature of measurements taken; if the nonphone population has very different values on the characteristics being measured, then the noncoverage bias could indeed be severe.

For most telephone sampling, the required materials are easily obtained. For local area studies, telephone directories either supply the listings or identify the prefixes that are used in the area. Boundary maps for exchanges are available either from telephone business offices or from state public service commissions. We describe procedures for using these materials in Chapter 2, but whatever method for telephone sampling is used, the sampling costs are generally much smaller than those for areal probability sampling.

We noted earlier that the need for personal visits to sample households in face-to-face interviews greatly influenced the division of labor within the research organization. Long distance telecommunication for telephone surveys frees the researcher from such restrictions and permits a wide variety of organizational plans. Some survey organizations that already had staffs of field interviewers have implemented telephone surveys by mailing interviewing materials and sample telephone numbers to their interviewers and having them telephone from their homes. This model closely resembles the personal interview organization and offers smooth transition from one mode to another for existing organizations. It also serves to maintain both telephone and personal interview capacities. Other national organizations have planned multiple telephone interviewing sites throughout the country to reduce toll charges, and use regional groups of interviewers, each of which administers the survey work from a central location in its region. The most prevalent organizational mode, however, has been a centralized staff of telephone interviewers located in the headquarters of the research staff. Such a design may offer reduction of costs by eliminating the need for long-distance communication among dispersed interviewers. It also promises greater control over the quality of the data collection through continual supervision of interviewers. Centralized interviewing facilities typically include a room with interviewer carrels, a telephone system (usually a WATS system for national or regional studies), and some capability to monitor interviewer behavior during interviews.

The proximity of research, interviewing, and data-processing staff members offers several advantages. Rarely in national personal interview surveys can research investigators interact with those who are collecting data, but such interaction can be easily built into the training sessions for telephone interviewers. A meeting can be scheduled with the research investigator to review the protocol question-by-question and to address any misunderstanding of the instructions for administering the questionnaire. Such contacts can also benefit the investigators by alerting them to problems in the questionnaire that were not discovered in the pretests.

Once the interviewing period begins, other quality control procedures unique to centralized telephone interviewing can be implemented. Interviewers who are having difficulty eliciting the cooperation of respondents or who are encountering problems with certain questions can be monitored and coached by supervisors. Monitoring of telephone interviews by the research staff can offer insights into the meaning of survey results that quantitative analysis would not reveal. Since the coding staff is also located in the same facility as the interviewers, the coding schedule need not be delayed until completed questionnaires are received by mail from the field. Coding can begin near the start of the interviewing period, and coders can watch for answers that are not codable and quickly relay that information to the interviewing staff or to the particular interviewers who are involved.

Thus freedom from the need to disperse an interviewing staff throughout the whole national population seems to facilitate greater control over data collection. We also observe that the personnel needs for a national telephone survey are smaller than those for an equivalent personal interview survey. For example, instead of about 200 interviewers, each conducting 7 or 8 interviews, national telephone surveys are often conducted in the same amount of time using about 30–40 interviewers, each doing 40–50 interviews. Supervisory and coordinating staffs are similarly reduced. With a smaller organization the quality of data per unit cost for telephone surveys could theoretically be higher.

Attempts to use the data from previous surveys to test these hypotheses, however, usually are complicated by the lack of comparability between the telephone and personal interview surveys being examined. Moreover, the cost of data collection efforts must be evaluated relative to the quality of the data collected, and quality is an elusive concept. Statisticians have constructed models of survey error containing error components from sampling, question form, interviewer administration, respondent behavior, and nonresponse. For most sets of data, however, only the errors that arise from sampling can be estimated with known probabilities. Until other sources of error are measured, a comparison of telephone and personal interview data merely tests whether the two methods give different results on statistics of interest to the investigator.

In an early study on the validity of responses in telephone and personal interviews Larson (1952) found that 80% of the reports of actions by those in face-to-face interviews were verified, but only 16% of those in the telephone survey could be supported. Although the two samples were not comparable in all other respects, results like this suggested that the telephone medium was more susceptible to measurement error than was personal interviewing. Later studies using validity checks, however, generally fail to find such discrepancies. Locander, Sudman, and Bradburn (1974), for example, find small, generally negligible differences between telephone and personal interviews on reports of embarrassing events such as personal bankruptcy or arrests for drunken driving.

The vast majority of studies comparing different modes of collecting data do not have access to data permitting validity checks on individual responses, but rather compare differences in response distributions among different modes. Many of these studies have concentrated on reports of embarrassing or sensitive data. Wiseman's comparative study (1972) of mail, personal, and telephone interviews generally found no differences among the three modes. There was, however, some slight tendency for women to respond on mail questionnaires with more favorable attitudes toward abortion and toward the distribution of contraceptives to unmarried women. Hochstim (1967), also in a three mode comparison, found greater tendencies for women, when questioned on the telephone, to admit drinking alcoholic beverages. Henson, Roth, and Cannell (1974) generally found only small differences among the three modes, but observed that telephone respondents were somewhat more likely to choose desirable qualities for themselves on the Lubin depression scale. Lucas and Adams (1977), in comparative personal and telephone surveys of two Pennsylvania cities, found that respondent reports on sensitive subjects was essentially the same in both modes. Colombotos (1965), in a comparison of tendencies to provide socially acceptable responses in a survey of physicians, found no differences between telephone and personal interviews.

A few studies attack the problem of method effects by examining differences between initial personal interviews and telephone reinterviews of the same respondents. Rogers (1976) reinterviewed respondents by telephone and, although hampered by small sample sizes, found no differences between the two modes in reports of income, education, and voting in recent elections. Schmiedeskamp (1962) found that respondents on the telephone were more reluctant to reveal data on their financial conditions than they were in previous personal interviews. Coombs and Freedman (1964) found that sensitive data on family planning and pregnancy could be obtained using telephone interviews on a sample previously contacted in personal interview.

The literature on the effects of mode of data collection thus contains a variety of results, some contradictory and not comparable because of differences in research design, populations studied, or kinds of data collected. It is likely that the differences between modes themselves vary by population studied or subject of the interview. A general statement on the method effects of telephone interviewing, therefore, is inappropriate. What is needed is a systematic research on response differences obtained in different modes, on several populations, and for a wide variety of measures. Such work could guide survey researchers in decisions concerning data collection methods.

1.2 THE DESIGN OF A RESEARCH PROJECT
INVESTIGATING METHOD EFFECTS

Much of what we have recently learned about the properties of telephone surveys resulted from an experimental comparison of personal and telephone interview surveys conducted at the Survey Research Center (SRC) in spring, 1976. That study, supported by the National Science Foundation, was designed to identify certain basic characteristics of telephone surveys and compare them to corresponding features of personal interview surveys.

The project involved three national surveys, two telephone and one personal interview. Of the two national telephone surveys, one used a stratified random (non-clustered) sample with phone numbers spread over the entire United States and the other (clustered) used the 74 primary areas of the SRC's national sample of dwellings. The telephone survey with the stratified random sample utilized a centralized interviewing staff and was conducted simultaneously with the companion personal interview survey, interviews for which were taken by members of the permanent field staff in the SRC primary areas. Identical questions were asked of all survey respondents.

The design of the project offers measurement of several characteristics of the various survey procedures, and they are illustrated in Figure 1.1. At the most basic level we can combine all cases sampled for the telephone survey and compare their results with those obtained in personal interviews. This analysis can compare response differences measured in the two modes, errors of administration, response rates, patterns of calling respondents, the people required to administer the surveys, and the costs of sampling and data collection. In order to increase the generalizability of response differences measured in the two modes, the questionnaire included items that differed in form (e.g., open and closed question formats), topic, sensitivity of content, and ease of asking the item over the telephone (e.g., items that utilize response cards in personal interview surveys).

We introduced the two different telephone samples into the project partly in order to test one possible future use of telephone surveys, the study of rare populations by means of mixed-mode techniques. The

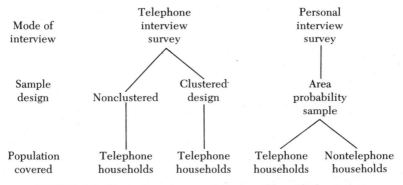

FIGURE 1.1. **Illustration of comparisons possible with the project.**

cost of sampling and screening large populations with personal interviews often prevents research on groups that represent only small
proportions of those populations. Some studies of rare groups, for
example, assessments of the health needs of handicapped persons,
may require personal interviews after eligible persons are located. If
telephone sampling could be clustered into the primary areas of an
existing national areal probability sample linked to a permanent staff
of field interviewers, then the results of telephone sampling and
screening could be given to the field interviewers for follow-up in
person. The entire design might make studies more feasible for small
subpopulations that have high coverage by telephone.

Such a clustered design, however, would have different sampling
errors than a telephone sample with numbers sampled individually.
By dividing the telephone survey into different sample designs we
were able to investigate the loss of precision due to the clustering in
this type of design. In addition, since the primary areas used in the
clustered telephone sample were identical to those used in the personal interview sample, we were able to investigate the loss of precision due to clustering on the telephone relative to that in the personal
interview survey.

Finally we take advantage of the larger coverage of the household
population in the personal interview survey and examine differences
between telephone households (covered by all telephone surveys)
and households without telephones (missed by all telephone surveys).

1.3 ORGANIZATION OF THIS MONOGRAPH

This monograph focuses on the results of the research previously
described and begins in Chapter 2 to describe in detail how personal
interview surveys and telephone surveys differ in the design of their
samples and in the organization of staff for collection of the survey
data. In that chapter we describe methods used to construct national
samples of randomly generated telephone numbers, how those samples are transmitted to the interviewing staff, and what facilities were
constructed for the telephone interviewers. We describe what steps
are necessary in matching a telephone sample to areal units (in our
case, counties) and how a clustered telephone sample is selected.
Finally, we review a study of alternative ways of selecting in an
objective fashion one respondent from each sample household.

By contrasting the design characteristics of telephone and personal
interview surveys in Chapter 2 we prepare for the discussion of Chapter 3, which describes the results of implementing survey designs in

the two modes. We discuss the dialing of randomly generated telephone numbers and the number of calls made on sample households in both modes. We evaluate the procedure used on the telephone for selecting respondents within households. Here also we first address one of the major questions regarding mode of interview, whether telephone surveys yield higher response rates than personal interview surveys. Finally, we examine the characteristics of respondents and sample households in both surveys, to assess differences that may be related to nonresponse in the two modes.

Chapters 4 and 5 are devoted to an analysis of response differences between the two surveys. In Chapter 4 we examine characteristics of the administration and of the respondent that may be associated with response differences. In Chapter 5 we explore characteristics of the question type that may produce different responses by mode of interview. There we examine in some detail the results of open-ended questions.

Chapter 6 attempts to quantify as many sources of error in the data as possible and to compare the two survey modes on the sizes of those errors. We begin by assessing errors of undercoverage, especially the results of deleting the nontelephone households in the telephone surveys. We then move to calculation of sampling errors, where we compare the effects of clustering in the two modes of surveys and note the relative efficiency of the cluster and single-stage telephone samples. Next, because we introduced an interpenetrating design for the assignment of sample telephone numbers to interviewers, we present estimates of interviewer variance, another source of error in the data. We also compare these interviewer effects in the telephone surveys with those previously found in personal interview surveys.

Chapter 7 describes the cost structure of the two survey modes and presents a detailed budget report on sampling and data collection costs. The results of this chapter can be juxtaposed to those of Chapter 6, to permit other investigators to judge whether the increased costs of personal interview surveys are justified for a particular survey.

The results of our investigations are summarized in Chapter 8 and our thoughts regarding the future of methodological research on mode of interview are presented.

1.4 SUMMARY

This study involves three national surveys:

1. A personal interview survey conducted in the Survey Research Center's national household sample of 74 counties and metropolitan areas

2. A telephone survey in the same sample areas, with telephone numbers selected by random-digit dialing (RDD) in each of the 74 counties and metropolitan areas
3. A telephone survey in which the numbers were selected by random-digit dialing throughout the entire United States rather than being clustered within sample counties

The same interview questions, representing a wide range of form and content, were included in all three studies. It is thus possible to compare two modes of data collection—telephone and personal interviews—and two methods of developing national telephone samples with random-digit dialing, single-stage stratified and multistage clustered sampling. Extensive data were collected on the costs of the three national surveys, since proponents of telephone interviewing have emphasized its relative economy. In addition, the randomization of assignments to the telephone interviewing staff makes it possible to estimate the magnitude of interviewer effects on costs, rates of completion, and on the substantive outcome of interview questions. Other points of methodological comparison between telephone and personal interviews are also evaluated.

Organizational and administrative matters are discussed in Chapter 2, comparative response rates and problems of coverage and omission in Chapter 3, methodological differences in response content in Chapters 4 and 5, nature and magnitude of sampling errors in Chapter 6, and relative costs in Chapter 7. Chapter 8 is both a summary of the research findings and a set of tentative recommendations to those who plan to use either or both of these approaches to sampling and data collection in survey research.

Chapter 2

Sample Designs for Personal and Telephone Interview Surveys

A variety of sample designs is currently in use for national and local personal interview surveys. Advances in sampling techniques in the early years of interview surveys allowed researchers to estimate the amount of error in their estimates arising from the fact that only a subset of the population was measured. Many current national personal interview surveys use areal probability samples which select geographically defined units as primary sample areas and select persons for interviews within these areas. Probability samples where each individual in a designated population has a known, non-zero chance of selection allow direct assessment of the amount of sampling error corresponding to sample estimates.

Many sample designs are possible for national and local telephone surveys. Not all of those available produce probability samples; some systematically exclude some telephone numbers assigned to residences. The major dimensions of variation for these designs are (a) the amount of information to be assembled about the quantity and characteristics of working household numbers in the population; (b) the extent to which all residential telephone numbers in the population are eligible for selection; and (c) the proportion of sample numbers that are not working household numbers.

15

In all sample surveys the sampling design and the organization of the interviewing are interrelated, and both are constrained by the desired level of precision of survey estimates and the amount of resources available to the project. In the following sections of this chapter we discuss the main features of some national personal and telephone interview sample designs and describe the designs used in this comparison of the two modes of data collection.

2.1 NATIONAL PROBABILITY SAMPLES OF HOUSING UNITS

Most national personal interview surveys are based on samples with more stages of selection and greater stratification than most telephone samples. Multistage designs often result from the absence of a list or sampling frame covering all housing units in the country. Such designs do not require a listing of housing units until the last stages of selection, when the number of units to be listed need not be far greater than the desired number of sample housing units. The greater stratification introduced into personal interview samples reflects the availability of census data on the characteristics of the sampling units of various stages and the desire to improve the precision of sample estimates.

A national probability sample of housing units, designed for personal interview, is maintained by the Survey Research Center.[1] The SRC national sample of dwellings is a multistage areal probability sample containing units at different stages selected with probabilities proportional to 1970 population and housing unit counts.[2] The primary sampling areas are counties or county groups. The 12 largest standard metropolitan statistical areas (SMSAs) are included with certainty; 62 other areas are chosen from 62 strata, each of which contained a total of about 2 million people in 1970.

Stratification is based on the following criteria:

1. Major geographical region: Northeast, North Central, South,.and West
2. SMSA classification: SMSA, non-SMSA
3. Size of largest city

[1] Kish and Hess (1965).
[2] The primary selections are updated every decade with the availability of decennial census data.

4. Rate of population growth
5. Major industry or major type of farming
6. In the South, proportion of nonwhite population

Each of the 62 primary areas is chosen from among those in the same stratum, with a probability proportional to its 1970 population. In personal interview surveys using the SRC sample, instead of sampling dwellings spread over the entire primary area the sample is further clustered by choosing secondary selections, which are cities, towns, and other smaller areas. Within primary areas the following stratification of these secondary areas is introduced:

1. *Primary areas that are SMSAs*
   Stratum 1 Urban places of 50,000 or more population
   Stratum 2 Urban places of 2500–49,999 population
   Stratum 3 Tracted areas entirely or partially in urbanized areas, exclusive of Strata 1 and 2
   Stratum 4 Tracted areas outside urbanized areas
   Stratum 5 Remainder

2. *Primary areas that are not SMSAs*
   Stratum 1 Urban places with 2500 or more population
   Stratum 2 Places under 2500 population
   Stratum 3 Remainder

The third and fourth stages of sampling choose "chunks," areas containing 20 to 30 dwellings within the secondary selections, and then "segments," containing an expected 4, 8, or 12 housing units, depending on the study. Some studies select every housing unit in a segment for interviewing; others sample further within segments, taking only a specified fraction of the housing units.

In short, the SRC dwelling sample design contains five stages of selection with the overall probability of selection determined as follows:

Probability of selecting a housing unit =

Prob. of Primary Area × Prob. of Secondary Selection × Prob. of Chunk × Prob. of Segment × Prob. of Housing Unit Within Segment

Clustering the sample into secondary, tertiary, and smaller areal units increases the sampling variance of estimates somewhat but is tolerated in order to reduce travel costs for interviewers.

2.2 ATTRIBUTES OF THE POPULATION OF TELEPHONE NUMBERS

Telephone numbers in the United States have three parts; for example:

$$313\text{--}555\text{--}1234$$

Each telephone number includes a three-digit *area code* (AC), a three-digit *central office code* (CO) or prefix, and a four-digit *suffix*. Currently, there are more than 100 area codes in use in the coterminous United States, with more than 30,000 total working central office codes in these areas. Central office codes are grouped into geographical units called *exchanges*. Some exchanges serving large metropolitan areas contain hundreds of central office codes, but 16,000 of the 30,000 central office codes are located in single code exchanges. Central office codes are assigned to one and only one exchange within a given area code.[3] Within an exchange containing multiple central office codes, numbers are usually assigned without geographical considerations; individual central office codes are usually not clustered into portions of the exchange.[4]

Area codes generally serve only one state. Earlier in the development of the telephone system, some exchanges crossed state lines, and some customers within the exchange paid interstate rates for calls to other numbers in the same state. This practice was largely eliminated by a ruling of the Federal Communications Commission and exchanges were split, giving distinct area codes and sometimes distinct central office codes to the parts of each exchange lying in two states.[5] Individual state samples can therefore be drawn without fear of including people living outside the state being sampled. The design of telephone numbers also permits stratification by state and area code for national samples. We have discovered one small area within coterminous United States that is served by a Canadian exchange. Although we have not investigated the full Canadian and Mexican borders, it is possible that other areas of the United States are served by foreign exchanges.

---

[3] Special arrangements can be made with some telephone companies to install a telephone line having a central office code from another exchange. Such cases seem most prevalent near large metropolitan exchanges where suburban users can reach a large area of service toll free if they import a number from the metropolitan exchange.

[4] Some large metropolitan exchanges are divided into zones which contain subsets of central office codes; such zones could be considered equivalent to exchanges.

[5] These two areas may still be served by the same business office. Some areas on the borders of Western states are still served by central office codes from another state.

The population of working telephone numbers is a dynamic one, but most changes over time take place within working central office codes. Area codes are rather stable over time, although new ones may be added over time as new numbers are needed within area codes that are densely filled. The number of central office codes generally increases at the rate of 10 to 20 per month, as indicated below.

	Central office code changes	
	Deleted codes[a]	New codes
September 1976	17	34
October 1976	13	63
November 1976	11	30
December 1976	13	25
January 1977	19	46
February 1977	9	31
March 1977	6	46
April 1977	10	38
May 1977	38	35
June 1977	12	58
July 1977	11	43
August 1977	20	52

[a] Based on information obtained from a type file of working central office codes supplied by A.T. & T. Long Lines Department.

2.3 ALTERNATIVE SAMPLE DESIGNS FOR TELEPHONE NUMBERS

Whether national or local surveys are being planned, there are various sources of information concerning telephone numbers:

1. Published telephone directories
2. Cross-index directory listings of phone numbers by address, or by numerical ordering
3. Information concerning local exchanges obtained from personnel at telephone company business offices
4. Listings of working area code—central office code combinations in the United States

Sample designs for telephone numbers probably began with selecting numbers from among those listed in telephone directories for exchanges covering the area of interest. For national telephone samples this would require the collection of over 4500 directories covering United States exchanges and detailed clerical work in selection of sample numbers from those directories. For local area surveys, obtaining the telephone directories would be a lesser task. The advantage of such a design is that all selected numbers, except those disconnected since the directory was published, will be working household numbers. The problem with selecting numbers from telephone directories is that many residential numbers are not listed in current directories, either because the subscriber requested an unlisted number or because service to the number was initiated after the publishing date of the directory. Over 20% of all residential numbers are not listed in current directories (Glasser & Metzger, 1972; see also Chapter 6, pages 153–155). The proportion unlisted is much larger in large metropolitan areas; recent data from Detroit estimate the unlisted percentage at greater than 35; in San Francisco it is about 40%. In rural areas one would expect a much lower rate of unlisted numbers. Overall, however, the proportion of unlisted numbers is increasing across the country.

One attempt to cover the unlisted numbers, suggested by Sudman (1973), alters sample numbers selected from a telephone directory by replacing their last three digits with three-digit random numbers. More than one set of three digits is appended to each selected number, as many as required so that a fixed number of *listed* household numbers are selected for each initial selection from the directory. This results in a two-stage design where the selection from the directory identifies thousand series of numbers within a central office code (e.g., 764-4424 is altered to 764-4 _ _ _). For each of these first-stage selections, enough random three-digit numbers (000 to 999) are used so that a prescribed number of listed household numbers is selected in each sample thousand series (e.g., 764-4424, 764-4014, 764-4972. . .). If an appended set of three digits forms a nonworking number or business number, another set is appended until a fixed number of household numbers is selected. This design can give equal chances of selection to each number whether listed or not, in thousand series that have at least one listed number. If for some reason an unlisted household number lies in a thousand series that has no listed numbers (perhaps because of recent initiation of service to such numbers) it will have no chance of being selected.[7] Although this design

----

[7] This design can be altered to replace only the last two digits or only the last digit of selected numbers, but would then incur even larger potential undercoverage of unlisted numbers.

includes most unlisted numbers, some numbers that are selected are not working numbers (a small overhead to pay for increased coverage).

Cross-index directories were used by Cooper (1964) to determine "working" blocks (thousand series) within exchanges in a study area. Some directories numerically order all listed telephone numbers, so that thousand series of numbers with listings can be readily identified. Three-digit random numbers were then appended to those seven digits corresponding to thousand series (313-764-4 _ _ _). The properties of this design are very similar to those of the design suggested by Sudman.

Cross-index directories have also been used for selecting phone numbers within small geographical areas (e.g., neighborhoods within exchanges). These designs utilize the ordering of listed numbers by address, which many cross-index directories present. Without a supplemental sample for unlisted numbers, such samples face the same problems of undercoverage as telephone book samples.

Although telephone books may not have current information on working banks of numbers within central office codes, the local business office of the exchange necessarily has this information. If all thousand series (or better, all hundred series) with any working numbers could be identified, the appropriate random digits could be appended without fear of excluding some unlisted numbers. For national surveys, obtaining this information could entail contacts with over 5000 separate offices, so some national designs utilize a first-stage selection of exchange areas (perhaps 100–200) with probabilities proportional to the number of central office codes. For each of the sample exchanges selected, the researchers then utilize current information on banks of working numbers, in order to reduce the number of nonworking numbers selected. With accurate information, sampling fractions within sample exchanges can be set to achieve a self-weighting sample. Obtaining information on banks of numbers that contain working numbers, however, is most easily done in local surveys, where personal contact with telephone company personnel can facilitate the acquisition of those data.

If the quantity of working numbers within each bank is also obtained, some designs can disproportionately select from banks densely filled with working numbers. The higher sampling fractions in densely filled banks assure a lower proportion of sample numbers that are nonworking but require that selection weights be used in data analysis. Although this design has the advantage of selecting only working household numbers, the loss of precision of sample estimates due to weighting may make it less attractive.

The designs described can obtain complete coverage of both listed and unlisted numbers only with current information on banks of working numbers. With the high costs of obtaining this information for national telephone surveys, two other approaches have been developed to assure complete coverage in the absence of that information. Both designs require a complete listing of all area code–central office code combinations (AC–CO) with working numbers. These designs append four-digit random numbers to the AC–COs to form the sample numbers. A magnetic tape listing of AC–COs is available through the Long Lines Department of A.T.&T. It is updated monthly and can be ordered through local telephone business offices. Each record on the tape contains the following information:

Area code
Central office code
Exchange name
V & H coordinates (vertical and horizontal)

Although the exchange names tend to be those of the largest city in the exchange area, they need not be so, and there are many exceptions. Technically, exchanges carry the names of the rate centers, the physical locations of the equipment through which all calls to or from numbers in the exchange are routed. Long distance charges between rate centers are calculated with the aid of a system of vertical and horizontal geographical coordinates (V & H coordinates). The vertical dimension lies Southwest–Northeast; the horizontal, Northwest–Southeast. Most exchanges are given unique pairs of V & H coordinates, although sometimes two neighboring exchanges share the same coordinate pair. For example, Minneapolis and St. Paul, Minnesota share coordinates.

If we view each record on the AC–CO listing as representing 10,000 telephone numbers (0000–9999), the listing provides a complete frame for all numbers. The vast majority of such numbers will not be working household numbers, but since the AC–CO listing is updated monthly, its use eliminates the undercoverage problem of alternative designs.

Designs that use the AC–CO records as a sampling frame differ in the nature of stratification they introduce and the existence of clustering in the selection procedures. We describe later a design that selects individual sample numbers from among all those having working AC–CO codes. This design will be labeled the "single-stage" telephone sample. Another design came into use after most of the data in this monograph were collected. This design, described in Waksberg

(1978), is a two-stage design that first selects hundred series of telephone numbers from AC–CO listings (e.g., 313-764-44 _ _) and then selects several numbers within each sample hundred series. This procedure increases the proportion of sample numbers that are working household-numbers but can still maintain a self-weighting sample with complete coverage of listed and unlisted numbers. These one-stage and two-stage designs are formally compared in Appendix III.

It is likely that telephone survey designs will continue to change as sampling statisticians are faced with different survey problems, as new information about the telephone system is made available, and as the technology changes over time. The designs will probably continue to balance the desire for complete coverage of the telephone population and for maximum precision of estimates with the need to reduce costs by minimizing the proportion of nonworking numbers sampled.

2.4 USING AN AREAL PROBABILITY DESIGN AS A BASE DESIGN FOR A TELEPHONE SAMPLE

Clustering is introduced into national samples of dwellings in order to decrease travel costs for personal interviewers visiting sample households. The effect of such clustering is an increase in the sampling variance of estimates. Clustering can be avoided in most telephone samples because no costs are reduced by concentrating sample numbers into primary areas. Some studies may benefit from clustering when a mixed-mode design would seem most efficient; for example, physical measures such as blood pressure taken from a subpopulation of elderly persons would require personal interviews of that subsample. Areal probability sampling to locate this subpopulation (since about 5–10% of the households might contain an eligible elderly person) would on the average require sampling and *visiting* more than ten households for each interview required. An alternative scheme would use a clustered telephone sample, with telephone interviews to determine eligibility (at a much lower cost), followed with visits to eligible households by personal interviewers located in the areas. We utilize such a design, called the "multistage" telephone sample, as part of the personal and telephone interview surveys described in this book.

By using a national sample of dwellings as the base design for a clustered telephone sample we can take advantage of the stratification introduced into the selection of its primary areas. (This is discussed in more detail in Chapter 6.) Adapting the design to sampling of telephone numbers requires a departure from areal sampling after the primary selections (counties or county groups). Instead, samples of numbers based on the list of all working central office codes are directly constructed, without selection of secondary areal units within primary areas.

The major task in utilizing the SRC areal design was identifying the telephone exchanges that serve any portion of the primary areas of the national sample. The primary areas of the SRC sample are defined by county boundaries, but telephone exchanges do not usually follow county boundary lines. Some telephone books contain maps in the first pages that list the exchanges and central office codes that serve various areas. Rarely, however, are these maps sufficiently accurate to identify those exchanges that serve any part of a specific county.

State public service commissions, public utility commissions, or state corporation commissions are generally given the responsibility of regulating the activities of telephone companies. These commissions make decisions on requests for rate changes and on definitions of service areas of the various companies. As part of their responsibilities, the commissions often require the submission of detailed maps exhibiting the boundaries of the companies' service areas. Since this information is in the public domain, exchange maps can be obtained from the public service commissions.

The quality of the maps obtained for the 74 primary areas of the SRC sample varied greatly. Most companies affiliated with larger systems (e.g., Bell, General) maintain up-to-date and fully detailed maps that either list county boundaries or other features which permit identification of the county boundary locations. Others, often smaller independent companies serving rural exchange areas, submit less detailed maps that are less helpful in locating exchanges within counties. Still other companies submit written descriptions of exchange boundaries, which yield the desired information only with tedious plotting. In addition to maps from state public service commissions, some independent telephone associations publish state maps listing exchange or company service boundaries. Sometimes these have sufficient detail to permit identification of exchanges serving any given county.

After maps for exchanges in the SRC primary areas were obtained, the exchange boundaries were plotted onto county base maps. The map of Washtenaw County, Michigan, treated as a primary area (Figure 2.1) is a typical example. The Britton exchange in the southern part of the county covers a small crossroads area that might contain only a few housing units. There are 10,000 possible numbers within the Britton exchange; the majority of the numbers have probably not been assigned, and only a handful lie in the county of interest. In the design used in this project, numbers from the border exchanges are included with probabilities equal to those for numbers from other exchanges in the primary area. Sample numbers from border exchanges require initial screening to avoid interviews with residents outside the primary area. The result is a self-weighting sample of telephone numbers attached to households in each primary area.

Although little external information on exchanges is available that might be useful for stratifying them within primary areas, observation of their placement in the area permits some grouping of exchanges whose subscribers are likely to share demographic characteristics.[8] The following stratification was introduced within primary areas:

1. Grouping together all central office codes in the same exchange
2. Ordering exchanges within the primary area geographically and by number of central office codes within the exchange
3. Ordering exchanges lying only partially within the primary area geographically

For example, the Washtenaw County central office codes might be ordered as in Table 2.1.

Systematic samples are drawn from the central office codes in each primary area. The order of the central office codes thus specifies the stratification implicit in the design. The number of central office codes within an exchange is a proxy variable for the population density of the exchange. Typically, the exchange of some large city of the primary area has the largest number of central office codes and thus is usually first in each ordering. By choosing exchanges close to one another geographically we form strata of neighboring suburbs which may have similar socioeconomic characteristics. By separating exchanges that lie only partially within the primary area, we attempt to ensure proper representation of residents on the border and in the interior of the area and to control the proportion of sample numbers that require screening.

Although we used the SRC national sample of dwellings as a base design, the clustered telephone sample is an element sample within primary areas and does not follow the secondary clusters of the per-

---

[8] In some large metropolitan areas it was possible to stratify central office codes within an exchange since their service was confined to certain areas within the city. In general, however, the different central office codes within an exchange serve customers scattered across the whole area.

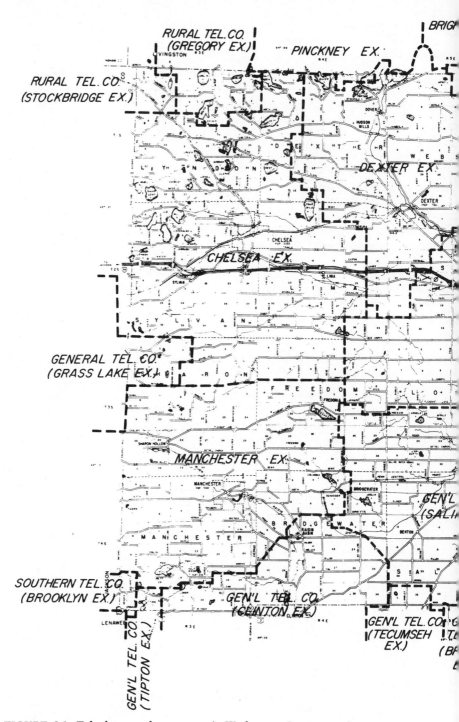

FIGURE 2.1. Telephone exchange areas in Washtenaw County, Michigan.

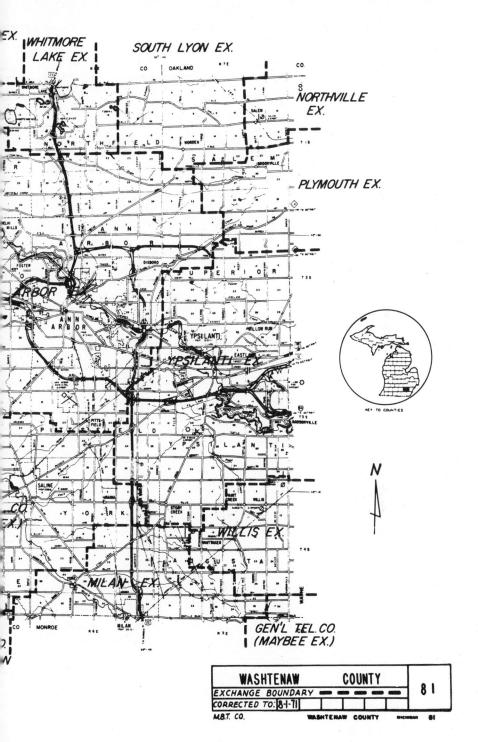

WHITMORE LAKE EX.

SOUTH LYON EX.

NORTHVILLE EX.

PLYMOUTH EX.

WILLIS EX.

MILAN EX.

GEN'L TEL. CO. (MAYBEE EX.)

KEY TO COUNTIES

N

WASHTENAW	COUNTY	81
EXCHANGE BOUNDARY	— — — —	
CORRECTED TO: 8-1-71		

M.B.T. CO.   WASHTENAW COUNTY   MICHIGAN   81

TABLE 2.1
Stratification Order of Telephone Exchange Areas in Washtenaw County, Michigan

Stratification order of exchanges	Number of central office codes	Completely or partially within Washtenaw County
1. Ann Arbor	12	Complete
2. Ypsilanti	7	Partial
3. Saline	1	Complete
4. Manchester	1	Partial
5. Chelsea	1	Partial
6. Dexter	1	Partial
7. Whitmore Lake	1	Partial
8. South Lyon	1	Partial
9. Northville	2	Partial
10. Plymouth	4	Partial
11. Willis	1	Partial
12. Milan	1	Partial
13. Clinton	1	Partial
14. Tipton	1	Partial
15. Brooklyn	1	Partial
16. Grass Lake	1	Partial
17. Stockbridge	1	Partial
18. Gregory	1	Partial
19. Pinckney	1	Partial
20. Brighton	2	Partial
21. Maybee	1	Partial
22. Britton	1	Partial
23. Tecumseh	1	Partial

sonal interview version of the SRC sample. An "element sample" within the primary areas selects the telephone numbers directly without introducing another stage of sampling, as opposed to first selecting exchanges or central office codes and then confining the sample numbers to those units. In contrast to the five stages of its personal interview analog, the clustered telephone sample is thus a two-stage sample:

$$\text{Prob. of Number} = \frac{\text{Prob. of}}{\text{Primary Area}} \times \frac{\text{Prob. of Number}}{\text{within Area}}$$

The investigation of matching a telephone sample to an areal sample can go on unimpeded by this feature, and it does allow an analysis of the effects of secondary clustering.[9]

[9] For mixed-mode studies using initial telephone screening and personal interview follow-up, subsampling of exchanges may be desirable to reduce travel costs of the personal interviewers.

   The ordered list of all central office codes serving any part of the primary areas was placed in computer files, and software was constructed to act on these files for the generation of sample telephone numbers. Since each primary area is selected with a probability proportional to its 1970 population, the probability of selection of numbers within primary areas must be inversely proportional to the 1970 population in order to give each telephone number in coterminous United States an equal chance of selection. Every non-self-representing primary area, therefore, has a different within-sampling fraction. Separate random starts are taken in each primary area. Each central office code is assumed to have 10,000 telephone numbers (0000–9999). For each primary area, an interval is calculated that is proportional to the probability of selection of the primary area. The first sample number is generated within that central office code indicated by the random start. For example, if the random start is 6323, in the case below

Stratification order			Cumulative count of numbers
1.	central office code	423	10,000
2.	central office code	809	20,000
3.	central office code	764	30,000
⋮	⋮	⋮	⋮

the first number would be in central office code 423. If the random start was 10,141, the first number would be in central office code 809. After the central office code for the sample number is identified by the random start, a four-digit random number is generated and appended to the central office code. For example, with a random start of 6323 and a four-digit randomly generated number of 0101, the first sample number would be

$$423\text{-}0101$$

The random number generation algorithm used is a standard IBM routine, URAND.

2.5 THE STRATIFIED RANDOM TELEPHONE SAMPLE

   An alternative to the clustered telephone sample is a stratified random single-stage sample, where telephone numbers are generated directly within working area code–central office code combinations.

Since the population of those working combinations is assembled on the Long Lines Department tape listing, the only remaining task for developing such a sample is stratifying the central office codes. As noted earlier, however, the tape records contain few variables useful for stratification.

The following design is used for this sample:

1. Using area codes, group central office codes by state and major region.
2. Within area codes, group together central office codes in the same exchange.
3. Within area codes, order exchange groups by the number of central office codes within the group.
4. Within those size categories, order exchange groups by the two geographical coordinates, rotating the order across size groups (Northwest to Southeast, Southeast to Northwest, Northwest to Southeast, and so on).

A systematic sample of telephone numbers is taken from this listing; the listing order specifies the stratification of the design. In contrast to the multivariate stratification of the clustered sample, geography and size of exchange are the only stratification dimensions utilized. The selection of sample numbers uses the same procedures as outlined for the clustered sample.

2.6 CONSTRUCTING SAMPLING FRACTIONS FOR THE SAMPLE DESIGNS

For the personal interview survey the following estimates were used to calculate a sampling fraction:

Estimated occupied HUs (households)	71,500,000
Coverage rate (proportion of HUs located by interviewers)	95%
Eligibility rate (proportion of households with eligible person)	100%
Response rate (from Field Office)	73%
Desired number of interviews	1500

The sampling rate is then

$$\frac{1500}{71,500,000(.95)(.73)} = \frac{1}{33,057}.$$

Since the estimate of occupied households in 1976 was subject to some error, the actual sampling fraction was raised to 1 : 32,000. Given the probabilities of selecting the primary and secondary areas, probabilities of selection for chunks, segments, and housing units within those areas were determined so that the product of probabilities for all stages was 1 : 32,000 for every housing unit.

For the telephone samples, previous research (Glasser & Metzger, 1972) suggested that approximately 20% of the numbers within working area code–central office code combinations are working household numbers. Since some time had passed since that research, and we had no knowledge of the proportion of good numbers in the clustered sample, the required sample size was not known. Instead, the sampling fraction was based on the following estimated parameters:

Total number of housing units in coterminous U.S.	71,500,000
Percentage of housing units with telephones	92.5%[10]
Expected response rate	75%
Desired sample size each sample	1000

The overall sampling fraction was, therefore:

$$\frac{1000}{71,500,000\,(.925)\,(.75)} = \frac{1}{49603}.$$

In the stratified random sample that fraction is applied directly to the listing of working area code–central office code combinations. In the clustered sample a different within-sampling fraction is used for each area, so that the product

$$\text{Pr(primary area)} \times \text{Pr}\left(\begin{array}{c}\text{number within}\\\text{primary area}\end{array}\right) = \frac{1}{49603}$$

is the desired constant.

Instead of drawing one sample at 1 : 49,603, small replicate subsamples were independently drawn, each utilizing a fraction of $1/(10)\cdot(49{,}603)$. Fourteen replicates were drawn, to provide for errors in estimating the needed sampling fraction. Since the replicate groups were independent samples, they could be distributed to interviewers in stages until the desired sample size was obtained. If time or cost constraints were heavier than expected, fewer than ten replicate groups could have been distributed without fear of bias.

[10] Derived from the 1975 SRC Fall Omnibus Survey.

In addition to dividing the sample into independent replicate groups, we also divided each replicate group into random subsets assigned to individual interviewers. This division permits analysis of interviewer differences, since each interviewer is in effect assigned a small national sample. The confounding of interviewer idiosyncracies and respondent characteristics has been avoided by randomization. (See discussion in Chapter 6, Section 6.4.)

2.7 SELECTING A RESPONDENT FROM SAMPLE HOUSEHOLDS

In personal interview studies conducted by the Survey Research Center the sample often consists of adults (persons 18 years or older) living in households. Since the majority of households in the United States contain more than one adult, procedures for objective selection of one respondent from among those eligible in the household have been developed (Kish, 1949). This sampling of respondents thus becomes the last stage of sampling, both in the personal interview sample and the telephone samples. Data records are weighted by the inverse of the probability of selection to achieve unbiased estimators.

In the personal interview survey, interviewers used a page like that shown in Figure 2.2 to list the adult household members at each sample housing unit. Interviewers are instructed to list male adults first, oldest to youngest, then female adults, oldest to youngest. A selection table assigned to each coversheet specifies the selected respondent for different numbers of eligible persons. There are eight selection tables in total and they are rotated systematically after a random initial assignment. The rotation scheme yields an equal expected number of chosen respondents from each position in the listing box.

Obtaining a detailed household listing in the first few moments of contact with a household member was thought to be difficult. That was, however, one of the options tried in early pretesting of respondent selection techniques. Two other techniques were pretested (see Figures 2.3, 2.4), both of which merely translate the selection tables of Kish (1949) into a different form. Figure 2.3 shows a selection technique that requires only one question of many households to determine the selected respondent. Half of such selection sheets would ask "Would you tell me how many *men*, 18 or older . . ." and the other half would replace "men" with "women." If there are one or more adults of the particular sex named in the question, the person to be

4.

9. List <u>all</u> members of the household 18 years and older by their relationship to the Head.

PART I (a)	(b)	(c)	(d)	(e)
				Enter "R" to
			Person	Identify
Household members by relationship to Head	Sex	Age	Number	Respondent
HEAD OF HOUSEHOLD				

SELECTION TABLE C	
If the number of eligible persons is:	Interview the person numbered:
1	1
2	1
3	2
4	2
5	3
6 or more	3

For (a) See pages 92-93 of the Interviewer's Manual (1976 edition).

For (d) Assign number "1" to the oldest male, number "2" to the next oldest male, and so on until all eligible males are numbered. Continue the number sequence, numbering eligible females from oldest to youngest; the oldest female gets the next number after the youngest male, etc.

For (e) Use the selection table on the right to determine the <u>number</u> of the person to be interviewed. In the first column of the selection table, circle the number of eligible persons--the highest number assigned in column (d). The corresponding number in the second column of the selection table denotes the person to be interviewed. In column (e) enter letter "R" to identify the respondent.

FIGURE 2.2. **Interview cover sheet.**

FORM **B1**

1. Sequence Number _____

2. Telephone Number _____

3. Would you tell me how many men 18 or older there are in your household?

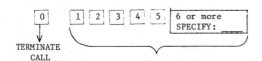

4. How many women 18 or older are in your household?

TERMINATE CALL

Number of men	Selected R is:
1	SOLE MALE
2	YOUNGER MALE
3	2nd YOUNGEST MALE
4	2nd YOUNGEST MALE
5	2nd YOUNGEST MALE
6 or more	4th OLDEST MALE

Number of women	Selected R is:
1	SOLE FEMALE
2	YOUNGER FEMALE
3	2nd YOUNGEST FEMALE
4	2nd YOUNGEST FEMALE
5	2nd YOUNGEST FEMALE
6 or more	4th OLDEST FEMALE

TELL THE PERSON ON THE PHONE WHICH MEMBER OF THE HOUSEHOLD IS THE SELECTED RESPONDENT AND ATTEMPT AN INTERVIEW.

5. DESCRIPTION OF FINAL RESULT:_____

_____

FIGURE 2.3. **Respondent selection form: telephone interview (alternative 1).**

FORM **A2**

1. Sequence Number _____

2. Telephone Number _____

3. First, could you tell me how many people 18 or older live there?

0 ⟶ TERMINATE CALL

4. How many of these are female?	3 → 1	2	3	4	5	6 or more SPECIFY
0	SOLE MALE	YOUNGER MALE	2nd YOUNGEST MALE	2nd YOUNGEST MALE	2nd YOUNGEST MALE	4th OLDEST MALE
1	SOLE FEMALE	SOLE MALE	OLDER MALE	2nd YOUNGEST MALE	2nd YOUNGEST MALE	3rd OLDEST MALE
2		YOUNGER FEMALE	YOUNGER FEMALE	OLDER MALE	2nd YOUNGEST MALE	2nd OLDEST MALE
3			2nd YOUNGEST FEMALE	YOUNGEST FEMALE	OLDER MALE	OLDEST MALE
4				2nd YOUNGEST MALE	YOUNGEST FEMALE	YOUNGEST FEMALE
5					2nd YOUNGEST FEMALE	2nd YOUNGEST FEMALE
6 or more SPECIFY: ___						4th OLDEST FEMALE

TELL THE PERSON ON THE PHONE WHICH MEMBER OF THE HOUSEHOLD
IS THE SELECTED RESPONDENT AND ATTEMPT AN INTERVIEW.

5. DESCRIPTION OF FINAL RESULT:_____

_____

_____

_____

_____

FIGURE 2.4. Respondent selection form: telephone interview (alternative 2).

interviewed is indicated in the instruction box. If there are no adults of that sex, a count of members of the other sex is obtained to choose a respondent.

All households with adults of both sexes of course require only one question before selecting a respondent and no household requires more than two questions. Several forms of the tables listing the selected respondent are randomly rotated among interviewers so that every adult has an equal chance of being selected in all households with the same number of adults (below six adults). Such efficiency might permit the interviewer to begin the questionnaire more quickly.

The selection procedure illustrated in Figure 2.4 presents another pretested technique that required two questions to select the respondent: first a count of all adults living in the household, then a count of either adult males or adult females. In this form, the sex for the second question is not randomly rotated over selection sheets. The project would use one of two alternatives for all sample numbers; one format would ask counts of males always, the other of females always. The answers to the two questions indicate a cell in the selection matrix of Figure 2.4, and that cell contains the identification of the selected respondent. As in the technique illustrated in Figure 2.3, different versions of the tables are randomly rotated over the sample to assure equal probabilities of selection within households with the same number of adults.

Several concerns were raised during pretesting that influenced our choice of respondent selection technique:

1. The fear of asking detailed household composition on the first contact made the full household listing less attractive.
2. Techniques that required a count of the number of adult males were thought to be sensitive to nonresponse or erroneous replies among single and widowed women living alone. We came to prefer techniques that asked about number of adult women.
3. There was also concern with the complicated nature of the labels for the selected respondent (see Figures 2.3, 2.4, e.g., 2nd Youngest Female, 4th Oldest Male). These fortunately are required only in households with many eligible respondents. The alternatives (see Troldahl & Carter, 1964 and Bryant's, 1975 comment on their selection scheme) assign unequal probabilities of selection to some eligible respondents.

The technique presented in Figure 2.4 was selected for use in this project. The form used required a count of all adults and all female adults in each household. We evaluate the performance of this technique in the following chapter.

2.8 SUMMARY

The basic design of this study involves a comparison of three national samples: the SRC national sample of dwellings and two telephone samples—a clustered telephone sample chosen within the 74 primary areas (counties and metropolitan areas) of the SRC national sample of dwellings and a stratified random sample of telephone numbers chosen nationwide without any clustering of numbers.

The SRC national sample of dwellings is a multistage area probability sample. Five stages of probability selection determine the overall probability of a dwelling unit being chosen: (a) probability of the primary area (county or county group); (b) probability of the secondary area within the county (cities, towns, and other areas); (c) probability of the "chunk" (areas of 20–30 dwelling units within the secondary areas); (d) probability of the segment (areas 4–12 dwelling units within chunks); and (e) probability of the dwelling unit within segment.

Telephone samples are constructed around the ten-digit system of telephone numbers in use in the United States—a three-digit area code, a three-digit central office code, and a four-digit number. The telephone sample drawn within the SRC national sample of dwellings took advantage of the deep stratification of the primary areas of that sample. Such a telephone sample lends itself to economical use in mixed-mode surveys, in which some data are collected by telephone and some by personal interview. The selection of any given number in such a telephone sample is the product of the selection probabilities of two stages—probability of primary area and probability of number within area. The selection of telephone numbers within each primary area was performed by means of a standard computer routine for random number generation.

The stratified random telephone sample is not a multistage sample. To select numbers for this sample, a nationwide state-by-state listing of central office codes (prefixes) was prepared, with exchanges within area codes ordered by size and (within size categories) by geographical coordinates. The selection of numbers was then done by applying the overall sampling fraction directly to all working central office codes and possible numbers within codes.

In personal interview surveys, the selection of respondents within households is done by the interviewer, who first records information about the composition of the household and then uses a selection table to choose the individual respondent. A variant of this, requiring only two questions before selection of the respondent, was developed for the telephone surveys.

Chapter 3

Administration of the Surveys

The administrative attractions of telephone surveys are many and obvious. Virtual elimination of interviewer travel costs, relative ease of supervision, the feasibility of repeated calls without the rising costs of increased sample dispersion, and the prospect of collecting data more fully from areas in which interviewers are unwelcome or reluctant to work constitute an impressive set of administrative advantages. Add to these the naive impression that every set of randomly chosen digits corresponds to a working telephone number, and the attractions become almost irresistible.

Like most Utopian descriptions, this one is more nearly perfect in prospect than in actuality, however, and it is actuality that must guide administrative choices. For this reason, and because little information has been available on the administration of telephone surveys using random-digit dialing, we will describe in detail the administrative arrangements for the telephone samples and the experiences of the telephone interviewers when they begin to dial the sample numbers. Where the contrast is instructive, we will compare the experiences of the telephone interviewers with the more familiar pattern of personal interviews at sample addresses.

3.1 DESIGN OF THE
SURVEY ADMINISTRATION

Taking personal interview surveys with national samples of any substantial size requires hundreds of interviewers dispersed across the sample areas, supervisors who oversee their work directly, and one or more field coordinators who monitor the progress of the field work from some central location and dispose of problems with the sample and the questionnaire. The field staff of the Survey Research Center is permanent; interviewers live in the sample area where they interview and they participate in each study the center conducts using the national household sample. Interviewing is a part-time job, and most interviewers do not want full-time work.

A national telephone survey could be organized in the same fashion as a personal interview survey, with telephoning done by interviewers located in each city and county included in the sample. Such an arrangement would have the advantage of using local instead of long-distance telephone lines, perhaps using the same staff for telephone and personal interviews, and making mixed-mode interviewing (telephone and personal interviews combined) administratively convenient. Several arguments, however, suggested that a centralized interviewing staff would be more efficient, at least for purposes of the present study:

1. *Interviewer training*—Many of the telephone interviewers were newly hired for this project. These were given initial training in the Ann Arbor offices to give them skills in general interviewing techniques, eliciting cooperation, following question wording, probing, pacing, enunciation, etc. This group was then combined with another group of telephone interviewers who had worked on a previous study,[1] and a 2-day training session (4 hours each day) was conducted to orient the combined group of 37 interviewers to the specific features of this study. These sessions were conducted by specialists in data collection, but one of the study directors was also present to answer questions about the interview schedule, the instructional materials, and the research design. The group studied the questionnaire item by item, discussing the format of each item, what it was attempting to measure, and any properties that made it difficult to administer.

---

[1] That study was a telephone reinterview of respondents to an earlier personal interview. Interviewing was done in the same facilities but did not involve random-digit dialing. The numbers called were given by the respondents at the end of their initial personal interview.

A practice interview was taken on the night of the first session. Individual sessions with the interviewing supervisor were held after the practice interview, and further discussions on the questionnaire were held.

A centralized interviewer training session is too costly for most national personal interview surveys. Gathering over 150 interviewers together is almost never attempted. Instead, for SRC surveys, conferences are held by groups of interviewers in the same sample areas with one of the more experienced designated as leader or local supervisor. A regional or "traveling" supervisor also attends these conferences whenever possible. Before the conference itself, each interviewer completes a worksheet, a written exercise designed to emphasize items that could cause problems in the interview situation. A practice interview is also taken; then the interviewers gather for the conference. Other survey organizations use different procedures for training specific to one study.

Centralized training for telephone interviewers seemed to permit an orientation program of higher quality (with the presence of the study director and interviewer supervisor for a 2-day session) and greater consistency. In most national personal interview surveys the prestudy conferences in sample areas are relatively uncontrolled, probably variable in their quality, and sometimes do not include interviewers located in small rural areas.

2. *Distribution* and *return of interview materials*—In a national survey with a dispersed interviewing staff, the distribution of materials from the research headquarters becomes a task of some complexity. Separate packets of questionnaires, sampling materials, coversheets, payroll forms, and the like must be assembled for each sample area. For safety, each packet must contain more than the expected number of each form required. After sampling households and interviewing respondents, interviewers must return the completed materials to the headquarters office. Delays and losses in mailing are inevitable in both directions.

With centralized interviewing the amount of extra materials required is smaller and their distribution is much simpler. All materials can be stored in the interviewing facilities and used as needed. The transmittal of completed interviews to the coding staff is equally convenient.

3. *Contact with research and coding staffs*—Unanticipated problems in question wording, interviewer instructions, or methods of administration often arise after interviewing has begun. When such problems are encountered in personal interview surveys, memoranda

must be sent or phone calls made to inform all interviewers of the possible difficulties and instructions for handling them. Some lag time usually exists between the first identification of a problem in the field, the notification of the research staff, and the alerting of the entire interviewing staff of the problem and its solution. When interviewers are centralized at the research center, the project directors can observe the administration of the questionnaire daily; a supervisor is present during all shifts, and problems can be identified and communicated to the research staff much more quickly than with a dispersed staff.

Locating telephone interviewers at the research headquarters has other benefits. Almost all questionnaires require some postinterview coding to reduce the data to a machine-readable form for analysis. Sometimes, because of carelessness or poor training, interviewers record answers that cannot be coded and yield missing data on individual items. In most personal interview surveys, such results are found only after the field period has ended and are rarely communicated to the interviewer. When coding is concurrent with interviewing in a centralized arrangement, coders can record interviewer errors and alert the interviewers to particular problems that they should avoid in future interviews. This feedback can be given to interviewers soon enough to improve their methods in later interviews on the same study. In this project, the practice interview and the first five interviews of each telephone interviewer were examined by the coding staff to locate coding problems. Questionnaires with errors were returned to the interviewers with notes attached calling for corrections.

4. *Exchange of information among interviewers*—The presence of other interviewers in a centralized interviewing room may permit informal transfer between interviewers of skills of persuasion and delivery. The spatial arrangement of the interviewing room for this project was as follows:

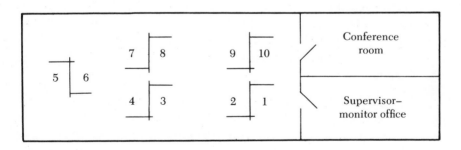

There were ten carrels, each with a five-line telephone and interviewing supplies. The carrels were open to one side and interviewers could hear one another during the questioning. To the extent that efficient techniques of introduction, questioning styles, and feedback were discovered by some interviewers, others on the same shift could observe this and might informally adopt those techniques.[2]

5. *Monitoring of interviewers' performance*—Telephone companies can provide simple monitoring equipment which permits supervisors to listen to ongoing interviews, hearing both the respondent and interviewer portions. Although tape recording such conversations is illegal without measures which would defeat their unobtrusive nature, the supervisor can listen for good and bad habits of individual interviewers and, after the interview is completed, offer suggestions for improvement.

In this project the monitoring equipment was located in the supervisor's office. Monitoring was concentrated on new interviewers and those having unusually low response rates. The monitoring was heavier at the beginning of the field period than at the end. No minimal level of monitoring for each interviewer was set.

6. *Assessing the progress of interviewing*—With centralized telephone interviewing a much closer monitoring of the data collection process can be implemented and much of it can be computerized. In this project all sample telephone numbers were punched and printed on computer cards. Every evening all numbers for which a final disposition had been obtained during the day were recorded in computer files. Every morning a computer-generated report was available summarizing the number of sample numbers outstanding, response rates, proportions of telephone numbers linked to households, and performance results for individual interviewers.

7. *Debriefing of interviewers*—After the data collection had been completed for the project, two sessions of 2 hours each were held with telephone interviewers and supervisors. The discussions touched on all aspects of the survey, with special emphasis on the introduction of the study at the time of the initial telephone contact, adaptation of response-card questions to telephone interviewing, length of the interview, and problems that led respondents to terminate the inter-

---

[2] This assumes some motivation to maximize the number of completed interviews. Although interviewers were not paid on the basis of number of completed interviews, there was an experience point system which rewarded interviewers with pay increases after certain numbers of interviews had been completed.

view before completion. Feedback on some of the same issues was obtained from the personal interviewers through short self-administered questionnaires that they returned after completing all their interviews.

In short, in addition to the elimination of travel costs, almost all the attractions of centralized telephone interviewing arise from two qualities, fewer people and easier communication among them:

1. One field office coordinator, one full-time supervisor, two part-time supervisors and 37 interviewers were able to perform the data collection work for the entire telephone survey of over 1700 interviews. One field office coordinator, 11 field supervisors, several "field contacts" who distributed materials, and 144 interviewers were required to complete the personal interview sample of about 1550 interviews. The ease of coordination of the telephone survey design relative to that of the personal interview survey permitted the close monitoring of the whole data collection effort.

2. In addition to the advantages of having smaller numbers of people engaged in data collection, the fact that those people are in the same location as the research, coding, and data-processing staffs permits interaction that is beneficial to the quality of the entire survey.

Some of these advantages were only partially realized in this project because it was our initial full-scale utilization of the telephone methodology. For example, supervisory monitoring of telephone interviewers became more routine in later surveys and thus assured that all interviewers received such evaluation early and regularly. Continued use of centralized telephone interviewing will almost certainly discover new ways to make the data collection process more efficient.

Some of these may come in the form of technological developments that combine into a single task sets of activities which were traditionally separated. For example, in terminal-based interviewing each interviewer reads the questions from a cathode-ray tube, codes the responses by pressing the appropriate numbered key on his or her terminal keyboard, and at designated points in the interview obtains consistency checks from the computer. If the checks indicate consistency, the computer enters the entire "chunk" of response information directly into machine-based files. Terminal-based interviewing thus transforms some of the coding and data-processing activities to machine processes and changes the interviewer's job of penciling responses on paper to keying them into a cathode-ray tube terminal. Machine-dialing systems free the interviewer from keeping track of sample telephone numbers and virtually eliminate misdialings. Other developments may simply improve the control over the quality of data collection—learning what interviewing techniques are best suited to telephone interviews, discovering types of measures that are most efficient for telephone surveys, and improving feedback between interviewers and the research staff.

3.2 RESULTS OF CALLS TO SAMPLE NUMBERS

One of the most dramatic differences between survey work in a random-digit dialing (RDD) telephone study and that in a personal interview study involves the match between the sampling frame and the actual population. In an areal household sample, actual physical spaces containing housing structures are sampled, and only vacant structures or the mistaking of business for residential units can cause the selection of nonpopulation elements. In a sample of telephone numbers generated randomly, however, there are many numbers that are not connected to residences. The initial experience of using such a sample serves to teach one about the structure of the telephone system in the United States.

To generate the two national telephone samples yielding a total of 1734 interviews required calling a sample of 12,898 randomly generated telephone numbers, 7710 of which were clustered into the primary areas of the Survey Research Center's multistage national sample and 5188 were distributed over the entire coterminous United States as part of a stratified element (single-stage) sample. The multistage national sample and the single-stage sample calls yielded 865 and 869 interviews, respectively.

Table 3.1 presents the results of these telephone calls for each of the two sample types. Definitions of the eight disposition categories appear in the first footnote below the table. In the single-stage sample, about 22% of the sample numbers randomly dialed were working household numbers. This is the figure comparable to the 20% found by Glasser and Metzger (1972). Except for the numbers that produced a ringing response but were never answered, the remaining types of numbers were confirmed as nonworking and nonresidential. If we assume that all of the "ring, no answers" are working numbers, the proportion of unassigned numbers in the national telephone system is 69.5%; if the "ring, no answers" are all nonworking numbers, the

TABLE 3.1

Final Disposition of All Sample Numbers by Telephone Sample Type

Disposition category[a]	Telephone sample type (percentage)	
	Single-stage[b]	Multistage[c]
1. Working household numbers	21.6	15.4 ⎫ 20.0
2. Out of primary area	—	4.6 ⎭
3. Nonresidential numbers	6.0	5.0
4. Nonworking numbers	53.3 ⎫	52.6 ⎫
5. Double wrong connection	4.7 ⎪ 69.5	5.1 ⎪ 70.9
6. No result from dial	6.3 ⎬	6.1 ⎬
7. Fast busys	5.2 ⎭	7.1 ⎭
8. Ring, no answers	2.9	4.0
	100.0	99.9

[a] Definitions of disposition categories: 1. Working household numbers—numbers answered by person who reported that number serves a residence; 2. Out of primary area—household numbers in the clustered sample which serve residences lying outside the primary area; 3. Nonresidential numbers—businesses and institutions not fulfilling the housing unit definition; 4. Nonworking numbers—numbers yielding nonworking number recordings at least twice consecutively; numbers with operator intercepts which told the caller that the number was nonworking; 5. Double wrong connection—numbers answered by people who reported a different number than that dialed; at least two calls; 6. No result from dial—numbers producing neither a ring, a busy signal, nor a recording; at least two consecutive calls; 7. Fast busys—numbers yielding a tone with 120 interruptions per minute, indicating circuit inability to complete call; at least five calls; 8.,Ring, no answers—numbers consistently yielding ringing without any of the above responses (majority with ten or more calls).

[b] $N = 5188$.

[c] $N = 7710$.

percentage of unassigned numbers in the telephone system is 72.4%. In either case, this large percentage of unassigned numbers causes increased costs of random-digit dialed telephone surveys over those using numbers sampled from directories.

The disposition categories for the multistage telephone sample have the additional class of "out of primary area." These numbers fall in telephone exchanges that are located partially within a primary sampling area. The actual numbers generated, however, are located outside the primary area. They are working household numbers but are ineligible for interview because their subscribers live outside the primary areas of the Survey Research Center areal sample—across a county line, for example. About 5% of the numbers in the clustered sample belong to households outside the primary areas. This 5%, however, also means that the single-stage sample yields significantly more eligible working household numbers than the multistage (21.6 to 15.4% of the two samples, respecively). To yield the same number of interviews in the clustered sample requires approximately 50% more generated sample numbers than the single-stage (7710 to 5188), all other things being equal.

In both designs the other set of numbers confirmed as working but ineligible is the nonresidential group. These represent 5 or 6% of all sample numbers and about 20–22% of all sample numbers identified as working. In other words, there are about five times as many working household numbers as there are working nonresidential numbers. Nonresidential numbers are thus a nuisance and a source of reduced efficiency in random-digit telephone samples of residential populations, but a random-digit telephone sample of businesses would be more severely handicapped by unwanted residential numbers—four out of five. Moreover a study of businesses or other nonresidences using an RDD sample would encounter many more difficulties than merely the time and cost of contacting many nonbusiness numbers. Many businesses have multiple phone numbers and would have disproportionately large probabilities of selection. In addition, most businesses have at least one listed phone number, so that directory sampling might be more efficient than RDD sampling.

Telephone numbers that apparently belong neither to residences nor nonresidential establishments make up Categories 4–7 of Table 3.1. Category 4, "nonworking numbers," contains those sample numbers that when dialed yielded a nonworking number recording or an operator intercept. In the latter case an operator answered the dialing, asked what number was dialed, then reported that the number had been changed, was a nonworking number, or was temporarily disconnected. Temporary disconnections sometimes occur because of delinquent payment or sometimes because residents are using another residence temporarily (e.g., summer homes). As we do in personal interview surveys, we defined the telephone sample as consisting of eligible units at the time of first contact. Since these nonworking numbers were not attached to households at the time of first contact, they were not pursued.

Ideally every dialing would yield a ringing tone, a busy tone, a nonworking recording, or an operator intercept. In practice a dialed number may produce any of several more ambiguous results (Categories 5–8, Table 3.1). One such outcome, the "double wrong connection," was surprising to us, although instances of it had been noted by Glasser and Metzger (1972). One of the first questions the interviewer asked when a dialed number was answered attempted to verify that the correct number had been reached (e.g., "Is this 313-764-4424?"). If the person said that the number dialed was not his or hers, the interviewer thanked the respondent for that information and terminated the call. We assumed that in most such instances the number had been misdialed, and the interviewers' instructions were to dial it again. A "double wrong connection" occurred when the second dialing again yielded the same wrong number. About 5% of all sample numbers were double wrong connections in this study.

At first there was some puzzle as to how a telephone could be reached by two different numbers without the subscriber's knowing it. Conversations with A.T. & T. staff members suggested a possible explanation. The switching systems used by telephone companies sometimes require a new piece of equipment for every "thousand series" (4000s, 5000s, etc.) served within a central office code. Often companies begin use of a central office code with numbers that lie in the 2000–3000 series, since these can be more quickly read by the equipment and can be more quickly connected. Central office codes serving rural areas sometimes require only a few thousand assigned numbers and need only the 2000–3000 series. Custom dictates, however, that several numbers in the 9000 series be devoted to telephone company service use in the central office. To maintain both the 2000 and 3000 series numbers for subscribers and the 9000 series for plant use *without* buying separate equipment for the 9000 series, the 9000 series is sometimes "bridged" to a working series. For example, if the 9000s were bridged to the 2000s, all numbers in the 2000s could also be reached by their corresponding number in the 9000s (e.g., 313-764-2112 could be reached by 313-764-9112). Since the corresponding 9000 numbers are nonworking, only dialing errors and random-digit dialed surveys reach them. The bridging is thus practically invisible to the subscriber. If the dialed number is not verified by the interviewer, these bridgings are not discovered and households reached in this way have two chances of falling into the sample, one for each number. Therefore, we classified the "double wrong connections" as nonworking numbers to reduce their chances of selection to equal that of other telephone households.

Sometimes when a sample number was dialed, nothing happened. There was no ringing, no busy signal, and no recording. Sometimes the response was static noise, screeching, or periodic clicks. When these responses occurred on at least two calls, the numbers were classified as "no result from dial." It is possible that a small percentage of these numbers were assigned to households but that a temporary equipment failure in the area prevented the completion of the call. However, equipment problems of that kind should trigger a recording stating "Your call cannot be completed at this time, please hang up and dial again later. . . ." Numbers yielding this recording were called repeatedly until their status was confirmed as working or nonworking. Early in the interviewing period, operators were called for assistance regarding the numbers yielding no response; they aided in confirming that some of these were nonworking numbers. In general, however, we have found that operators do not provide this assistance.

The busy signal received when the phone being called is in use is a tone interrupted by silence 60 times per minute. Sometimes when a sample number was dialed, the interviewer received a similar signal but with 120 interruptions per minute. This signal, often called a "fast busy" or "reorder" tone, is given for working numbers if the circuits into the area are temporarily overloaded, and that is the cause most familiar to operators. Unfortunately for telephone interviewers, the same signal is sometimes given for nonworking numbers that are not connected to nonworking number recordings. In order to distinguish between the two cases, numbers yielding a "fast busy" signal were called at least five times over several days. If five consecutive calls yielded that same result, no further calls were made; 5–7% of the sample numbers yielded five or more "fast busy" signals. It is our belief that all of these numbers are nonworking numbers.

The final category of disposition includes numbers that gave a ringing tone whenever called, but were never answered. It was our naive understanding at the beginning that all these numbers were working, but when many numbers yielded the result, we became doubtful. Calls for assistance to WATS lines operators provided few answers; local business offices of the central office code often refused, "for security reasons," to disclose whether such numbers were working or not. When we examined these numbers, we noticed that many of them fell in one rural primary area in the multistage sample. A call to the business office of the central code revealed that there were no working numbers in the thousand series of those sample numbers. These numbers were merely switched into a ringing machine instead of a nonworking number recording or an operator intercept mode. It is the impression of some telephone company representatives that this problem is largely a rural one concentrated in central offices that cannot afford enough nonworking number recordings to handle all nonassigned numbers. The vast majority of these "ring, no answer" numbers were called ten or more times.

Some insight into the telephone system can be gained by examining the disposition of groups of numbers from each of the ten thousands series. For example, 313-764-4424 belongs to the 4000s series, 313-764-6563 to the 6000s series. Table 3.2 presents the disposition of sample numbers of this project in each series. The percentage of working household numbers varies across the groups from a low of 12.5% in the 9000s series to a high of 32.4% in the 2000s series. The proportion gradually declines after the 2000s series. The 0000s and 1000s have proportions of working numbers intermediate in magnitude.

When we presented these figures to representatives of the telephone company, they offered several possible explanations. Older telephone switching equipment, called "step-by-step" equipment, processes the last four digits dialed by having selector arms climb number banks until the correct digits are located. For example, the digit 5 requires the arm to go to the fifth level. Although this type of switching takes only a few seconds, it is slower for higher digits in each location of the four-digit number; a 6 takes longer to locate than a 1. The numbers are ordered in each bank from 1 to 9 and then 0. This may explain the general trend to smaller proportions of working household numbers among the higher thousands series and the 0000s. It does not explain why the 0000s have relatively few working household numbers. One explanation offered was that some exchanges have equipment that gives callers a new dial tone if they interrupt the dialing of a number for 30 seconds or more. If, for example, one wanted to dial 764-4424 and paused for 30 seconds after dialing 764, a new dial tone would be received and the four-digit number 4424 might be viewed as the first four digits of a new dialing. If the last four digits of a number fell in the 0000s and a 30-second pause occurred before they were dialed, the operator would be reached by the first zero. If the last four digits fell in the 1000s, a 30-second pause in some exchange areas would route the call to the direct distance dial network. Local telephone exchange offices can avoid these unfortunate results by beginning the assignment of numbers in the 2000s, and Table 3.2 suggests that some exchanges may have done just that.

Table 3.2 also shows that the largest proportion of wrong connections (15.3%) is found in the 9000s series. This thousand series contains some numbers that are standardized for company use throughout the telephone system. This standardization may permit company per-

TABLE 3.2
Disposition of Total Telephone Sample Numbers by Thousand Series of Generated Four-Digit Numbers

Thousand series	Working household numbers	Non-residential numbers	Ring, no answer	Non-working number	Fast busys	Wrong connection	No response	Total	N
				Percentage					
0000	16.8	3.1	1.9	57.2	4.6	3.5	13.1	100.2	1272
1000	21.2	5.0	1.1	57.1	6.3	2.0	7.4	100.1	1223
2000	32.4	6.6	6.0	40.4	4.9	4.8	4.9	100.0	1310
3000	25.5	7.6	5.0	44.6	8.5	4.5	4.3	100.0	1257
4000	23.3	7.3	4.3	50.0	7.0	4.1	4.1	100.1	1305
5000	22.4	5.0	3.0	52.9	8.0	3.9	4.9	100.1	1342
6000	17.7	5.2	2.8	58.5	7.3	2.9	5.5	99.9	1334
7000	17.2	4.2	2.6	59.3	6.5	4.3	6.0	100.1	1333
8000	17.5	4.2	2.7	59.1	5.8	4.3	6.2	99.8	1270
9000	12.5	6.5	6.4	49.7	4.2	15.3	5.4	100.0	1252
Total	20.7	5.5	3.6	52.9	6.3	4.9	6.2	100.1	12,898

sonnel outside the exchange to access the numbers with assurance that they fulfill the same test functions in all exchanges. If no other 9000s numbers are in use and especially if the exchange equipment is designed for servicing an area of low population density, bridging between the 9000 and some thousands series in use (e.g., 2000s) may be implemented, as we have seen. Thus if 9637 is a standard plant number, 2637 will not be assigned to a subscriber but will ring when both 9637 and 2637 are dialed. The bridging affects all 9000 and 2000 numbers. For example, if we generate 313-764-9424 as a sample number and dial it, the subscriber of 313-764-2424 reached by the call will not verify the number. The table suggests that one of the most prevalent causes of bridging is the need for use of 9000s series numbers.

To demonstrate how problems of the phone system tend to be concentrated in nonmetropolitan areas we examined the disposition of sample numbers separately for three groups of primary areas in the clustered telephone sample: the 12 self-representing areas (the largest metropolitan areas in the United States), the non-self-representing primary areas which are SMSAs, and those primary areas that are not SMSAs. The first two columns of Table 3.3 show that percentages of working household numbers both within and without the primary area are much higher in the large metropolitan areas (35.7 + 1.8 = 37.5%) than in the nonmetropolitan areas (7.7 + 5.3 = 13.0%). The nonresidential working numbers are also more prevalent in the metropolitan areas. In sum, metropolitan central office codes are more densely assigned than are others, a larger proportion of sample numbers are working household numbers, and, therefore, RDD samples are more efficient in metropolitan areas.

The small proportion of working household numbers in nonmetropolitan areas implies that the control over sample size is very poor in these areas. Although, for example, 7.7% of the sample numbers in the non-SMSAs are eligible for interviews, there is considerable variation in the size of that group over different primary areas. This variation is related to a loss of control over sample size and a loss of precision of sample estimates.

Table 3.3 also demonstrates how nonmetropolitan exchanges exhibit the largest problems of unconfirmed nonworking numbers and strange results. Wrong connections are three times more frequent (6.2–1.9%) in the non-SMSAs than in the largest metropolitan areas. Dialings yield no result five times more frequently (7.9–1.5%), nonworking numbers connected to fast busy signals are almost nonexistent in the metropolitan areas, but form 9.5% of the dispositions in

TABLE 3.3
Disposition of Sample Numbers by Primary Area Type in Clustered Sample

Primary area type	Household numbers		Non-residential Numbers	Ring, no answer	Nonworking number	Fast busys	Wrong connection	No response	Total	N
	Within primary area	Outside primary area								
Self-representing	35.7	1.8	13.3	1.6	43.3	.8	1.9	1.5	100.0	943
Non-self-representing SMSAs	25.0	4.6	8.4	1.8	48.8	4.0	3.7	3.7	100.0	1885
Non-self-representing non-SMSAs	7.7	5.3	2.2	5.3	55.9	9.5	6.2	7.9	100.0	4882
Total	15.4	4.6	5.0	4.0	52.6	7.1	5.1	6.1	99.9	7710

Percentage

non-SMSAs. Finally, the sample numbers that yield constant ringing over many calls are three times as prevalent in the non-SMSAs. In short, all of the aberrations of expected functioning in the telephone system occur with greater frequency in the nonmetropolitan areas. From examining exchange maps for several states, we learned that these areas are often served by independent companies responsible for single exchanges. Although the Bell System, for example, has developed guidelines for exchange area practices, these are evidently not always followed by the small independent companies. This also implies that random generation of sample numbers is a more efficient sampling design in the metropolitan areas.[3]

The generation of household population samples by random-digit dialing of telephone numbers is a relatively new development in survey technology, and a promising one. It might also be called an adjunct or secondary technology, since it depends so heavily on the much larger technology of the telephone system itself. The automatic dialing and switching methods of the telephone system make RDD samples possible, and survey technicians sometimes come to think of those methods as being extensions of survey procedures. The telephone system is not operated for the convenience of survey researchers, however, and some of the technical arrangements made for economy or convenience within the telephone system itself have quite opposite implications for the adjunct technology of survey research. The disposition categories summarized in Table 3.1 and discussed thereafter illustrate this point. Survey technicians who seek the advantages of random-digit dialing and telephone interviewing must be prepared to encounter and deal with the technological traps created unintentionally by the larger system as it seeks to maximize its own convenience and efficiency.

Working household numbers are only a modest proportion of all number combinations that are randomly generated. Telephone exchange boundaries do not correspond to the boundaries of census areas or political subdivisions. Business and other nonresidential numbers are not segregated or otherwise identifiable in advance. Nonworking numbers may or may not produce a recorded message that so identifies them. Equipment bridging, in no way detectable to the caller, may produce double wrong connections—households that can be reached by more than one number even though the household-

---

[3] We also note that the stimulus to random generation of sample numbers is weaker in rural areas where unlisted numbers often form a small proportion of all numbers and mobility in and out of an exchange area may be smaller. In such cases, directory sampling may be preferable.

ers are not aware of that fact. Some numbers may produce a ring audible to the caller even if there is no connection to any household or business. Other such "unconnected" numbers may produce a fast busy signal or merely a great silence. All these outcomes, which reduce the efficiency of RDD sample surveys, are incidental consequences of problems and solutions within the larger technology.

3.3 NUMBER OF CALLS MADE TO SAMPLE NUMBERS

About 44,300 calls were made to the 12,898 sample numbers in the two telephone samples; the mean number of calls was thus about 3.4, but the median was less than 2. The overall distribution (Table 3.4, Column i) fails to reveal the large differences in the number of calls required to determine the status of each type of number. Since about half of the sample numbers were confirmed as nonworking, the overall results generally reflect the experiences with these numbers. Most nonworking numbers (76%) received a nonworking number recording on the first call and were called once again to protect against misdialings (Table 3.4, Column d). On the other hand, most numbers that rang without answer (Table 3.4, Column h) were called 16 times or more, in an attempt to confirm them as working or nonworking.

The column of most interest in Table 3.4 is the first, listing the distribution of calls made to working household numbers. For these numbers, we see that 2 or 3 calls are usually enough for final disposition. The cumulative percentage distribution for both samples is presented in Figure 3.1. This shows that about three-quarters (74.5%) of the working household numbers are disposed of in 5 or fewer calls, but that at least 9 calls are required to complete the next 15% and thus to reach 90% of the working household numbers. If the number of calls is limited to 10, the survey would have completed work on about 93% of the working household numbers. About 2% of the numbers required 17 or more calls before an interview was taken, a final refusal was obtained, or some other conclusive outcome reached.

Two things should be considered in comparing these figures to the callback distribution for personal interview surveys. First, the ease and economy of making calls in a telephone survey are much greater than in most personal interview surveys. Second, the callbacks of personal interviewers may be guided by better information about the sample household, the neighborhood, and times when the residents are more likely to be at home.

TABLE 3.4
Disposition of Total Telephone Sample Numbers by Number of Calls to Number

Number of calls	Working household (a)	Outside primary area (b)	Non-residential (c)	Non-working (d)	Wrong connections (e)	No result from dial (f)	Fast busys (g)	Ring without answer (h)	Percentage for all categories (i)
					Percentage				
1	23.7	50.1	43.4	9.6	11.6	15.1	0	0	14.6
2	18.0	23.7	22.6	76.0	48.8	59.9	.2	.4	51.4
3	13.7	9.0	12.1	5.9	13.7	7.9	0	0	7.7
4	11.1	5.4	6.5	3.1	8.3	5.2	.1	0	4.9
5	8.0	2.8	4.0	1.6	3.9	3.5	67.5	.2	7.3
6	6.0	3.1	2.8	1.2	3.1	3.3	16.7	0	3.4
7	5.0	1.1	2.1	1.0	2.5	.4	7.2	1.1	2.2
8	2.9	2.0	1.4	.5	1.4	.6	3.8	2.8	1.3
9	2.6	1.1	1.7	.4	1.4	.6	1.0	4.6	1.1
10	1.8	1.1	.7	.1	.9	.3	1.0	1.1	.6
11	1.3	0	.4	.2	.6	.4	.4	3.0	.6
12	1.2	.6	.6	.2	1.1	.1	.2	2.6	.5
13	1.1	0	.7	.1	.5	.3	.5	9.1	.7
14	.8	0	.1	.1	.9	.4	.1	10.2	.6
15	.3	0	.4	.1	.5	.5	.2	8.7	.5
16	.5	0	.3	.1	0	.9	.2	14.6	.7
17 or more	1.9	0	0	.1	.6	.8	.7	41.5	2.0
Total %	99.9	100.0	99.8	100.3	99.8	100.2	99.8	99.0	100.1
Total N	2311	355	703	6821	637	795	816	460	12,898

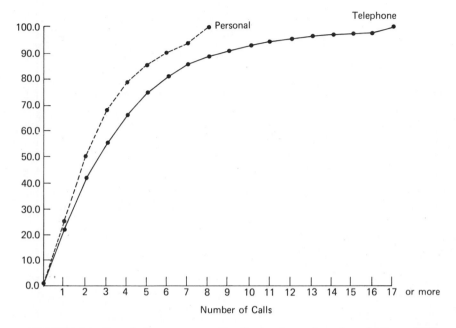

FIGURE 3.1. Cumulative percentage distribution for total number of calls made for each sample household by mode of interview. The 8-call category of personal interviews includes cases with 8 calls or more; the 17-call category in the telephone survey includes cases with 17 calls or more.

The telephone interviewer merely looks at the sample card, checks that it is an appropriate time to call, and punches out the phone number. In contrast, the personal interviewer must leave home, travel to the sample segment of the housing unit, and attempt to make contact with a household member. Sometimes, of course, the interviewer may be in a segment to contact a sample household and at the same time can make callback visits to other houses in the segment. Even with such attempts at economy, callbacks in personal interview surveys are time consuming and expensive.

On the other hand, callbacks on personal interviews are more likely to yield contact than those in telephone surveys. Personal interviewers are able to observe characteristics of the neighborhood or of the housing unit and make inferences about appropriate times to call. Sometimes the interviewer can ask neighbors when a member of the sample household might return; notes can be left at the door of sample households stating when the interviewer will return. In contrast, the telephone interviewer knows nothing about uncontacted numbers except that they were not answered on previous calls. This lack of knowledge, and the ease of making callbacks on the telephone, makes the yield or quality of repeated calls on the phone somewhat lower than those in a personal interview. For both these reasons, the call distribution of sampled households takes a different form in the personal interview counterpart.

Given this reasoning, we would expect a lower average number of calls in the personal interview sample than in the telephone samples. Table 3.5 presents the distribution of total number of calls on sampled housing units for the personal interview sample. The median number of calls is somewhat less than two, compared to two or three on the telephone. If we limit our comparison to those households that yielded an interview, the median number of calls per interview is 2.2 for the telephone sample and 1.8 for the personal interview sample. The cumulative percentage distribution in Figure 3.2 shows that 78% of the telephone interviews and 91% of the personal interviews are obtained with five or fewer calls. Six times as many telephone interviews as personal interviews required eight or more calls. This probably reflects both the lack of information guiding telephone callbacks

TABLE 3.5
Number of Calls to Sample Cases for Personal Interview Survey by Result

| Number of calls | Percentage [a] | | | |
	Interview	Non-interview	Non-sample[b]	Total
0	0	.8	7.0	1.0
1	28.4	13.8	68.3	30.0
2	27.5	18.5	15.3	24.0
3	18.5	14.9	5.2	16.1
4	10.6	11.9	2.1	9.8
5	5.7	11.9	.7	6.5
6	4.1	6.1	.7	4.1
7	2.3	5.9	.3	2.9
8 or more	2.9	16.3	.3	5.6
Total	100.0	100.1	99.9	100.0
N	1515	523	287	2325
Not ascertained	33	12	3	48

[a] Noninterviews with zero calls consist of four cases where no visit was made to the unit. Nonsample units with zero calls were classified immediately as noneligible units (e.g., vacant dilapidated houses, businesses).

[b] Nonsample cases include all structures listed that were not occupied housing units or were occupied housing units listed in error outside the boundaries of sample area.

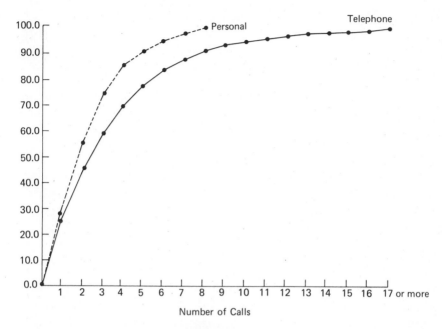

FIGURE 3.2. Cumulative percentage distribution for total number of calls made for each interview by mode of interview. The ·8-call category for personal interviews includes cases with 8 calls or more; the 17-call category in the telephone survey includes cases with 17 calls or more.

and the fact that, regardless of mode, many calls are required to reach some respondents. Many repetitive calls to a household are more likely to be made in the telephone sample than in a personal interview sample. In that view, the travel costs of the personal calls are partly balanced by the benefits of informed callbacks, which reduce the number of required calls for most interviews. For respondents who are very rarely home, however, the information available about their "at-home" patterns may be insufficient to prevent an unacceptably large number of personal callbacks. These cases may be more cheaply interviewed in a telephone survey.

3.4 SELECTION OF THE RESPONDENT IN THE TELEPHONE SAMPLE

In a personal interview survey, the smallest "area" in the sample design is the dwelling unit, a space occupied by a household. When a sample of individuals rather than households is wanted, the interviewer makes contact with some responsible member of the household, lists the persons who are included in it, and then selects the respondent from them. The procedures for accomplishing this final stage in the multistage sample for personal interviewing have been described in Chapter 2.

The adaptation of these definitions and procedures to telephone surveys involves several problems. To begin with, dwelling units and telephone units are not identical. People who share a telephone line are not always members of the same household, and members of one household may have more than one telephone line. If dwelling units and households were of no significance for a given study, telephone units might be used in their own right. In this study, however, the comparison of survey data from telephone and personal interviews was one of the major objectives, and as part of the telephone interview it was therefore necessary to identify dwelling units and households.

Let us designate as *informant* the first person to whom the interviewer speaks at the door or on the telephone, and as *respondent* the person within the household who is subsequently chosen for interview. The procedure for respondent selection in the telephone survey required two questions of the informant: "We need to talk to a man in some households and a woman in others. First, could you tell me how many people 18 years or older live there?" and after that question was answered, "How many of these are female?" In the body of the interview we asked the chosen respondent (who may have been a different person than the one who answered the initial questions) to provide a listing of all occupants of the household. At that point, we utilized the rules applied in personal interviews for defining membership in the household. The telephone interviewer was reminded of this fact by means of the following instruction, which appeared on the same page as the box in which household members were to be listed:

Interviewer: Remember that R's household includes those people who

1. Live together with R in rented or owned quarters separate from others in the building.
2. Share with R the same entrance from outside *or* share with R complete kitchen facilities separate from the other units.

Define "household" to R in these terms when necessary.

There are three reasons that different results might be obtained from the informant and the respondent in the telephone interviews:

(a) The informant identifies the number of adults by answering one question; the respondent is asked to enumerate the adults in the household and a count is derived when the interviews are coded. (b) The question is asked of the informant after very little interaction with the interviewer has been experienced; the respondent is asked the question after several minutes of questioning. (c) Finally, the household is relatively undefined in the informant's question, but the interviewer is explicitly asked to follow the standards of personal interview surveys in defining the respondent's household in the body of the interview.

Despite these differences we maintained the form of the two-question series because examination of other organizations' techniques and review of the literature on telephone respondent selection suggested that most organizations were using a simplified selection technique like that used with our informants. The listing box in the body of the interview was viewed as a method of analyzing the correspondence between households selected in a telephone sample and those selected in a personal interview sample. The listing also permits a comparison of the two techniques for identifying numbers of adults in a household.

Table 3.6 compares the number of adults in the household identified by the informant with the number of adults mentioned by the respondent. We will view the respondent's report (in the interview listing box) as more accurate and look at the percentage distribution of informant's answers (on the selection sheet) within categories of number of adults. Within every household size category there are discrepancies between the two counts; the larger the number of adults in the listing box, the more prevalent are discrepancies between the two modes. The majority of households contain only two adults, and in total 9% of the sample households had errors on the selection sheet. When we analyze the types of errors made, we find that households containing young adults—sons and daughters 18 to 21—have higher rates of discrepancies. An examination of the cases with errors suggests that there were few large discrepancies, that the most prevalent error was in adding or deleting a female adult, and that the numbers here balance one another. In addition, there is some tendency for the selection procedure to underestimate the number of members in larger households.

Two alterations of the selection procedure have been attempted since the project was conducted. The first added a question, "How many people in total live there?" and then "How many of those are 18 years old or older?" Although this appeared to reduce some of the errors, there were still discrepancies between the selection sheet

TABLE 3.6
Number of Household Members 18 Years or Older Recorded on Selection Sheet by Number Recorded in Interview Listing Box

Number of adults in interview listing box	Number of adults on selection sheet (percentage)									Missing[a] data	Total N
	1	2	3	4	5	6	7	8 or more	Total		
1	93.8	4.6	1.6	0	0	0	0	0	100.0%	32	400
2	1.9	94.0	2.4	1.4	0.3	0	0	0	100.0%	66	1000
3	1.3	10.9	78.7	7.5	1.3	0	0.4	0	100.1%	17	256
4	0	11.1	11.1	74.1	1.9	1.9	0	0	100.1%	1	55
5	7.1	21.4	7.1	7.1	57.1	0	0	0	99.8%	1	14
6	0	0	0	0	0	0	0	0	—	0	0
7	0	0	100.0	0	0	0.	0	0	100.0%	0	1
8 or more	0	0	0	0	50.0	50.0	0	0	100.0%	0	2
Missing data	5	1	0	0	0	0	0	0			6
											1734

[a] Missing data includes records of broken-off interviews.

report and the number of adults in the household. Our current selection procedure for telephone interviews is precisely that used in the personal interviews; a complete household listing is taken before identifying one adult as the respondent. This has been accomplished without reduction in the response rate. Moreover, the telephone interviewers seem to prefer the complete enumeration as a means of introducing the study gradually to the sample household and as a vehicle to develop some rapport with an informant before rushing into the interview. We have thus completed a full circle in selection procedures since we began, from the folk knowledge that quick, impersonal respondent selection was desirable, to attempts to lengthen the acquaintance process and improve the efficiency of the selection procedure through complete enumeration of the household.

3.5 RESPONSE–NONRESPONSE ANALYSIS OF THE SURVEYS

Judging from the previous comparisons of telephone and personal interview surveys, we expected that the telephone response rate would exceed that of the personal interview survey (Ibsen & Ballweg, 1974). Although most past work did not use random-digit dialing techniques, the evidence stimulated our interest in evaluating telephone surveys as a methodology to avoid the current low response rates in personal interview surveys.

Before we examine the response rates of the two modes, we must define what we mean by the term "response rate." In both modes we define the response rate to be the ratio of

$$\frac{\text{Number of completed interviews}}{\text{Total number of eligible sample units}}.$$

The numerator of the ratio is the number of completed interviews and excludes those interviews only partially completed (a considerable problem in telephone interviews). In the personal interview sample, the denominator includes all sample housing units containing an eligible respondent, whether or not an interview was obtained. It excludes housing units improperly listed, unoccupied, or occupied only by people less than 18 years old. In the telephone sample the denominator should include only those sample telephone numbers that were working household numbers.

Unfortunately, as we have seen in Chapter 2, some numbers ring without answer on every call and determining their actual status is difficult. Early in the interviewing period we called the local telephone business offices of these numbers in an attempt to determine their status. This effort was largely unsuccessful; office personnel refused "for security reasons" to tell us whether a number was working or not. Colleagues in other settings have been successful in obtaining this information when sampling a restricted geographical area, where time can be well spent in developing a relationship with the office and discovering which employees to call for this information. Because the status of unanswered numbers is ambiguous, we calculated two different response rates for the telephone survey, one including those numbers in the denominator, the other excluding them. Thus, we offer a range of the response rates that could have been achieved depending on how many of the unanswered numbers were really working numbers.

The response rate for the total telephone sample is presented in Table 3.7, and shows a range from 59–70%, depending on whether or not the unanswered numbers are included in the base. The comparable rate for the personal interview survey is 74.3%. Work on a later project found that 19 of 20 unanswered numbers that were each called over 12 times were nonworking numbers. This and other data would suggest that the telephone survey response rate is closer to 70% than to 59%, but even the higher figure is lower than that achieved in person.

TABLE 3.7
Response–Nonresponse Components for Total Telephone Sample[a]

Disposition	N	Results including unanswered numbers (%)	Results excluding unanswered numbers (%)
Complete interviews	1618	58.6	70.4
Partial interviews	116	4.2	5.0
Refusal by R[b]	203	7.4	8.8
Refusal by other HU[b] member	133	4.8	5.8
Noninterview (other)	208	7.5	9.0
R absent	21	.8	.9
Ring, no Answer	460	16.7	99.9
	2759	100.0	

[a] Table 3.8 has similar figures for the personal interview survey.
[b] R = respondent; HU = household.

There is also a difference between modes in components of the nonresponse rate; "break-offs," interviews prematurely terminated by the respondent, are a negligible problem in personal interviews but they characterize over 4.2% of the telephone sample cases. Break-offs in personal interviews are infrequent, probably because of the difficulties involved in asking the interviewer to leave the home—in contrast, it is much easier to hang up the telephone receiver. If all partial interviews had been completed, the response rates for the two modes would be similar.

The response rate on the telephone fell much below our expectations, and at first we blamed the poor performance on our lack of experience in "cold" telephone interviews. After this first project, we anticipated higher response rates as trial and error identified better techniques of initial contact with sample households, of maintaining the respondent's interest in the questioning, and of constructing telephone questionnaires. Some time has passed since the interviewing began on this project, and the achieved response rates for later national random-digit dialed surveys have rarely exceeded 70%, despite alterations in our training, monitoring, and administrative techniques. The low response rates of telephone and personal interview surveys demand formal examination, but analysis of the data from this project must be limited by the response rates obtained. Similar rates are likely to be achieved in replications of this project, and so our comparisons of the two modes are probably accurate characterizations of what others might find. The low response rates do prevent full identification of differences in the results solely attributable to the method of interview, as opposed to differential proportions or types of nonrespondents. For that reason and with the purpose of guiding further research, we will devote some further discussion in this chapter to the examination of respondents, nonrespondents, and response rates within different categories of sample elements.

The level of urbanization of an area has often been associated with achieved response rates in personal interview surveys, with population size inversely related to completion rates. The SRC national household sample stratifies areas into the 12 largest SMSAs, other SMSAs, and non-SMSAs, and this categorization provides a simple trichotomy related to level of urbanization. One of the two telephone samples in the project was clustered in the same primary areas as those of the personal interview sample, and therefore offers the best basis for comparison of response rates.

Table 3.8 compares the response–nonresponse components for that

TABLE 3.8
Response–Nonresponse Components for Clustered Telephone Sample and Personal Interview Survey, by PSU Type

	Percentage								
	Complete interviews	Partial interviews	Refusal by respondent	Refusal by other	Non-interview (other)	Respondent absent	Ring, no answer	Total	N
Telephone survey—including "Ring, no answers" in base									
Self-representing	62.7	4.0	8.8	6.0	13.1	1.1	4.3	100.0	351
Non-self-representing SMSAs	69.8	3.2	8.5	4.7	7.1	0	6.7	100.0	506
Non-self-representing non-SMSAs	41.3	3.3	6.1	3.1	4.8	.6	40.7	99.9	641
Total	55.9	3.4	7.5	4.3	7.5	.5	20.7	99.8	1498
Telephone survey—excluding "Ring, no answers" from base									
Self-representing	65.5	4.2	9.2	6.3	13.7	1.2		100.1	336
Non-self-representing SMSAs	74.8	3.4	9.1	5.1	7.6	0		100.0	472
Non-self-representing non-SMSAs	69.7	5.5	10.3	5.3	8.2	1.1		100.1	380
Total	70.5	4.3	9.5	5.5	9.5	.7		100.0	1188

TABLE 3.8 (*Continued*)

	Percentage						
	Complete interviews	Refusal by respondent	Refusal by other	Noninterview[a] (other)	No one contacted	Total	N
	Personal interview survey						
Self-representing	61.6	15.3	2.5	14.6	6.0	100.0	596
Non-self-representing SMSAs	78.2	10.8	1.7	7.0	2.3	100.0	872
Non-self-representing non-SMSAs	81.1	7.0	1.6	8.3	2.0	100.0	615
Total	74.3	10.9	1.9	9.6	3.3	100.0	2083

[a] Category includes: Refusal (R not determined), Noninterview (permanent condition), Noninterview (R determined, other), Noninterview (R not determined).

67

telephone sample and the personal interview sample. Three panels of results are presented, each containing a separate row for the sample in the 12 largest SMSAs (self-representing), primary areas which were SMSAs (nonself-representing), and the areas which are not SMSAs (nonself-representing). The first two panels list results for the multistage telephone sample, first including unanswered numbers as working household numbers, then deleting them. The third panel presents results for the personal interview survey, and we will discuss those first. Although the overall personal interview response rate is 74%, the largest metropolitan areas yield interviews in only 62% of the sample households. The rate in the smaller areas that are non-SMSAs is 81%. All categories of nonresponse are higher in the largest metropolitan areas—refusals, sample households where no contact was ever made, as well as noninterviews for other reasons. The differences in response rates produce a significant underrepresentation of urban households in personal interviews.

Response rates in the three types of primary areas vary in a different way for the clustered telephone sample. As with the personal interviews, the lowest response rates (63–66%) are achieved in the largest metropolitan areas, but the rates do not increase uniformly with decreasing urbanization. Instead, the highest response rates are achieved in the middle group, primary areas that are SMSAs, with 70–75% of the sample households yielding an interview. The least urban areas have relatively low response rates (41–70%).

The components of telephone nonresponse rates also have different patterns over the primary area types. First, as we noted earlier, the least urban areas suffer from the largest problems of "unanswered" numbers. If we classified them as working household numbers, they would form over 40% of the group. In contrast, the same table shows that unanswered numbers form only 4% of eligible numbers in the largest metropolitan areas. Hence, the response rate varies only from 63–66% in the largest areas but from 41–70% in the smallest areas, depending on whether the unanswered numbers are included in the base. This distribution itself suggests that the majority of these numbers are nonworking. It is unlikely that the least urban areas have dramatically higher not-at-home rates. Indeed, the opposite is more plausible. In discussing components of nonresponse, we prefer to use the rates excluding these numbers from the base.

Whereas in the personal interview survey all categories of nonresponse were higher in the largest metropolitan areas, in the telephone survey most categories of nonresponse are larger in the least urban areas. Some of the categories differ in their content; for example, partial interviews do not appear in the personal survey, but in the telephone survey are slightly more prevalent (5.5%) in the least urban areas than in the largest metropolitan places (4.2%). Telephone refusals by the respondent are also more prevalent in the small areas, but two other categories of noninterviews exhibit a different pattern. In both surveys the metropolitan areas have the largest proportion of cases where another household member refuses after a respondent has been selected and cases where refusals occur even before a respondent has been selected. These are the categories of nonresponse that occur most quickly after initial contact is made. These groups permit little exercise of the interviewers' persuasive skills: the immediate "hang-ups" when the interviewer describes the purpose of the call, the husband who says that his wife is not interested and refuses to permit direct contact with her, and also those respondents who refuse to reveal personal information over the telephone and view the questions used for respondent selection as too sensitive to answer.

To some extent, the table contains a meaningful pattern of nonresponse components; the longer the interaction occurring before the nonresponse, the greater the likelihood that the household was located in a nonmetropolitan area. Nonresponse that occurs immediately after initial contact is more prevalent in larger metropolitan areas. The problem of telephone nonresponse in metropolitan areas thus may center on the first few moments of interaction, when the interviewer introduces himself/herself and the research organization, reviews the research goals, and attempts to establish rapport with the household member answering the call. Improvement in these aspects of telephone interviewing would contribute significantly to rates of response.

Several other analyses offer insight into influences on nonresponse. Table 3.9 separates clustered telephone sample numbers into two groups, those in exchanges located completely within a primary area and those in exchanges located only partially in a primary area. Exchanges lying partially within a primary area generally serve more rural areas than those lying completely within it, and the higher proportion of unanswered numbers for these partial exchanges is consistent with a similar finding for rural primary areas. Furthermore, when we classify the "unanswered" numbers as nonworking, the response rate for the numbers in partial exchanges (72.8%) is greater than that within complete exchanges (69.6%). This result resembles

TABLE 3.9
Disposition and Response Rates for Clustered Sample Numbers by Whether Number's Exchange Is Located Partially in Primary Area

	Percentage					
	All categories		Working household numbers only			
			Including ring, no answers		Excluding ring, no answers	
Disposition	Numbers in partial exchanges	Numbers in complete exchanges	Numbers in partial exchanges	Numbers in complete exchanges	Numbers in partial exchanges	Numbers in complete exchanges
Complete interview	6.3	17.4	45.1	64.1	72.8	69.6
Partial interview	.2	1.3	1.7	4.7	2.8	5.1
Refusal by R	.8	2.4	5.7	9.0	9.1	9.7
Refusal by other	.5	1.4	3.3	5.1	5.3	5.6
Noninterview (other)	.8	2.4	5.5	8.8	8.9	9.6
R absent	.1	0.1	.6	.5	1.0	.5
Ring, no answer	5.3	2.1	38.1	7.9	—	—
Out of primary area	7.8	—	—	—	—	—
Nonresidential numbers[a]	3.3	7.6	—	—	—	—
Nonworking numbers	55.4	48.7	—	—	—	—
Double wrong connection	5.5	4.5	—	—	—	—
No result from dial	7.1	4.6	—	—	—	—
Fast busys	6.9	7.4	—	—	—	—
Total	100.0%	99.9%	100.0%	100.1%	99.9%	100.1%
N	4546	3164	636	860	394	792

[a] Includes two household numbers with no member 18 years or older.

the typical findings for personal interview surveys, with higher response rates for suburban and rural areas, and lower rates for central cities.

Another possible cause of the different response rates in partial exchanges is the fact that households in these areas were first asked, "We need to talk with people in certain counties. Would you tell me what county you live in?" If they answered with the name of a county included in the particular primary area, the interviewer continued; if not, he or she terminated the call. The addition of a county filter question may have helped to convince some respondents of the authenticity of our affiliation, that we were not selling on the telephone, and that procedures were specified for the interviewer to follow. This difference may have contributed to a higher response rate for the partial exchanges.

Another categorization of response rates may be useful for research workers planning local and state random-digit dialed surveys, and for those comparing our results from national surveys with surveys conducted more locally. Table 3.10 presents response rates for different WATS bands. As Figure 3.3 shows, our WATS bands form a rough categorization of numbers by their distance from the Ann Arbor office. From Ann Arbor, WATS band 0, the cheapest type of WATS line, permits calling only to the state of Michigan. WATS band 5, the most

TABLE 3.10
Response Rates for Total Telephone Sample by WATS Band[a]

	Percentage	
WATS band	Including ring, no answers	Excluding ring, no answers
0[b]	67.4	79.8
1	56.2	68.8
2	57.6	66.5
3	58.6	64.0
4	50.3	70.0
5	67.4	74.6

[a] Response rate:

$$\frac{\text{Number of Complete Interviews}}{\begin{array}{c}(\text{Number of Complete and Partial Interviews} + \text{Number of Refusals} + \\ \text{Number of R absent} + \text{Number of Ring without Answers})\end{array}}$$

[b] State of Michigan.

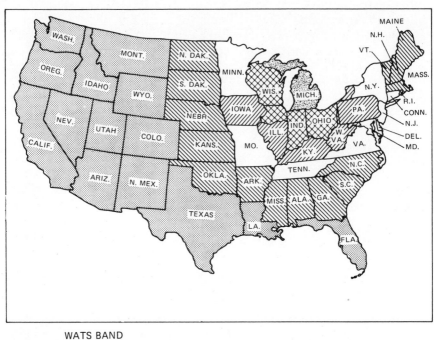

WATS BAND

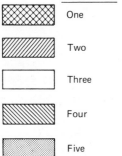

One

Two

Three

Four

Five

FIGURE 3.3. **WATS band areas for service originating in Ann Arbor, Michigan.**

expensive, allows calls to any point in coterminous United States. The rates presented in Table 3.10 include numbers for both telephone samples. For the state of Michigan, the maximum response rate is about 80%, the highest of all bands. This resembles the information obtained informally about the performance of statewide RDD surveys conducted by other organizations. Comparing the different values of Table 3.10, we find a curvilinear relationship of response rate with distance, with high rates both near and far from Ann Arbor. Two different influences may be producing this trend. For residents of Michigan, knowledge of and respect for the University of Michigan may heighten cooperation. In contrast, persons far from Ann Arbor may be impressed with a long distance call from Michigan and consider the purpose of the call more favorably.

We noted in Chapter 2 that we achieved the desired sample size for the telephone survey by creating small national samples of replicated design and calling as many of them as required. Our final investigation into response rate differences looks at the individual rates across the 9 different replicate groups of the 14 originally drawn. Figure 3.4 plots the minimum response rates (including unanswered numbers in the denominator). The replicate groups were distributed at different times during the interviewing period, in order of their replicate group number. The highest response rates were achieved for those replicate groups distributed in the middle of the interviewing period, after the interviewers had gained some experience with cold telephone inter-

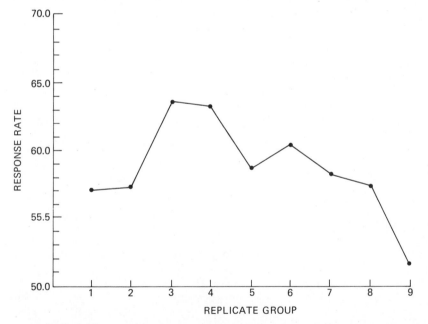

FIGURE 3.4. Response rates for individual replicate groups. Response rate = No. of interviews/No. of interviews + No. of refusals + No. of rings without answer + No. of R absent. Replicate groups were given to interviewers in order of replicate group number. Replicate group 9 cards were first called on May 13. The planned end of interviewing was May 23. Undisposed cards were followed up past that date; the last interview was taken on July 2.

views but before the pressure of the ending date of the survey period. This form of the response rate curve was unexpected; we anticipated a gradual increase in the rate over time. The especially low response rate in replicate group nine prompted us to examine some of the results separately by replicate group, and we report that analysis in Chapter 4. The differences across replicate groups provide a handy check on the effects of variation in nonresponse and we attempt to use the separate samples for this purpose.

3.6 SUMMARY

Differences between telephone and personal interview surveys are very great with respect to organization and administration, and the advantages lie heavily with the telephone procedure. A nationwide survey based on personal interviews with 1500 households is likely to involve hundreds of interviewers, as many as 20 supervisors, and several additional staff members performing functions of liaison and coordination. Training and supervision are necessarily decentralized, and contact with the central office is made by mail and telephone. By contrast, the interviewers for the telephone surveys were trained together in a single location, where they subsequently worked. Supervision was direct, with supervisory monitoring of some interviews, especially during the earlier stages of interviewing. Telephone interviewers were located in sound-absorbent carrels in a single large room and were thus able to exchange information with each other on an informal basis. Coding of telephone interviews began almost concurrently with interviewing, and thus provided very rapid feedback to interviewers regarding consistency, completeness of entries, and other indicators of quality.

The potential economies of RDD telephone surveys relative to those conducted by personal interviews are considerably reduced by the large proportion of randomly generated telephone numbers that are not actually connected to residences. More than one-half of all numbers generated in both the stratified and the clustered telephone samples were reported as nonworking by an operator or a recording, and many others were judged to be nonworking after repeated unanswered calls or fast busy signals. Some working numbers were, of course, found to be nonresidential; algorithms for generating random numbers do not distinguish homes from businesses. On average, about five numbers were called to locate one working household number.

Most nonworking numbers were disposed of in two calls; the first received a nonworking number recording and the second was made to check against the possibility of misdialing. Most working household numbers were disposed of in three calls, and about three-quarters of them were disposed of within five calls. Increments thereafter reduce gradually, but even at the 17th call some additions to the response rate were being made.

Completion rates per interview are somewhat higher for the personal interview survey than for the telephone. The median number of calls per interview was 2.2 for the telephone and 1.8 for the personal interview survey. Seventy-eight percent of the interviews obtained by telephone were completed within five calls; 91% of the personal interviews were completed within five calls. The greater efficiency of the personal interview in this respect is more than offset, of course, by the relatively low cost of callbacks by telephone.

In some surveys the sampling procedure is complete when contact has been made with any adult member of the chosen household; in other surveys a respondent must be selected within the household. Such selection within households was required for both telephone and personal interview surveys in this study, but different procedures were used for the two modes of interviewing. In the personal interview survey, the person with whom contact was first made in a household was asked to provide a complete listing of all household members. The interviewer then selected the respondent from this list by means of a selection table designed to approximate random choice.

In the telephone surveys we were reluctant to require a full listing of household members at the beginning of the interview and therefore developed a simpler procedure, in which the interviewer made the selection of the respondent after only two questions—one to determine the total number of adults in the household and a second to determine the number of those adults who were female. Subsequent analyses, however, showed this procedure to be underestimating household size and biasing the selection of respondents because of a tendency to omit young adults, especially sons and daughters 18–21 years of age. In other telephone studies we tried variations of the two-question procedure to correct for this underreporting, but without real success. We have now made the telephone procedures identical with those in personal interview surveys and require a complete listing of household members from the person who first answers the telephone. This procedure improves the selection of respondents within households and it appears not to reduce response rates.

Comparisons of response rates between telephone and personal interview surveys are complicated by some indeterminacies inherent in telephone procedures. Numbers that ring without answer in spite of many calls may be nonworking numbers or may be the working numbers of unusually elusive respondents. Local telephone companies can, of course, resolve such questions, but often refuse to do so on the grounds of protecting the privacy of subscribers. In the present study, response rates were 74% for personal interview survey and 70% for the corresponding (clustered) telephone survey (assuming the never-answered telephone numbers to be nonworking).

Contrary to expectations, the nonresponse rates were thus higher in the telephone than in the personal interview surveys. Partial interviews, in which the respondent terminated the conversation before completion, were also more frequent in the telephone survey—4% on the telephone as compared to a negligibly small proportion in personal interviews. The telephone completion rate of 70%, while less than we had predicted and less than we want, has remained stable over many subsequent surveys in which variations in training, supervisory monitoring of interviews, and other administrative procedures were introduced in attempts to increase response rates.

Patterns of nonresponse were somewhat different for telephone than for personal interview surveys. Completion rates for personal interviews were lowest in the largest metropolitan areas (62%), considerably higher in other standard metropolitan areas (78%), and highest in rural and nonmetropolitan areas (81%). The telephone survey showed its highest completion rate in non-self-representing SMSAs, and its lowest in the largest metropolitan areas, although the differences are not large.

These and other differences in the pattern of telephone response rates appear to result from the interplay of many factors. These factors include positive acquaintance with the University of Michigan among people in nearby areas, the persuasive effect of long-distance telephone calls on people most distant from caller, the growing experience of the telephone interviewers during the course of the study, and the pressure of time as the deadline date for completion approached.

Chapter 4

Response Differences between the
Two Modes of Data Collection

It is easy to describe an ideal comparison of the telephone and personal interview as modes of data collection for survey research—identical questions, broadly representative of the universe of survey measures and balanced in their appropriateness to the two modes; identical or identically qualified interviewers; equivalent training and experience; identical and well-designed population samples; respondents unaffected by previous exposure to one or the other mode of interview; complete fulfillment of sample design—and so on down the list of which researchers' dreams (and textbooks) are made.

Reality, of course, is different. One set of interviewers, the permanent field staff of the Survey Research Center, conducted the personal interviewing; another and relatively new staff conducted the telephone interviewing (Chapter 2). The telephone sample design included several independent replicates or random subsamples that were given to interviewers at successive times during the interviewing period; we use these replicate subsamples to investigate time effects on response patterns in the telephone survey data that may reflect interviewer learning or fatigue.

Both surveys are subject to the large nonresponse rates that plague much of current survey research (Chapter 3). Moreover, response rates were very different for the large metropolitan areas and the smaller areas and differently distributed for the two survey modes. Gross differences in method effects might be related to types of nonresponse in the different areas. To put it more broadly, the method effects we measure are really differences between *respondents* to the two surveys; they may arise merely from differences between the types of people who grant interviews in the two different modes. Moreover, comparisons of different variables as reported in the two survey modes have different meanings; some variables are subject to larger sampling and interviewer variance than others.

Finally, not all households in the United States have telephones and thus a telephone survey cannot represent some parts of the household population. To a smaller degree, not all households are covered by personal interview surveys (Chapter 6). Using telephone survey data for inference to the entire household population is biased to the extent that the population not covered has different values on the characteristics of interest. To eliminate that source of differences in response patterns, this discussion will compare telephone survey results with personal interview results for respondents in households with telephones.

In short, the analyses that follow report differences in results obtained by two "bundles" of survey methods—telephone and personal interview. The telephone bundle of methods was applied to two independent national samples, one selected with maximum dispersion to take full advantage of the telephone technology, the other selected within the sample areas of the personal interview survey in order to investigate the sampling precision of alternative designs. Even so, our comparison does not empirically estimate the net effect of mode of data collection on the quality of survey data. For two questions in the data set we *do* have independent population data that permit some estimate of the bias in survey estimates, but even in these cases we are prevented from labeling any differences as method effects alone because of possible nonresponse and interviewer effects. The differences that we do observe, however, should be useful for other researchers evaluating study designs that could utilize either telephone or personal interviews for data collection. In that view these data may be most helpful to those comparing centralized telephone interviewing of national samples with dispersed personal interviewing of household samples. Obviously, the comparisons will also be more useful for those asking questions similar to those we asked in the survey, in interviews of similar length, and subject to the same response and nonresponse characteristics.

4.1 PREPARING FOR METHODOLOGICAL COMPARISONS

The Omnibus Surveys of the Survey Research Center combine separate question sets from several researchers into a single interview schedule. This format allows participants to collect data on the national household population even though they may lack the funds for an independent national sample or may be using a set of measures too small to justify an independent national study. In the Omnibus Surveys, personal interviews are conducted with approximately 1500 adults, 18 years or older, selected from an areal probability sample of households in the coterminous United States.

The flexibility of this structure permits supplementation of the Omnibus interview schedule with measures that are thought to be differentially susceptible to telephone and personal interview effects. The project we have been describing purchased 17 minutes of the approximate hour-long interview schedule of the 1976 Spring Omnibus. To illustrate the context of the various questions we analyze later, we present the other sections in the Spring Omnibus below:

Section A

This section contains economic questions asked every quarter. They ask respondents to view their own economic situation in comparison to what it was last year and to report their expectations about the next 12 months. There are parallel questions about the economy of the country as a whole.

Time: 11.7 minutes in personal interview.

Sections D, F

These sections contain a standard set of demographic questions.

Time: 9.7 minutes in personal interview.

Section J

This is a group of questions on plans for and attitudes toward retirement and on satisfaction with retirement among people already retired. Some measures examined the respondent's awareness and evaluation of the "trade off" between earlier retirement and larger retirement income.

Time: 4.4 minutes in personal interview.

Section K

This group of questions asks respondents about their cars and other vehicles currently owned and about future purchase plans.

Time: 8.2 minutes in personal interview.

Within these sets of questions were a variety of measurement types—closed-ended and open-ended questions, attitudinal and factual items, abstract and concrete issues. The variation in subject content, however, appeared to be insufficient to gain insight into method differences on the many types of items asked by social science surveys. In order to introduce particular types of questions into the Omnibus interview schedule, we added another group of questions. In addition we dropped Sections J and K from the telephone questionnaire in order to reduce its length.

The criteria used for selection of items into the supplement included

1. Previous use in a personal or telephone survey; the more uses the better.
2. Representativeness of different types of questions commonly used in surveys.
   —closed-ended, open-ended questions
   —factual items, attitudinal items
   —short and long wordings
   —check lists
   —lists of items using the same response scale
   —adaptations of questions using response cards in personal interviews
   —items thought to be sensitive to some respondents
   —questions requiring factual recall
3. Lack of overlap with subjects already included in the Omnibus questionnaire.

Based on these criteria we added questions on life satisfaction, attitudes toward political issues, racial attitudes, reports on voting intentions and on filing tax returns. (See Section B of the telephone survey questionnaire reprinted in Appendix I.) In addition to a mix of factual and attitudinal questions, experimental variations in question format were introduced to measure sensitivity of method to wording changes. For example, random half-samples were assigned different versions of several questions on life satisfaction, one using a seven-point scale with all seven points labeled from "Terrible" to "Delighted." The other half-sample was asked to respond to the same questions in terms of a seven-point scale with three labeled points from "Completely Dissatisfied" to "Completely Satisfied."

Each of these scales was presented to the personal interview respondents on response cards (Figure 4.1). Since the presentation of visual stimuli is impossible on the telephone, we were particularly interested in the adaptations of such questions for the telephone. The seven-point "Delighted–Terrible" scale was altered to produce an "unfolding" measure. The following introduction was given:

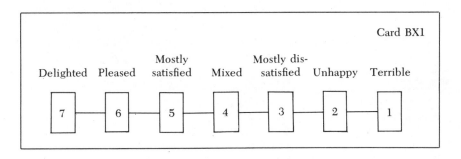

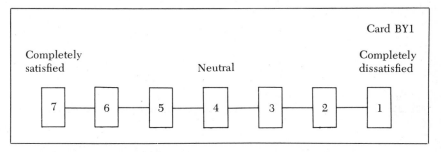

FIGURE 4.1 **Examples of response cards.**

The next questions ask how you feel about different parts of your life. Please take
into account the last year and what you expect in the near future. Of course, if you
don't have any feelings on a question, tell me. If your feelings are on the good side,
I'll ask you whether you feel *"delighted," "pleased,"* or just *"mostly satisfied."* If
they are on the bad side, I'll ask whether you feel *"terrible," "unhappy,"* or just
"mostly dissatisfied." Let's start with one about your housing: How do you feel
about your house or apartment? *Good, bad,* or *mixed?*

For each item the respondent was asked a similar question. In this
way the respondent was prompted for a more specific response after
replying in terms of three general categories. The properties of this
adaptation that may affect the responses are (*a*) the introduction of two
new words, "Good" and "Bad," in the respondent's first estimate of
his or her feelings; these are different from the labeled stimuli on the
seven-point show card; (*b*) the absence of a follow-up question for a
"Mixed" response; and (*c*) the repetition of the initial and follow-up
question over several items, with potential respondent fatigue effects.
Another response card question, this one in the economic section, was
also adapted for telephone by "unfolding" the responses (Question
A10, Appendix I).

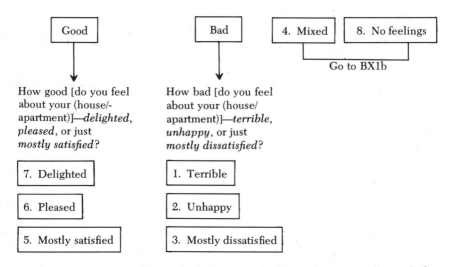

The seven-point "Satisfied–Dissatisfied" scale was adapted for telephone use in a different way, beginning with the following introduction:

> The next questions ask how you feel about different parts of your life. Please take into account the last year and what you expect in the near future. Of course, if you don't have any feelings on a question, tell me.
>
> I'll give you a number from one to seven that describes how you feel— "one" stands for "completely dissatisfied," and "seven" for "completely satisfied." If you are neutral, answer "four." So the low numbers indicate you are dissatisfied; the high numbers, you are satisfied.

The respondent was thus required to understand and recall the continuum underlying the scale and to reply in numbers from 1 to 7. This format uses a single question where the "unfolding" format uses two. Another response card question in the personal interview utilized a thermometer scale from 0–100° to measure how the respondent felt about various political figures. This was adapted for the telephone in much the same fashion as the "Satisfied–Dissatisfied" scale.

Personal and family income are viewed by some respondents as sensitive information, and direct questions about income typically have the largest missing data rates in survey research. In many personal interview surveys, therefore, a card containing income categories is shown to the respondent (Figure 4.2), who is then asked to identify the appropriate category for his or her income. Locander and Burton (1976) have examined several ways of asking income on the telephone and prefer a measure that uses a series of questions, which would look something like the following example:

Was your approximate total family income in 1976 before taxes 15,000 dollars or more, or was it less than 15,000 dollars?

15,000 dollars or more		less than 15,000 dollars

Was it 20,000 dollars or more or was it less than 20,000?

Was it 12,000 dollars or more or was it less than 12,000?

20,000 dollars or more	less than 20,000 dollars	12,000 dollars or more	less than 12,000 dollars

Was it 25,000 dollars or more or was it less than 25,000?

Was it 8,000 dollars or more or was it less than 8,000?

25,000 dollars or more	less than 25,000 dollars	8000 dollars or more	less than 8000 dollars

Was it 35,000 dollars or more or was it less than 35,000?

Was it 5000 dollars or more or was it less than 5000?

35,000 dollars or more	less than 35,000 dollars	5000 dollars or more	less than 5000 dollars

A. Under $2000
B. $2000–$2999
C. $3000–$3999
D. $4000–$4999
E. $5000–$5999
F. $6000–$7499
G. $7500–$8999
H. $9000–$9999
J. $10,000–$10,999
K. $11,000–$12,499
L. $12,500–$14,999
M. $15,000–$17,499
N. $17,500–$19,999
P. $20,000–$22,499
Q. $22,500–$24,999
R. $25,000–$29,999
S. $30,000–$34,999
T. $35,000 and over
X. Didn't work in 1975

FIGURE 4.2. Card F18.

This format requires respondents to answer two, three, or four questions, depending on the amount of their total income. Parallel questions would be required for each income component to be estimated separately in the study. Since three income estimates are asked of most respondents in SRC surveys, we were interested in telephone measures requiring fewer questions for each income component. We therefore decided on the following contingent combination of specific and categorical income questions:

Finally, how much income did *you (and your family living here)* receive in 1975, not just from wages *but from all sources*, before taxes and other deductions were made? (Just tell me the figure to the nearest thousand dollars.)

_____ dollars

(Ask only if R refuses to give dollar figure)

F19a.   We don't need the exact dollar figure; could you tell me which of these three broad categories it falls in?

1. Less than 7500 dollars	2. Between 7500 and 15,000	3. More than 15,000?

The reasoning in support of this version of the income questions begins with the fact that most people are willing to give their income in direct, dollar-specific terms; they do not insist on categories. In order to minimize the length of the question sequence for that majority, therefore, we began by asking simply for their total income. If the respondent hesitated either because of lack of knowledge or reluctance to reveal an exact income figure, the interviewer reduced the difficulty and threat of the task by asking the respondent to choose one of three broad income categories. It was our hope that those hesitating on the first question would answer the second and that the missing data rate for the resulting trichotomous measure would be much lower than that for alternative approaches.

In later work we used an unfolding procedure, like that suggested by Locander and Burton (1976), both in a telephone survey and in a companion personal interview survey. Personal interviewers familiar with the response card method found the unfolding method easier to administer. We found that the proportion of missing data in the telephone interviews was higher than that in the personal interviews, but the discrepancy was smaller than that experienced with the methods used in the first study.

4.2 AN OVERVIEW OF RESPONSE DIFFERENCES BETWEEN MODES

There are several ways of evaluating response differences between sets of survey data. In the present case, for example, one can begin by looking at the gross differences between the marginal or univariate data obtained by personal interview and those obtained by telephone, as we have done for demographic characteristics. Since more than 200 measures were obtained in common to both modes, these comparative data are presented as appendix material. Appendix II displays them in full, for respondents interviewed by telephone and for those interviewed in person. To facilitate comparison between the two modes, responses obtained by personal interview are shown separately for households with telephones and for those without telephones.

On inspection, few of the differences between modes are large. We can, of course, use statistical criteria for making such judgments about differences between modes. An approximate standard error of the difference between telephone survey results and the personal interview survey results for those living in telephone households is estimated as follows:

Standard error of difference of proportions between telephone survey and phone households of personal interview survey

$$= \left(\frac{(1.05)^2\,.25}{800} + \frac{(1.19)^2\,.25}{865} + \frac{(1.24)^2\,.25}{1618} \right)^{1/2} = .03149.$$

This assumes that the proportion estimated in each survey has the value .5, and that the average design effects estimated in Chapter 6 apply to the variables at hand. The value slightly overestimates the actual standard error because it ignores a covariance term between the clustered telephone sample and the personal interview sample. Using a confidence interval of 95% would require differences between the telephone and personal interview results of 6.3% or more for statistical significance. Very few of the differences in the Appendix II tables are this large. Such comparisons can be refined by controlling for differences between the two respondent groups. One such control—possession of a telephone—is included in the appendix tables, and others are described in later sections of this chapter.

A different and broader approach to the analysis of differences over many measures does not require that each difference meet the standards of statistical significance. Rather, it looks for trends in the data that by their consistency across different situations and question-naire items suggest that later studies are likely to experience the same results. We will employ this strategy often in this chapter to identify possible effects of interview mode.

We devote this chapter to an examination of response differences across different variables and various types of measures. There are several results of our comparisons, however, that are related to the interaction of interviewer and respondent on the telephone: (a) greater amount of missing data in the telephone survey; (b) lack of expressed enjoyment of the interview by telephone respondents; and (c) greater optimism expressed on some items by telephone respondents.

One of the most visible of such trends in the Appendix II tables is the larger proportion of missing data in the telephone surveys, that is, entries of "not ascertained" for specific questions. Part of the missing data is associated with telephone interviews that were terminated by the respondent before completion; incomplete interviews occur more often in the telephone mode. We have separated these from the other sources of missing data in the appendix tables.

We did not anticipate the larger missing data rate in telephone interviews and hesitate to insist on its generality. We can, however, compare the missing data rate on this project with those of later surveys, at least for some items. Questions about economic attitudes were repeated in later telephone surveys with randomly generated sample numbers. Table 4.1 presents the proportion of respondents with response codes of "not ascertained" on 12 different economic questions, as obtained in four surveys—one personal interview and three telephone. Interviews broken off before the given question was asked are excluded from these calculations. In general, the percentage of this type of missing data is larger in all three telephone surveys, but the problem is largest in the data obtained by this project (Spring). For these 12 questions, the personal interview data have the lowest aver-age percentage of missing data (1.4%), and the first telephone survey has the largest (2.7%). The subsequent telephone surveys gradually reduce this percentage to a value very similar to that of the personal interview survey.

This reduction of missing data over time suggests that our experi-ence with centralized telephone interviewing might lead to fewer nonsubstantive responses. We cannot say with certainty that a de-crease in the missing data rate reduces overall response error, because the substantive responses given by those that would have produced missing data may create even larger errors in estimates. Factors that

TABLE 4.1
Percentage of Respondent Cases with "Not Ascertained" Codes on 12 Economic Attitude Measures for the Personal Interview Survey and Three Telephone Surveys[a]

Variable number	Description	Personal (phone households) (%)	Telephone surveys		
			Spring (%)	Summer (%)	Fall (%)
13002	Better/worse off financially than 1 year ago	.1	.6	.6	.6
13006	Better/worse off financially than 3 years ago	.8	.9	.4	1.3
13007	Better/worse off financially in 1 year	.5	1.0	.1	.7
13008	Good/bad business conditions next 12 months	1.1	6.7	5.7	3.1
13009	Business better/worse now than 1 year ago	1.0	6.2	3.8	3.4
13013	Business better/worse in 1 year	.7	2.4	1.8	1.2
13015	Good/bad time to buy a house	1.5	2.3	2.1	0
13019	Good/bad time to buy a car	2.5	2.9	2.9	1.2
13025	When buy a new car	.9	1.4	4.1	2.8
13026	How long before buy new car	4.2	3.7	1.8	.8
13027	Buy a new or used car	.2	.6	1.5	2.0
13028	Good/bad time to buy household durables	3.4	4.1	4.6	1.0
	Mean over 12 variables	1.4	2.7	2.5	1.5

[a] Data weighted by reciprocal of selection probability.

may have created this reduction in missing data in later surveys are more efficient interviewer training prior to the study period, increased monitoring of interviews, objective coding of interviewer performance by the monitor, and immediate feedback to the interviewer about desirable adjustments of behavior.

The second general finding of the mode comparisons is the sensitivity of questions using response cards to the labeling of points on scales and to the adaptation of these questions used in the telephone survey. The distribution of responses from the personal interview and the telephone interview were affected by the response categories explicitly offered the respondent on a show card or verbally presented by the telephone interviewer, the order in which responses were offered (in those cases where more specific categories were sought after the initial response on the telephone), and the possible differences between reading a response on a card and hearing it spoken by a telephone interviewer. (These differences are analyzed more fully in Section 5.1.)

Our third general observation is that respondent reactions to the interview mode show two main tendencies—some tendency to prefer the mode one has experienced but also a tendency to prefer the personal interview to the telephone. Table 4.2 presents the responses

TABLE 4.2
Preference for Questioning Mode, Respondents in Phone Households by Interview Type[a]

		Personal interviews in phone households (%)		Telephone interviews in phone households (%)
Preference				
Face-to-face interview		78.4		22.7
Telephone interview		1.7		39.4
Mailed questionnaire		16.9		28.1
Mixed opinion		1.5		1.8
Don't know		1.5		8.0
Total		100.0		100.0
Missing data		14		69
Total *N*		1437		1696
Reason for choice				
Reasons for face-to-face		47.3		23.2
More personal, like to see person I'm dealing with	17.6		11.6	
Can give better answers	10.7		5.2	
Reasons against face-to-face		.7		6.9
R[b] rarely home, may be busy	.4		2.5	
R may not let stranger in HU[c]	.1		1.8	
Some interviewers are pushy, R wouldn't feel comfortable	.2		1.1	
Reasons for telephone interview		1.0		24.3
Easier, quicker to do	0		10.6	
Doesn't require visit by interviewer	.3		3.2	
Reasons against telephone interview		20.0		2.8
Don't know who you are talking to	6.8		1.0	
Don't like to talk on phone	6.0		.7	

(Continued)

TABLE 4.2 (*Continued*)

		Personal interviews in phone households (%)		Telephone interviews in phone households (%)
Reasons for mailed questionnaire		15.8		27.8
Gives you more time to think about questions	7.6		17.8	
Can fill out at your conven- ience	5.9		6.9	
Reasons against mailed questionnaire		14.5		12.9
Wouldn't fill it out	12.4		10.9	
Get too much junk mail	.8		.4	
Other		.6		2.1
Total		99.9		100.0
Missing data		26		34
Total *N*		1400		1694

[a] Data weighted by reciprocal of selection probability.
[b] R = respondent.
[c] HU = household.

to a question about how the respondent might prefer to answer the questions in the survey, in person (face-to-face), on the telephone, or by mail. The question was asked with the same wording in telephone and personal interviews. The top portion of the table shows that a large percentage of personal interview respondents expressed a preference for the mode they were experiencing (78.4%), but that a much smaller percentage of telephone respondents favored the telephone mode (39.4%). At least three interpretations of these differences seem plausible:

1. The satisfactions of the respondent role may differ by mode; telephone respondents may enjoy the experience less than personal interview respondents enjoy a personal interview.

2. The willingness of the respondents to reveal that they prefer another mode may differ in the telephone and personal interview surveys. For example, the physical presence of the interviewers may make respondents more reticent to reveal that they prefer another mode.

3. The commitment of respondents who agree to be interviewed at all may differ by mode. For example, only those preferring personal interviews may consent to them; because the telephone interview requires less intrusion into their homes, respondents who are less enthusiastic might nevertheless grant the interview.

Indeed all of these influences and others may combine to create the results shown in Table 4.2. For whatever reason, however, telephone survey respondents are much more likely to report preferences for personal or mailed questionnaires than respondents in the personal interview survey are to choose another mode. We asked respondents directly why they made their particular choice of mode; their reasons are summarized in the lower section of Table 4.2. The reason given most often by personal interview respondents involved positive feeling about the face-to-face interview (47.3%). Telephone respondents were more likely to mention the undemanding nature of the telephone interview mode. Feelings about mailed questionnaires were more divided, with telephone respondents more likely to cite reasons for preferring the mail mode.

The single reason most frequently mentioned by personal interview respondents in support of any preference favored personal interviews and involved the enjoyment of seeing the person who was asking the questions and of the personal contact that is part of the interview. Telephone respondents most often praised mailed questionnaires because they allowed more time to think about the questions. These reported preferences for different data collection modes, along with a self-reported tendency among telephone respondents to feel more uneasy about discussing some sensitive topics, suggest that feelings of respondents about the interviewing experience as a whole may depend on the mode used.

Finally, careful readers of the appendix tables will note some tendency toward greater optimism among telephone respondents compared to personal interview respondents. This is evident for some economic attitudes (V13006, V13008 in Appendix II) and for some of the life satisfaction items (V11039–V11044, V11050–V11055). Some of these variables show differences that achieve statistical significance, but most are below that level. Initially we thought that this tendency toward greater expressed optimism might be characteristic of the telephone mode of data collection, but later surveys suggest that this may not be the case.

Questions on economic attitudes are asked quarterly of household samples. For the two quarters following the present (Spring 1976) administration, part of the Survey Research Center sample used households newly drawn by random-digit dialing and part consisted of telephone reinterviews of respondents who originally had been interviewed in person. Several years of such experience has suggested negligible method effects for telephone reinterviews of respondents originally contacted in person. In these later comparisons the newly contacted telephone respondents do not appear to be more optimistic than those being reinterviewed. With such evidence we caution against believing the greater reported optimism by telephone respondents in this data set.

The simplest, most succinct characterization of observed method effects in this project is that they appear to be small for most statistics. Some exceptions to this rule are investigated in the later sections of this chapter, and most of that analysis results from searching for differences across question types or among certain types of respondents. It is clear that discrepancies between the survey modes that *may* exist are not so large that we should question the use of either mode in general. Future methodological investigations should choose more specific types of measures or respondent subpopulations to investigate, attempting to discover areas where these general conclusions do not apply. Only with more detailed analysis can future researchers be guided to proper matching of data collection methodologies to desired limits on survey error.

After noting these general conclusions from comparing telephone and personal interview survey data, we spend the remainder of this chapter in a more detailed search for differences. Section 4.3 checks on whether or not the two survey modes yield different distributions on basic demographic characteristics of respondents. Section 4.4 presents an examination of respondent reaction to certain sensitive items in both questionnaires. In the final three sections of the chapter we compare subsets of the respondents, searching for different reactions to mode of interview. In Section 4.5 we look at responses on the telephone survey by groups that were interviewed at different times and that have different response rates. In Sections 4.6 and 4.7 we check the effect of mode differences by level of urbanization of the respondents' residence and various demographic characteristics of respondents.

4.3 CHARACTERISTICS OF THE RESPONDENTS

Let us begin the study of response difference between modes by looking at the demographic characteristics of the respondents selected by the two multistage procedures—telephone and personal interview. Tables 4.3–4.8 on the following pages present weighted distributions for six demographic characteristics: age, sex, race, education, occupation, and income. We choose these measures because they provide basic descriptions of respondents and because they are "factual" items alleged to be less susceptible to measurement error than measures of attitudes, beliefs, and the like.

Table 4.3 compares the weighted age distribution of respondents in both modes, with separate figures for personal interviews in telephone households and in nonphone households. There are substantial differences in the age distribution of the two modes. Comparing respondents in telephone households (Columns b and c) in order to focus on the same population, we see that the telephone respondents are decidedly younger than those interviewed in person. More of the telephone respondents than personal interview respondents (68–53%)

TABLE 4.3
Age of Respondent by Sample Type Using Weighted Data[a]

Respondent category (a)	Phone (%) (b)	Households with phone (%) (c)	Households with no phone (%) (d)	Total Personal (%) (e)
		Personal		
18–24	16.2	15.1	31.5	16.0
25–29	14.0	12.0	15.2	12.2
30–34	10.3	9.5	11.2	9.6
35–39	10.3	8.2	6.7	8.1
40–44	9.4	7.5	7.9	7.5
45–49	7.9	9.5	5.6	9.2
50–54	7.8	7.8	5.6	7.7
55–59	7.2	7.7	5.6	7.5
60–64	6.1	6.8	6.7	6.8
65–69	4.7	6.0	2.2	5.7
70–74	3.2	4.9	.6	4.7
75–79	1.4	2.6	.6	2.5
80–84	.9	1.4	0	1.3
85–89	.5	.8	.6	.8
90–94	0	.2	0	.2
95 or more	0	.1	0	.1
Total				
%	99.9	100.1	100.0	99.9
Unweighted N	1575	1421	106	1527
Missing data				
Terminated	103			
Other	56	18	3	21

[a] Data weighted by reciprocal of selection probability.

are less than 45 years old. From our sampling error calculations (Section 6.3), we estimate that a confidence interval of two standard errors on either side of a sample estimate of the difference between modes would be a little less than six percentage points for this variable. Thus the difference observed in the age distributions is statistically significant. If we employ the entire personal interview sample for purposes of this comparison, the percentage difference between the two modes (Columns b and e) declines somewhat because of the large proportion of young adult households without telephones (Column d).

Race of the respondent is usually observed by personal interviewer and not asked of the respondent; in the telephone interview we asked "Would you mind telling me your race? (Are you White, Black, . . .)." The differences between the recorded racial distribution of respondents in the two modes never exceed one full percentage point in any category (Table 4.4, Columns b and c). Similarly small differences exist between modes on the sex distribution of respondents. Males form a slightly larger proportion of telephone survey respondents than of personal interview respondents (Table 4.5). This may reflect greater

TABLE 4.4
Race of Respondent by Sample Using Weighted Data[a]

| | | Personal | | |
Respondent category	Phone (%)	Households with phone (%)	Households with no phone (%)	Total personal (%)
White	87.1	86.7	68.5	85.6
Black	9.3	9.7	24.5	10.6
Chicano; Puerto-Rican; Mexican or Spanish-American	2.3	2.6	7.1	2.8
American Indian	.2	.1	0	.1
Oriental	.5	.8	0	.7
Mixed	.3	0	0	0
Other	.3	.2	0	.2
Total				
%	100.0	100.1	100.1	100.0
Unweighted N	1600	1436	109	1545
Missing data				
Terminated	103			
Other	31	3	0	3

[a] Data weighted by reciprocal of selection probability.

TABLE 4.5
Sex of Respondent by Sample Type Using Weighted Data[a]

		Personal		
Respondent category	Phone (%)	Households with phone (%)	Households with no phone (%)	Total personal (%)
Male	46.8	43.5	45.0	43.7
Female	53.2	56.5	55.0	56.3
Total				
%	100.0	100.0	100.0	100.0
Unweighted N	1625	1439	109	1548
Missing data				
Terminated	101			
Other	8	0	0	0

[a] Data weighted by reciprocal of selection probability.

scheduling flexibility in the telephone surveys, so that men are more likely to be found at home and interviewed in a telephone survey.

Smaller proportions of grade school educated respondents appear in the telephone survey (Table 4.6) than in the personal interview data. When categories are collapsed, there appear to be tendencies for those with more education to grant telephone interviews relative to those with less education. Two other possibilities, however, are consistent with the data: There may be a tendency to miss higher educated groups in personal interview surveys, and there may be differential overreporting of educational attainment in the two modes.

Other indicators of socioeconomic status, respondent's occupation and total family income, further delineate differences between modes. In the occupational table (Table 4.7) the proportion of "housewives—not currently working" is larger as estimated by personal interview than by telephone. This is consistent with the somewhat lower overall proportion of female respondents on the telephone, as noted earlier. Other differences show larger proportions of professionals and skilled workers in telephone surveys. The occupational distributions, however, do not show clear, smaller representation of lower status groups in the telephone mode, as did the educational distributions.

Differences in total family income distribution across the two modes (Table 4.8) resemble those for the educational level of respon-

TABLE 4.6
Education Summary of Respondent by Sample Type Using Weighted Data[a]

		Personal		
Respondent category	Phone (%)	Households with phone (%)	Households with no phone (%)	Total personal (%)
8 grades or less	8.2	12.7	34.1	14.0
8 grades or less, plus nonacademic training	1.3	1.7	1.1	1.6
9–11 grades, no diploma	10.7	11.5	21.8	12.1
9–11 grades, no diploma, plus nonacademic training	3.5	3.6	5.0	3.7
High school diploma	21.6	21.6	17.9	21.4
High school diploma, plus nonacademic training	14.1	12.9	10.6	12.8
Some college— 6 months–3 years	22.3	19.5	6.1	18.7
Junior or community college	1.6	1.9	2.2	1.9
B.A. level degrees	11.9	10.7	.6	10.1
Advanced degree, including LL.B	4.9	3.9	.6	3.7
Don't know	0	0	0	0
Total				
%	100.1	100.0	100.0	100.0
Unweighted N	1607	1431	107	1538
Missing data				
Terminated	103			
Other	24	8	2	10

[a] Data weighted by reciprocal of selection probability.

dents. There are larger proportions of respondents in households earning more than $15,000 in the telephone survey (50.1%) than in the personal interview survey (45.2%). As with some of the other demographic measures, there is the possibility that some of this difference arises from differential response error. Personal interview respondents chose the letter of an income category on a response card; respondents on the telephone either reported their income in a dollar figure or, if reluctant to do so, chose one of the three categories in Table 4.8. Requesting a dollar figure may produce overreporting rela-

TABLE 4.7
Occupation Summary of Respondent by Sample Type Using Weighted Data[a]

		Personal		
			Households	
		Households	with no	Total
Respondent	Phone	with phone	phone	personal
category	(%)	(%)	(%)	(%)
Professional, technical,				
and kindred workers	12.6	9.9	1.1	9.3
Managers, officials, and				
proprietors (except				
farm)	7.1	7.0	0	6.5
Clerical and kindred				
workers	12.0	10.1	1.7	9.6
Sales workers	4.2	4.5	2.2	4.3
Craftsmen, foremen, and				
kindred workers	9.8	8.0	7.7	8.0
Operatives and kindred				
workers	7.3	7.3	19.9	8.0
Laborers	2.2	1.6	5.5	1.8
Service workers	7.5	9.2	12.7	9.4
Farmers and farm				
managers	1.7	.9	2.2	1.0
Students—not currently				
working	2.1	3.7	0	3.5
Housewives—not currently				
working	16.4	21.4	19.3	21.3
No occupation	0	0	0	0
INAP., Temporarily laid				
off, looking for work,				
retired	17.1	16.5	27.6	17.2
Total				
%	100.0	100.1	99.9	99.9
Unweighted N	1632	1435	107	1542
Missing data				
Terminated	91			
Other	11	4	2	6

[a] Data weighted by reciprocal of selection probability.

tive to category selection. Alternatively, telephone surveys may be more successful in obtaining interviews with higher income respondents than are personal interview surveys.

In short, the demographic characteristics of the two samples present no major surprises. Households without telephones differ in predictable and income-related ways from those with telephones. Demo-

TABLE 4.8
Respondent's Total Family Income by Sample Type Using Weighted Data[a]

| | | Personal | | |
| | | Households with phone (%) | Households with no phone (%) | |
Respondent category	Phone (%)			Total personal (%)
Less than $7500	19.6	23.5	69.5	26.5
$7500–$15,000	30.3	31.3	21.6	30.6
More than $15,000	50.1	45.2	9.0	42.9
Total				
%	100.0	100.0	100.1	100.0
Unweighted N	1365	1247	101	1348
Missing data				
Terminated	112			
Other	257	192	8	200

[a] Data weighted by reciprocal of selection probability.

graphic differences between the two modes of data collection for equivalent samples (households with telephones) are not large. The pattern of such differences, however, suggests several possibilities for further investigation, including the differential availability of older and younger respondents to be interviewed in person or by telephone, and the tendency for higher income groups to form larger proportions of telephone respondents. It is plausible to regard the obtained differences in demographic distributions as differences in nonresponse rather than response. Let us turn to comparisons that are more specifically response-related.

4.4 REACTIONS OF THE RESPONDENT TO THE INTERVIEW

A further measure of respondents' reactions to the interview was introduced at the end of the questionnaire. People were asked if they felt uneasy about discussing several of the topics in the interview. The topics included income, racial attitudes, income tax returns, health, jobs, voting behavior, and political opinions. Table 4.9 presents the proportion of respondents who admitted that they felt uneasy about discussing each of these topics for the two interview modes. Larger proportions of telephone respondents said they felt uneasy about each

TABLE 4.9

Percentage of Respondents Who Reported Feeling Uneasy about Discussing Specific Topics by Mode of Interview[a]

	Percentage	
Topic	Telephone	Personal interview (phone households)
Income	27.9	15.3
Racial attitudes	9.2	8.8
Income tax return	14.1	8.6
Health	3.0	1.6
Job	3.1	1.9
Voting behavior	9.1	8.0
Political opinions	12.1	8.5

[a] Data weighted by reciprocals of selection probabilities.

of the topics mentioned; the largest differences appear for questions about financial status and political opinions. Over one-quarter of the telephone respondents (27.9%) admitted feeling uncomfortable about answering questions regarding their income, and this report is consistent with the higher missing data rates for income in the telephone data set.

These attitudinal measures gauging the respondent's reaction to the interview can be compared with the observations of respondent behavior that reveal discomfort with the interview. Refusal to answer questions concerning financial matters is one example of such action. Table 4.10 presents the percentages of respondents who refused to answer, replied "don't know," or failed to give any response to questions about the amount of income or tax refunds received in the past year. The three income questions used in the survey (spouse's, personal, and total family income) were first asked using an open-ended format, and if the respondent was reluctant to answer, a simpler trichotomous response format was used. In the personal interview, a response card was used. The table shows that the proportion of telephone respondents not providing a dollar figure is twice to three times the proportion of personal respondents who fail to choose an income category from the presented card. When those who are willing to choose one of the three gross categories are included, however, the missing data rate on the telephone appears very similar to that obtained in person. A similar rate of missing data can be attained in both modes, but in our experience the telephone survey data that corresponded to this response rate were coarser measurements of income.

TABLE 4.10
Percentage of Respondents Who Did Not Supply Answers to Income Questions
by Mode of Interview[a]

	Percentage	
	Telephone[b]	Personal (phone household)
Spouse's income		
Open-ended	37.4	13.3
Three category	13.5	
Respondent's income		
Open-ended	24.1	8.3
Three category	8.7	
Total family income		
Open-ended	36.7	13.3
Three category	16.8	
Entitled to tax refund	5.3	2.5
Size of tax refund		
Open-ended	22.1	11.6
Approximate	13.0	6.9

[a] Don't Know, Refused, and Other not ascertained codes included.
[b] Percentages exclude from the base those interviews terminated before the question was asked.

A better comparison of respondents' sensitivity to revealing financial data in the two modes may come from the question (Q. B17a) that asked respondents about the size of their tax refund if they were eligible for one. The same wording was implemented in both modes for this question, an open-ended initial probe followed by a prompt "It is about $5, $100, $200, or what?" Missing data on the first question *and* missing data on both the first and the follow-up are about twice as large in the telephone survey.

This behavioral and attitudinal evidence consistently implies that the reaction of the respondent to the interview, to individual questions, and to the interviewer differs by mode and favors the personal interview.

4.5 REPLICATE GROUP DIFFERENCES
WITHIN THE TELEPHONE SURVEY

Any comparison between a new technology and an established one involves a built-in problem. The established technology has been subjected to a long period of development and "debugging." Those who supervise it are thoroughly familiar with its workings, and those who operate it are well practiced in its procedures. The new technology, on the other hand, is likely to show the typical problems of newness—improvisation, unfamiliarity, awkwardness.

This holds to some degree for the comparison of personal and telephone interviews. The very concept of the interview transaction—that is, the presentation of topic and interviewer, the request for cooperation, and the norms regarding duration and format—have been developed in the context of personal interviewing. There is probably no way of compensating perfectly for these extraneous differences, or of knowing when one has done so. Moreover, in making the attempt one risks overcompensating and thus reaching exaggerated judgments about the potential of the new technology.

In the present study we attempted to deal with these problems as much as possible by advance preparation of the telephone installation and training of the telephone interviewers. We had also divided the telephone sample into nine subsamples, or replicate groups, that were assigned to interviewers at several successive times. Data from these groups can thus be expected to show the effects of increasing interviewer familiarity with the telephone mode, although other factors are operating as well.

Since these nine groups of sample numbers are themselves independent national samples, they can be analyzed separately for estimates of variation in results within the telephone survey data. This is especially useful in this project because replicate groups do exhibit two important differences: response rate variation and different placement in time within the interviewing period. Not all numbers in the sample received calls on the first day of the interviewing; instead replicate groups were distributed to the interviewers when they had processed one group of numbers and were free to call new sample numbers. The date on which the first interview of each replicate group was taken reveals this procedure more clearly:

Replicate Group	Date of First Interview
1–5	April 23
6	May 5
7	May 10
8	May 12
9	May 13

The response rates for replicate groups fall essentially into three categories. (See Figure 3.4, Chapter 3, page 73.) Replicate groups 3 and 4 have the highest response rate, groups 1–2, 5–8 have a somewhat lower rate, and replicate group 9 has by far the lowest rate.[1] By contrasting the results of groups 1–2 with those of groups 5 or 6–8 we may obtain some estimate of the effect of interviewer experience while controlling for response rate; by comparing replicate groups 7–8 with 9 we can reduce differences in interviewer experience between comparison groups and gain some idea of the effects of response rate on differences between modes.

We have chosen five different measures, some factual, some attitudinal, and have examined differences across replicate groups in terms of three characteristics of the response patterns: the proportion of respondents who fall within the modal answer category, the proportion of respondents who answer "don't know" to the question, and the proportion of respondents who have missing data of other kinds on the measures. For example, interviewer failure to ask the question or record the answer, or a respondent's answer that could be coded only as "not ascertained" would fall into this category of "missing data." For the interviewer experience comparison, we expected that familiarity with the questionnaire and the interviewing procedures that is obtained over time would improve the performance of the interviewer. Interviews from respondents in the same replicate group were taken at different points in the interview period, however, so that the replicate group is probably only a proxy variable for the interviewer's experience at the time of interview.

Given those limitations to our analysis, let us first summarize the graphs in Figure 4.3. Figure 4.3 presents two plottings for each of five proportions, one a solid horizontal line which denotes the proportion of respondents in the personal interview survey who gave the modal response. This is the constant to which the nine separate replicate group figures are compared, nine joined together with dotted lines. The question that asked for a listing of the most important problems facing the country (Q. B6, V22073) will be analyzed in more detail in Section 5.3; in the first panel we present the proportion of respondents who mentioned two or more problems. About 70% of the personal interview respondents do so, but the percentage on the telephone is always smaller, ranging mostly between 55–60%. The other estimate

---

[1] Only two interviewers terminated their employment during the course of the survey so that the response rates are the product of essentially the same group of interviewers throughout the study.

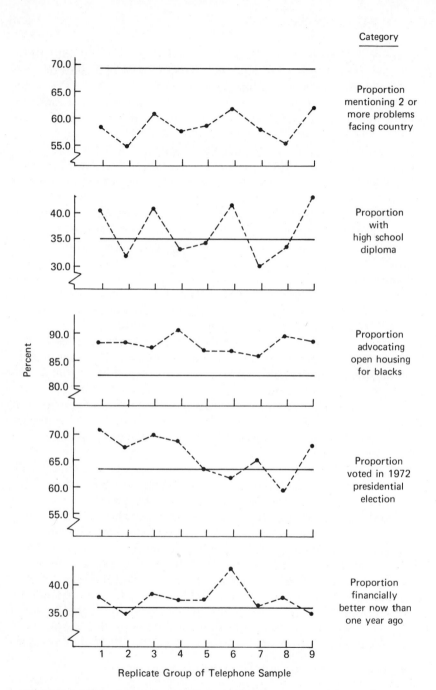

FIGURE 4.3. **Proportion of respondents in specific categories of several measures, overall proportion for the personal interview households with telephones, proportion by replicate group for telephone sample.**

that exhibits a similar form is the proportion favoring open housing for blacks (Q. B7, V12085), where larger percentages of respondents on the telephone over all replicate groups favor the more liberal position. In the other three proportions shown in Figure 4.3, the results for individual replicate groups fluctuate about the sample proportion of the personal interview survey.

Concentrating on the effect of interviewer experience, we can examine the five graphs for evidence that replicate groups 1–2 yield estimates that depart from those of groups 6–8. There is no evidence of large or consistent departures of replicate group 1–2 estimates from those of the other groups. The two measures where we might most expect to see the effects of interviewer experience would perhaps be the number of national problems mentioned and the reports on voting behavior in the 1972 presidential election. We would hypothesize that over time more problems would be elicited by interviewers through better utilization of probing and that a reduced overreporting of voting would be obtained. Only the vote report seems to indicate some effect of interviewer experience. Although the overall response rates of replicate groups 6–8 are similar to those of groups 1 and 2, the proportion of people reporting that they voted is consistently smaller. Since both the personal and the telephone survey results overestimate actual participation in the election, the trend in the data would imply that more accurate data are being collected in the later replicate groups. Since we are dealing with sample sizes one-ninth the size of the total sample, few of the differences in any of the graphs are statistically significant.

In attempting to use the graphs of Figure 4.3 to investigate the effect of response rate on survey results, we compare replicate groups 7–8 with 9. Since replicate group 9 was the last distributed to interviewers, we suspect that a large source of nonresponse in that set is the inability to follow-up sample numbers with as many calls as the other replicate groups received. Respondents in replicate group 9 are disproportionately those easy to reach by home telephone. Once again we look at the two variables where we can hypothesize a desired outcome (i.e., large proportions of respondents giving two or more problems, fewer respondents reporting that they had voted in the 1972 election). A larger proportion of respondents mention two or more problems in replicate group 9 than in groups 7–8, and a larger proportion report that they voted in the 1972 election. If respondents reached relatively quickly have greater interest in political affairs, both of these results could be explained without the need to hypothesize response errors. Although there is some evidence of nonresponse effects for the two "current affairs" questions, none of the other graphs in Figure 4.3 reveals any effects.

Figures 4.4 and 4.5 present the proportion of respondents who answered "don't know" to each of four different measures in the survey, and those with both "don't know" and "not ascertained" codes on the same questions. As with our previous discussion, telephone survey results are presented separately for each replicate group. In

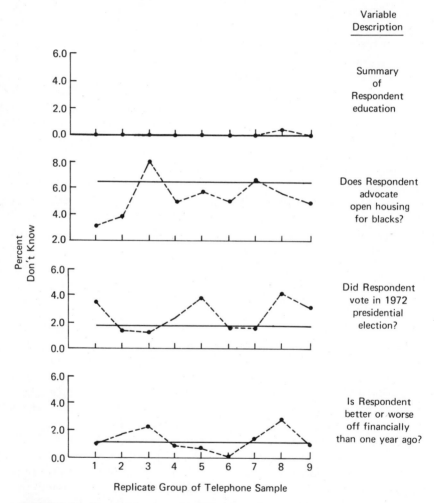

FIGURE 4.4. Proportion answering "don't know" on various measures, overall proportion for personal interview households with telephones, proportion by individual replicate group for telephone sample.

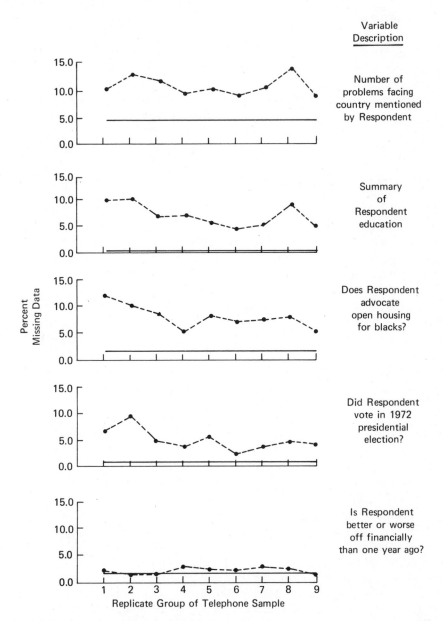

FIGURE 4.5. Proportion of cases with missing data on various measures, overall proportion for personal interview households with telephones, proportion by individual replicate group for telephone sample.

general, the proportion with "don't know" answers seems to be more a function of the question than of interview mode. Respondent's education, a factual self-report, has almost no such responses; the attitudinal measure about open housing for blacks yields 5–7% "don't know." Although the telephone respondents seem more willing to express an opinion on the open housing question, for the other measures in Figure 4.4 the two modes of interview yield about the same rate of "don't knows." There is no evidence that interviewer experience (as measured by comparing replicate groups 1–2 with 5–8) has any effect on the proportion giving such answers. Similarly the effect of response rate (comparing groups 7–8 with 9) on proportion "don't know" seems to be negligible.

Figure 4.5 reveals a persistent difference between the two modes, one which is confirmed by most of the tables in Appendix II. For all of the variables the amount of missing data on the telephone exceeds that on the personal interview data. Part of this effect results from interviews that were terminated by the respondent before completion; this source accounts for at most 6.7% of the telephone interview sample. The remaining missing data occur because of failure of interviewers to ask the questions, to elicit a meaningful response from the respondent, or to record the answer on the questionnaire. Although these sources of missing data are combined in the figure, a glance at the tables in Appendix II confirms that, even with the removal of interviews terminated by the respondent before completion, the rate of noncodable answers is higher on the telephone. We suspect that this higher rate reflects some limitations in training and monitoring procedures, as well as the sensitivity of some subjects to the telephone mode. The relatively high proportion of missing data for questions asking the respondent's opinions about political figures or current political issues appears to be an effect of such differential sensitivity to the two interviewing media. We will note later the greater reticence of respondents to reveal personal and family income on the telephone. We must be cautious in generalizing these results, however, especially since we lack coded data on the causes of nonresponse to individual items.

The graphs of Figure 4.5 do suggest that interviewer experience reduces the level of missing data; on the final four measures in the figure, missing data for replicate groups 5–8 is somewhat smaller than that for groups 1–2. This is consistent with our analysis in Table 4.1, which showed a reduction in missing data rates over successive surveys asking the economic attitude questions. The relationship of overall response rate to missing data rates on specific items (comparing replicate groups 7–8 with 9) is not easily discerned from the figure. There is some evidence that the group (9) with the lowest response rate also has the lowest missing data rate, but the differences are usually small.

4.6 METHOD EFFECTS IN DIFFERENT RESIDENTIAL GROUPS

Our comparisons between telephone and personal interviews have thus far made no attempt to take account of the possibility of differential reactions to mode by various population subgroups. Yet we know intuitively that such differentiation exists. Some people are experienced and at ease with the telephone; others are not. Some people are reluctant to admit strangers to their homes, whatever their credentials and identification; others look forward to such breaks in the day's routine.

Size of community is an obvious candidate for explaining such differences; difficulties of personal interviewing in the large central cities have become notorious. For our two multistage (clustered) samples we can readily compare response patterns in three broad residential categories—the 12 large "self-representing" metropolitan areas, the other standard metropolitan statistical areas (SMSAs) in the sample, and the relatively rural "non-SMSAs."

The self-representing areas had the lowest response rate in both modes, although the telephone survey in those areas seems to produce a slightly higher cooperation rate than the personal interview survey. In the telephone survey the highest response rate (about 75%) was achieved in the strata containing "other SMSAs," but for the personal interview survey the response rate rose monotonically across the three categories—lowest in the self-representing areas, intermediate in the "other SMSAs," and highest in the non-SMSAs (about 81%). Once again, therefore, the differences across mode that we will observe reflect two components—differences associated with method of data collection and differences in the types of person willing to cooperate with the survey.

We choose nine different variables for this analysis and will summarize the general tendencies that they exhibit. The first noticeable difference across the three residential or area groups is in the proportion of respondents replying "don't know" to questions. Table 4.11

TABLE 4.11

Difference between Percentage "Don't Know" for Various Measures (Telephone–Personal) by Primary Area Type[a]

Variable number	Variable description	Percentage difference		
		Self-representing	SMSAs	Non-SMSAs
13002	Better/Worse off financially than 1 year ago	1.9	.2	− .1
13006	Better/Worse off financially than 3 years ago	−1.2	1.7	1.8
13008	Good/Bad business conditions next 12 months	−3.5	5.7	−4.8
32061	Vote/No vote in 1972 election	.1	2.1	.5
12085	Open housing	0	2.3	−5.3
11043	Feel Terrible/Delighted about life	−1.3	1.5	− .1
11054	Feel Dissatisfied/Satisfied about life	1.7	.8	− .3
12047	Liberal/Conservative	−2.0	10.1	−5.9
12058	Liberal/Conservative/Middle of Road	.8	1.7	−8.5

[a] Data weighted by reciprocal of selection probability; personal data are for households with phones.

presents the difference between the proportion of "don't knows" in the telephone survey and the proportion in the personal interview survey, separately for the three primary area categories. The list of measures includes some economic attitudes and political attitudes, a report on voting behavior, and two life satisfaction items. In general, the results show that the respondents within SMSAs respond with more "don't knows" on the telephone than they do in person. In contrast, respondents in the non-SMSAs seem to respond "don't know" more often in personal interviews.

None of these item differences is larger than that expected by sampling variation but the consistency of the comparison over different measures suggests that the results may be replicated by other surveys. These cross-tabulations do not provide us with reasons for the differences observed. At this point we can merely note that these three types of areas, which differ in level of urbanization and population density, seem to produce different behavioral adjustments to the mode of data collection. We will keep these results in mind when we begin to examine method effects for different demographic groups.

There we may identify personal characteristics that are associated with these different behaviors.

The observation that mode differences in the proportion of "don't knows" vary over the three primary area types is easily made; substantive differences between modes in response patterns over the three primary area types are more difficult to assess. Table 4.12 suggests, however, that the tendency toward greater optimism in telephone interviews may be area specific. The results for the total sample on the question of the family's current financial status compared with their status 3 years ago (Q. A2, V13006) show that respondents on the telephone more frequently note that they are better off now (50.1%) than do respondents in person (45%). When we separate the results by type of primary area, however, we find that the greater optimism on the telephone is really centered in the large and small primary areas; in the SMSAs, the middle group, differences between the two modes of interview are negligible. This result is also true for the other economic attitudes examined in the analysis. Response rates are the highest on the telephone in these other SMSAs, but we probably cannot attribute the smaller method effect differences to lower nonresponse bias alone.

TABLE 4.12

Attitudes about Family Financial Conditions Relative to Three Years Ago by Primary Area Type and Mode of Interview[a]

| Primary area type | Mode of interview | Percentage present status versus three years ago | | | | |
		Better	Same	Worse	Don't know	Total
Self-representing SMSAs	Telephone	48.8	18.1	31.3	1.8	100.0
	Personal	42.6	20.3	34.1	3.0	100.0
Other SMSAs	Telephone	47.7	17.1	31.9	3.3	100.0
	Personal	47.8	21.4	29.2	1.6	100.0
Non-SMSAs	Telephone	52.7	15.0	29.0	3.2	99.9
	Personal	43.2	25.0	29.4	2.4	100.0
Total	Telephone	50.1	16.5	30.5	2.9	100.0
	Personal	45.0	22.3	30.5	2.2	100.0

[a] Data weighted by the reciprocal of selection probability; personal data are for households with phones.

4.7 DIFFERENCES AMONG DEMOGRAPHIC SUBGROUPS IN OBSERVED METHOD EFFECTS

We have already observed that the difference between personal and telephone modes on estimates from the total sample rarely exceeds that expected by sampling variation. The possibility remains, however, that different *subsets* of the population may exhibit more significant differential effects related to mode of data collection. To investigate this possibility, we utilize four demographic characteristics: age, education, income, and race.[2] Throughout the analysis we employ gross categories on these measures in order to maintain some control on the sampling variance of our comparisons. Method effects across these categories are examined for a diverse group of variables which are representative of those concerning economic attitudes, political attitudes and behavior, racial attitudes, and measures of perceived life satisfaction.

Since there are over 40 different tables involved in this analysis, we have chosen to limit our presentation of results to categories which exhibit the largest percentage differences between mode on the *total* sample. For these categories we compare the differences within various subgroups to differences in the total sample. In limiting our presentation to single categories of variables there is some danger that we will ignore different patterns of effects for various demographic groups. The actual analysis was performed on full cross-tabulations of demographic and response variables, and we will present examples of these which exhibit variation in patterns of effects over groups.

First we examine age differences in responses. We have already noted that the telephone respondents are disproportionately young relative to the personal interview respondents. If differences on the total sample are related to the respondent's age, then the cross-classifications by age may show reduced method differences (telephone–personal) for 11 different estimates. Only three estimates have differences on the total sample that exceed requirements of statistical significance. Telephone respondents are less likely than personal interview respondents to answer that their financial status is the same as 3 years ago (a 6.6% difference between modes), and more likely to choose one or the other of the two extremes. Telephone respondents also foresee good business times ahead more frequently

---

[2] Sex differences in method effects were also investigated but yielded no significant differences.

than do personal interview respondents (8.8% difference). Finally, telephone respondents appear more likely to have extreme or mixed feelings about their "life as a whole," and less likely to give the conventional responses of "Mostly Satisfied." (This particular result may merely be an artifact of the adaptation of this show card question to telephone use.)

Table 4.13 allows us to examine how method differences within specific age groups vary around those on the total sample. The simplest pattern would be one in which one age group would exhibit larger mode differences over all variables examined or where differences within age groups would all be smaller than those on the total

TABLE 4.13
Percentage Differences between Modes for Specific Categories of Several Variables by Age Groups[a]

			Percentage difference (telephone–personal) by age group			
Variable description	V	Category	18–29	30–49	50 or more	Total
Better/Worse off financially than 1 year ago	13002	Better	– .1	4.1	.4	3.1
Better/Worse off financially than 3 years ago	13006	Same	–2.7	– 6.8	–6.2	–6.6
Good/Bad business conditions next 12 months	13008	Good times	7.6	8.4	8.8	8.8
Voted in 1972 election	32061	Voted	7.0	2.4	3.4	2.5
Carter feeling thermometer	12067	Mean value	–5.3	– 8.1	–5.9	–6.5
Open housing	12085	Black rights	4.2	2.7	7.9	5.3
Delighted–Terrible scale— "Life as a whole"	11043	Mostly satisfied	–5.1	– 9.5	–9.4	–8.6
Satisfied–Dissatisfied scale—"Life as a whole"	11054	Completely satisfied	3.0	10.3	3.1	4.9
Dichotomous Liberal– Conservative measure	12047	Liberal	8.0	1.1	–4.1	2.1
Trichotomous Liberal– Conservative measure	12058	Middle of Road	5.2	–11.0	–6.0	–4.1
		Liberal	–6.0	8.2	2.4	2.7

[a] Data weighted by reciprocal of selection probability; personal data are for households with phones.

sample. No consistent differences of this sort exist over the estimates; the average difference between modes for the three age groups all lie within two percentage points of one another.

A more complex characterization of differences among age groups hypothesizes an interaction effect between age group differences and type of measures. For example, older respondents may exhibit larger method effects on items about their health than do younger respondents but the reverse might be true for other variables. The three economic attitude questions as a group, however, provide no evidence of homogeneity of effects within that topic area. Each of the three economic variables shows a different pattern of effects over the three age groups. Examination of the complete cross-tabulations for these variables produces the same conclusion. Another group of variables contains measures of political attitudes and voting behavior. There is also little homogeneity within that set of questions, with respect to the pattern of mode differences across the age groups.

Given all this evidence, we have little reason to suspect that different age groups are disproportionately affected in major ways by mode of data collection. Because we have utilized only a trichotomous measure of age, this analysis does not confirm that there is no relationship between age and behavior differences between modes. Further analysis and later designs may identify smaller age groups that show large method differences. At the present level of analysis, however, no visible differences exist.

Although we discovered only negligible differences between the two modes in the proportion of respondents in various racial groups, much survey analysis presents separate results for whites and nonwhites. Table 4.14 presents percentage differences between modes separately for whites, nonwhites, and the total sample for the measures examined above. The average difference for individual racial groupings is very similar to that on the total sample over all measures in the table, but there does seem to be some tendency for nonwhites to exhibit larger mode effects on questions about political attitude and behavior. Among nonwhites larger proportions reported on the telephone that they voted (4.2% difference) and that they were conservative (15.7% difference), and smaller proportions that they were "Middle of the Road" in political orientation (4.3% difference). The dichotomous form of the "Liberal–Conservative" question produced the largest difference between the race groups, as Table 4.15 illustrates. Whites appear more liberal on the telephone than in person (4.2% difference between modes); nonwhites appear more conservative (15.7% difference). Despite these large differences, the nonwhite

TABLE 4.14
Percentage Differences between Modes for Specific Categories of Several Variables by Race Groups[a]

Variable description	V	Category	Percentage difference (telephone–personal) by race group		
			White	Nonwhite	Total
Better/Worse off financially than 1 year ago	13002	Better	1.9	5.3	2.4
Better/Worse off financially than 3 years ago	13006	Same	−5.6	−11.9	−6.4
Good/Bad business conditions next 12 months	13008	Good times	9.5	1.4	8.5
Voted in 1972 election	32061	Voted	2.0	4.2	2.4
Carter feeling thermometer	12067	Mean value	−6.7	− 6.5	−6.7
Open housing	12085	Black rights	6.5	2.1	5.9
Delighted–Terrible scale— "Life as a whole"	11043	Mostly satisfied	−9.1	− 8.6	−9.1
Satisfied–Dissatisfied scale—"Life as a whole"	11054	Completely satisfied	5.9	7.8	6.2
Dichotomous Liberal– Conservative measure	12047	Conservative	−5.1	15.7	−2.3
Trichotomous Liberal– Conservative measure	12058	Middle of road	−2.4	− 4.3	−2.7

[a] Data weighted by reciprocal of selection probability; personal data are for households with phones.

method effects are not significantly different from zero, and we should seek additional evidence before concluding that race specifies the nature of method effects for this variable.

Table 4.16 presents separate effects for three different educational groups, those not completing high school, those receiving a high school diploma, and those continuing their education past high school. As with the other two demographic variables, none of the three education classes exhibits effects that are consistently larger than the others, and the average effect for each education group resembles that for the total sample. Within the groups of questions measuring the related at-

TABLE 4.15
Responses on Dichotomous Liberal–Conservative Measure by Racial Group by
Mode of Interview[a]

Racial group	Mode	Percentage						Unweighted N
		Liberal	Middle of Road	Conser-vative	Other	Don't know	Total	
White	Personal	25.8	12.0	54.7	.9	6.7	100.0	644
	Phone	30.0	12.1	49.6	1.5	6.9	100.0	658
Nonwhite	Personal	44.8	7.3	29.2	2.6	16.1	100.0	93
	Phone	33.6	10.4	44.9	0	11.0	100.0	94
Total	Personal	28.3	11.3	51.3	1.1	7.9	100.0	737
	Phone	30.4	11.9	49.0	1.3	7.4	100.0	752

[a] Data weighted by reciprocal of selection probability; personal data are for house-holds with phones.

titudes, there seem to be no consistent patterns of differences across the three education subclasses. One of the larger effects in Table 4.16 occurs in the "Satisfied–Dissatisfied" version of one life satisfaction variable (Q. BY1e, V11054). The low education group shows no effects (.3%), but the highest group exhibits a 12.6% difference in the percentage answering "Completely Satisfied." Table 4.17 presents the entire cross-tabulation for this variable and shows that all three education groups have somewhat larger proportions of respondents choosing "Completely Satisfied" in the telephone mode and usually smaller proportions choosing the points "5" and "6." This tendency is most pronounced among those in the highest education class and is an important source of the differences observed on the total sample. (We will examine the heaping on labeled points in Section 5.1.) We did not expect that the higher educational classes would be greatly dependent upon the show card for their answers; rather we hypothesized that those with lower educations would be most sensitive to the visual presentation of responses.

Finally, Table 4.18 presents the results by category of total family income, $0–$7500, $7500–$15,000, $15,000 or more. In general, the lower income group exhibits the largest method effect across the different variables (average difference over ten proportions equals 6.5%). The differences between mode are successively smaller for the two higher income classes (5.8% and 3.9% average). Indeed, for every variable except the two life satisfaction measures and reports on voting, the percentage differences are larger in the lowest income group

TABLE 4.16
Percentage Differences between Modes for Specific Categories of Several Variables by Education Groups[a]

| | | | Percentage difference (telephone–personal) | | | |
| | | | Education group | | | |
Variable description	V	Category	−HS	HS	HS+	Total
Better/Worse off financially than 1 year ago	13002	Better	2.3	.6	1.7	2.5
Better/Worse off financially than 3 years ago	13006	Same	−8.2	−3.3	−7.1	−6.6
Good/Bad business conditions next 12 months	13008	Good times	6.0	6.3	8.3	8.3
Voted in 1972 election	32061	Voted	− .8	6.7	−1.6	2.7
Carter feeling thermometer	12067	Mean	−7.1	−5.6	−8.0	−6.5
Open housing	12085	Black rights	7.7	7.3	1.7	5.8
Delighted–Terrible scale— "Life as a whole"	11043	Mixed	9.1	10.4	8.5	9.0
Satisfied–Dissatisfied scale—"Life as a whole"	11054	Completely satisfied	.3	4.5	12.6	6.1
Dichotomous Liberal– Conservative measure	12047	Liberal	−5.6	3.6	3.4	2.4
Trichotomous Liberal– Conservative measure	12058	Middle of Road	− .6	−3.8	−2.2	−2.8
		Liberal	.4	2.2	2.2	2.3

[a] Data weighted by reciprocal of selection probability; personal data are for households with phones.

than in the highest. This remains true when all categories of the response variables are examined (using coefficients of dissimilarity) on the full cross-tabulations. The method effects across the income groups are not significantly different from zero but the consistency of their direction suggests that similar results might be found in replications of this design. Describing the influences that might be producing these results, however, is a larger task than merely observing that method effects are specified by income.

We had suspected that education might be a key variable in explaining the ability to communicate in both modes; this was not the case. It may be the case that the crucial influence on method effects is not learning or ability reflected by education but rather lifestyle of the

TABLE 4.17
Responses on Satisfied–Dissatisfied Scale for "Life as a Whole" by Mode by Education Class[a]

| Education | Percentage | | | | | | | | | Unweighted N |
	Completely dissatisfied	2	3	Neutral	5	6	Completely satisfied	Don't know	Total	
Less than high school										
Personal	1.8	1.3	3.9	12.1	6.2	28.9	44.3	1.5	100.0	195
Phone	2.2	3.0	1.6	13.5	15.0	19.8	44.6	.3	100.0	136
High school diploma										
Personal	0	1.1	4.1	13.1	17.0	26.1	38.6	0	100.0	226
Phone	1.1	.5	1.6	11.7	14.8	25.5	43.1	1.6	100.0	217
More than high school										
Personal	.8	.6	2.8	7.2	20.7	43.7	24.3	0	100.0	250
Phone	.2	.2	2.0	10.4	13.6	36.6	36.9	.2	100.0	306
Total										
Personal	.8	1.0	3.6	10.6	15.3	33.5	34.9	.4	100.0	671
Phone	1.0	1.0	1.8	11.6	14.4	28.6	41.0	.7	100.0	803

[a] Data weighted by reciprocal of selection probability; personal data are for households with phones.

TABLE 4.18

Percentage Differences between Modes for Specific Categories of Several Variables by Income Groups[a]

Variable description	V	Category		Percentage difference (telephone–personal) by income group				
			0–7500	7500–15000	15000+	DK	Total
Better/Worse off financially than 1 year ago	13002	Better	7.5	.1	-1.4	6.6	1.8
Better/Worse off financially than 3 years ago	13006	Same	-13.5	-5.6	-4.0	-6.1	-5.9
Good/Bad business conditions next 12 months	13008	Good times	7.9	10.5	6.3	5.5	7.6
Voted in 1972 election	32061	Did not vote; no reason	-5.3	.6	-3.3	-.2	-2.5
Carter feeling thermometer	12067	Mean value	-5.3	-8.4	-4.2	-19.9	-8.9
Open housing	12085	Black rights	7.2	4.8	3.4	10.5	5.5
Delighted–Terrible scale—"Life as a whole"	11043	Mostly satisfied	-2.7	-10.1	-8.9	-13.6	-9.0
Satisfied–Dissatisfied scale—"Life as a whole"	11054	Completely satisfied	2.0	6.9	4.2	14.1	6.4
Dichotomous Liberal–Conservative measure	12047	Liberal	-6.3	13.3	1.3	-4.4	1.9
Trichotomous Liberal–Conservative measure	12058	Middle of Road	-6.5	-4.3	-2.2	1.6	-2.9

[a] Data weighted by reciprocal of selection probability; personal data are for households with phones.

respondents in terms of willingness to reveal personal information over the telephone or to be candid in their expressed attitudes. For example, the variables where the lowest income group exhibits the largest method effects are the economic attitude questions. On these questions, the lower income telephone respondents are much more optimistic about their own financial status and the country's than those in personal interviews. This answer might be considered the socially desirable response, and we might suspect that the increased choice of that answer reflects measurement error in the telephone survey data. Similarly, on the open housing question, the larger method effects for the lower income group reflect a greater tendency on the telephone to favor blacks' right to choose where they live. More detailed analysis is needed on the nature of these findings, and the answers may lie in measures that reflect the lifestyle of the respondent.

4.8 SUMMARY

Discrepancies between response distributions to the telephone and the personal interview surveys cannot be interpreted as due solely to inherent differences between telephone and face-to-face conversations. Different amounts of nonresponse, the unavoidable exclusion (from telephone surveys) of households without telephones, the adaptation of some questions to provide to telephone respondents certain cues that were provided visually in the personal interviews, combine to make interpretation of differences between the two sets of responses always difficult and often tentative. Such comparisons are nevertheless instructive, because personal interview surveys of probability samples have been taken as standards for many purposes. And the comparisons become additionally useful for those variables for which data independent of both telephone and personal interviews are available.

More than 200 measures were obtained on both the personal interview and telephone surveys, and few of the differences between the two modes are large enough to be statistically significant. Certain trends are nevertheless consistent between the two: (a) a greater tendency toward missing data (response not ascertained) in the telephone mode; (b) a tendency of respondents to prefer the personal to the telephone interviews (although this tendency is partially counteracted by a tendency of respondents to endorse the mode of interviewing that they are experiencing); and (c) a tendency toward greater expressions of optimism in the telephone interviews. This tendency, however, while it was manifest across a number of measures and sectors of life experience in the present surveys, was not replicated in subsequent telephone studies.

Demographic comparisons between the two modes of interviewing are more notable for their similarities than their differences. The largest difference was in the age distributions, with telephone respondents significantly younger than those in the personal interview survey. Racial distributions between the two modes were within one percentage point in every category. Differences in sex distribution are also small, with some tendency toward a larger proportion of male respondents in the telephone mode, a tendency that probably reflects the greater flexibility of telephone scheduling. Reported socio-economic characteristics are somewhat higher for the telephone respondents—more education, more professionals, more incomes above $15,000.

To investigate the possibility that some of these differences might reflect the relative lack of interviewer experience with the telephone mode, the telephone samples were divided into nine random subsamples, each assigned to interviewers only when they were nearing completion of the previous group. There was no consistent evidence of an "experience effect," although the tendency toward greater amounts of missing data in the telephone mode did decline somewhat in the later replicate groups.

Differences between the telephone and personal interview surveys were not uniform throughout the two samples. For example, response rates were higher overall in the personal interview survey, but that difference was concentrated in the least urbanized areas (the non-SMSAs). Response rates in the largest metropolitan areas (self-representing SMSAs) were higher in the telephone mode than in the personal interview survey. Other response characteristics also show such residential differences, too small for statistical significance in any one instance, but consistent. For reasons not fully understood, people in areas of different urbanization and population density sometimes react differently to the two modes of data collection.

Responses of various demographic subgroups to the telephone and personal interview modes were compared to see whether method differences might be concentrated demographically. No such differences are apparent within age groups, but nonwhites exhibited larger methods effects than whites on questions of political attitudes and behavior. In comparison to personal interview data, telephone responses show more nonwhites reporting that they voted and that their political preferences were conservative. Whites, on the other hand, reported themselves somewhat more liberal in the telephone interviews than in person. These tendencies were not statistically significant, however.

Different education groups showed no significant differences in the effects of interview mode, although the general tendency to report higher life satisfaction in the telephone interviews was most pronounced in the highest education class—an outcome difficult to explain. Lower income groups exhibited more effects of mode, and the highest income groups showed the least such effects on almost all characteristics measured. Again, however, this pattern is consistent without the specific comparisons being statistically significant. The overall findings of differences between the two modes thus show small differences, with some consistency of pattern but few instances of statistical significance.

Chapter 5

Method Effects Associated with Specific Types of Measures

Survey researchers over the years have developed a variety of question forms to gather data. Some items ask the respondent to agree or disagree with a statement or to choose one of a small number of response categories. Other measures ask the respondent to sort lists of items according to some dimension (e.g., preference, difficulty). Some seek numerical answers; others ask for words that describe feelings or behaviors. Some questions let respondents form their own answers; others restrict responses to prespecified categories.

In this chapter we focus our attention on three different kinds of measures: (a) questions that utilize response cards to aid the respondent in selecting an answer; (b) questions that permit external validation; and (c) open-ended questions that permit the respondent to phrase his or her own answer. Since response cards cannot be presented visually to telephone respondents, some adaptation of questions using those aids was required on the telephone surveys. Two different techniques were attempted and their results are discussed later. A few questions asked in surveys of a household sample permit measurement of overall bias; in this survey we examine published statistics on voting in the 1972 presidential election and compare them with estimates from the two survey modes. Finally, we examine in some detail the differences between modes in the responses to open-ended items, identify subgroups that have different effects, and use multivariate analyses to identify major correlates of the differences.

5.1 ADAPTING RESPONSE CARD QUESTIONS FOR USE IN A TELEPHONE SURVEY

Any question that contains some visual stimulus, such as a response card, as part of the measurement process must be transformed for use in a purely audio medium. We used the following methods on the telephone for such questions:

1. Verbally presenting major categories of the scale, having the respondent choose one, and on the basis of that choice, presenting a set of more specific alternatives for respondent selection. This results in a process of unfolding the respondent's answer. Two scale questions used the unfolding technique—the probability of the respondent's buying a car in the next 12 months, and one version of the life satisfaction items.

2. Verbally communicating the nature of the scale by describing what certain points on the scale meant, and then asking the respondent to choose a numbered point on the scale. Personal and family income questions, political attitude "thermometer" items, and one version of the life satisfaction scale used this technique.

In examining the results for questions where we asked the telephone respondent to give a numbered point as a response, it seems clear that labeling a point on the response card can cause some heaping of answers on labeled points and avoidance of the nonlabeled points. Figures 5.1 and 5.2 present histograms for the political thermometer items for Jimmy Carter and Gerald Ford; on the left side of each figure the results for the telephone survey are plotted; on the right, those for the personal interview survey appear. The labeled points on the response card given to the respondent were 0, 15, 30, 40, 50, 60, 70, 85, and 100°. The ranges and points mentioned in the telephone interviews were 0–50°, 50°, and 50–100°. (See Appendix I for the exact wording of the introduction on the telephone.) On neither of the modes are all possible points from 0 to 100° mentioned, but the clustering of respondents on points differs across mode. In telephone interviews, respondents tend to give numbers divisible by 10 (e.g., 10, 20, 30, 40, 50, and so on) or numbers representing quarters

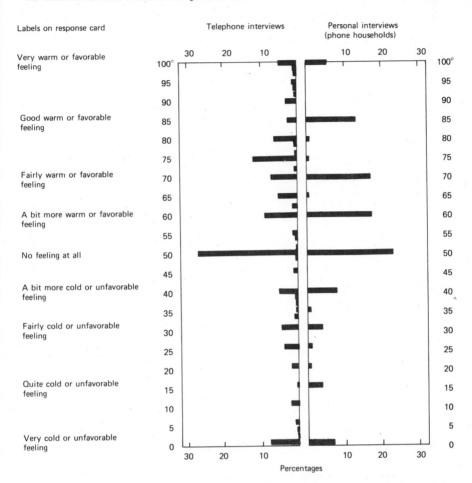

FIGURE 5.1. Histogram of responses for feeling thermometer toward Carter, by mode of interview. Data are weighted by reciprocals of selection probabilities.

of the 0 to 100 range (25, 50, 75, 100). The large remainder of their answers are divisible by 5 (15, 35, 45, 55, and so on). Indeed, the percentage of telephone respondents that provides numbers not divisible by 5 or 10 is only 3% on the Carter item. In personal interviews, however, the clustering of answers is almost completely dominated by labeled points on the show card. Only 2.7% of respondents provide answers outside those nine points. The findings for the feeling thermometer on Ford and other public figures were similar.

Five questions measuring respondent satisfaction with different parts of his or her life were asked in different ways on half-samples

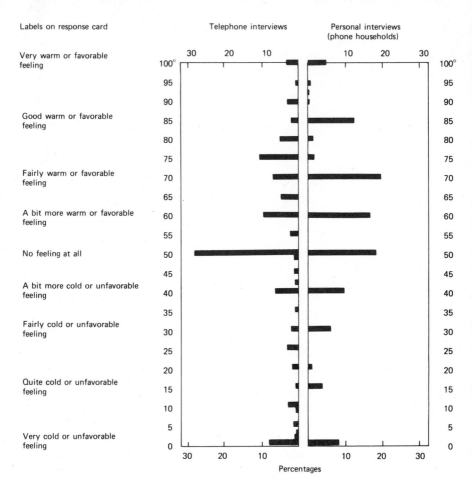

FIGURE 5.2. **Histogram of responses for feeling thermometer toward Ford, by mode of interview. Data are weighted by reciprocals of selection probabilities.**

within both modes. The ones that utilized a "Satisfied–Dissatisfied" scale asked the respondent for a numbered point on the scale (Q. BY1 and Figure 5.3) after the three labeled points were described. The proportions are generally about the same for the two modes on all seven points, the largest difference being a greater tendency for telephone respondents to answer "Completely Satisfied" (41.9% on the phone and 35.1% in person so characterizing their "Life as a Whole").

The other form of the questions unfolded the respondents' original response in terms of "Good, Bad, or Mixed" into seven more specific categories (Figure 5.4 and Q. BX1). Those who originally replied

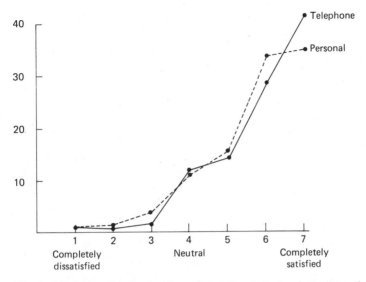

FIGURE 5.3. **Response distribution for satisfied-dissatisfied scale on "Your life as a whole," by mode of interview. Data are weighted by reciprocal of selection probabilities. Personal data are for households with phones.**

"Mixed" were not asked for a more specific response. Figure 5.4 presents the marginal distribution on a measure about "Your Life as a Whole" using this technique. In addition to the unfolding technique, there is another difference between this scale and the "Satisfied–Dissatisfied" scale. In this "Delighted–Terrible" scale all seven points are given labels, so neither the telephone nor the personal interview respondent answered in terms of a number. The differences between modes for this version of the question are somewhat larger and may be the result of two different influences. First, we note that a larger proportion of respondents on the telephone choose "Mixed" as a response (18.5%) than is the case in personal interviews (9.9%); "Mixed" is the only initial response (among "Good," "Bad," or "Mixed") that does not receive a probe for a more specific answer in the telephone measurement. There is no evidence from the use of the "Satisfied–Dissatisfied" scale that telephone respondents choose a middle or neutral point to avoid choosing one side of the scale or the other. It may be the case that some of those replying "Mixed" on the telephone, had they been faced with more specific alternatives than "Good" or "Bad," would have moved to the points adjacent to "Mixed" ("Mostly Dissatisfied" or "Mostly Satisfied").

In describing the second influence on method differences, we first

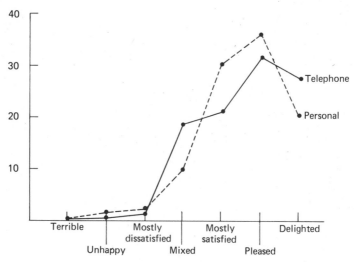

FIGURE 5.4. Response distribution for delighted-terrible scale on "Your life as a whole," by mode of interview. Data are weighted by reciprocals of selection probabilities. Personal data are for households with phones.

note that the distributions for "Mostly Satisfied," "Pleased," and "Delighted" are different in the two modes. In the telephone interviews these responses were read to those who replied that their feelings were on the "Good" side in response to the initial question. In the personal interview the respondent was faced with all seven alternative answers at the same time, and the interviewer verbally described the end and middle points of the scale only in introducing the question series. The proportion choosing "Delighted" is much larger on the telephone (27.3%) than in person (20.4%).

We have already noticed some tendency for telephone respondents to choose the extreme satisfaction point in the other scale used. The larger proportions of "Delighted" responses on the telephone may be more evidence for higher optimism and satisfaction in this group of telephone respondents. Alternatively, the differences on the "Delighted–Terrible" scale may also be the result of the telephone interviewer's verbally presenting the three alternatives "Mostly Satisfied," "Pleased," and "Delighted" for each of the five items. The word "delighted" may not be frequently used by some respondents to characterize their own feelings, and they may not readily choose it from among printed alternatives.[1] Hearing another person offer that as

[1] We note that both in telephone and personal interviews smaller proportions of respondents chose "Delighted" than the end point of the other scale, "Completely Satisfied."

an alternative may reduce this avoidance somewhat. Our interpretation of larger method effects on the unfolding technique versus the presentation of the entire scale thus rests on two observations: (a) the possible need for elaboration on all initial answers; and (b) possible differences between hearing and reading labels that are not natural expressions for the respondent.

Since these two scales were used for five different items, the data set offers an opportunity to investigate whether or not the relationships among the scale items are similar in the two modes of data collection. We examine two measures: (a) the number of times respondents gave the same answer to different items in the scale (estimating tendencies of response set); and (b) empirical estimates of association among responses to the different items. Tables 5.1 and 5.2 measure the number of times that each response was chosen for the five items. For example, 97% of the telephone respondents never chose the response "Terrible" for any of the five items; the remaining 3% chose it only once.

Two summary statistics can be examined from these tables, the proportion of respondents who never choose one of the alternatives, and the proportion of respondents who choose one of the responses many times. (We use three of the five items as the criterion.) For the "Delighted–Terrible" scale the largest difference between modes is centered on the "Mixed" category, which more personal respondents completely avoid (69.1%) than telephone respondents (56.0%). On the positive side of the scale ("Mostly Satisfied," "Pleased," and "Delighted") personal respondents exhibit more avoidance of the term "delighted" than telephone respondents. When we look at the percentages who gave the same answer on three or more items, only three categories show large differences between modes, "Mixed," "Pleased," and "Delighted." About 5–6% more of the telephone respondents chose "Mixed" and "Delighted" three or more times than did personal respondents. More personal respondents chose "Pleased" many times than did telephone respondents. Overall on the five different items, more telephone respondents (59.0%) chose the same answer three or more times in this version of the scale than did personal interview respondents (52.9%).

The differences for the "Satisfied–Dissatisfied" scale are generally much smaller across the two modes. The largest discrepancies involve the category "Completely Satisfied." Telephone respondents seem to choose this category more frequently than personal interview respondents, but even this difference is smaller than many of those for the "Delighted–Terrible" scale. That single category (completely satisfied) is the only one of seven to have nonnegligible differences

TABLE 5.1
Number of Times Same Response Category Was Chosen for Five X Version Life Satisfaction Measures by Response Category for Phone and Personal Interviews in Phone Households

Response	Number of times response chosen (percentages)						Total[a] (%)	Percentage with three or more times
	0	1	2	3	4	5		
Terrible								
Phone	97.0	3.0					100.0	
Personal	93.9	5.9	.1				99.9	
Unhappy								
Phone	95.8	3.8	.2	.1			99.9	.1
Personal	91.7	7.4	.8	.1			100.0	.1
Mostly dissatisfied								
Phone	91.8	7.6	.5	.1			100.0	.1
Personal	87.2	10.4	2.2	.1			99.9	.1
Mixed								
Phone	56.0	24.9	11.5	5.5	1.9	.2	100.0	7.6
Personal	69.1	23.6	5.3	1.8	.3		100.1	2.1
Mostly satisfied								
Phone	42.5	27.4	16.6	8.9	3.6	1.1	100.1	13.6
Personal	30.8	29.7	26.2	10.5	2.2	.5	99.9	13.2
Pleased								
Phone	31.8	30.4	20.3	11.9	4.5	1.2	100.1	17.6
Personal	20.9	31.4	24.6	13.2	7.9	2.0	100.0	23.1
Delighted								
Phone	40.5	23.5	16.0	10.3	5.8	3.9	100.0	20.0
Personal	47.9	25.1	12.6	7.5	5.1	1.7	99.9	14.3
No feelings								
Phone	98.1	1.7	.1	0	.1		100.0	—
Personal	98.8	.9	.1	.1			99.9	—
NA								
Phone	95.5	3.0	.9	.4	.2	—[b]	100.0	—
Personal	97.5	2.1	.1	.1	.1	—[b]	99.9	—
Total phone								59.0
Total personal								52.9

[a] N for phone = 824; N for personal = 677.

TABLE 5.2

Number of Times Same Response Category Was Chosen for Five Y Version Life Satisfaction Measures by Response Category for Phone and Personal Interviews in Phone Households

Response	Number of times response chosen (percentages)						Total[a] (%)	Percentage with three or more times
	0	1	2	3	4	5		
Completely dissatisfied								
Phone	93.2	5.8	.7	.1	.1		99.9	.2
Personal	89.8	8.4	1.2	.4	0	.1	99.9	.5
2								
Phone	94.4	4.6	1.0				100.0	.0
Personal	90.8	7.5	1.3	.3			99.9	.3
3								
Phone	84.5	13.5	1.7	.4			100.1	.4
Personal	82.0	14.9	2.7	.4			100.0	.4
Neutral								
Phone	64.2	23.8	8.3	2.9	.6	.2	100.0	3.7
Personal	61.7	26.4	8.6	2.1	.9	.3	100.0	3.3
5								
Phone	55.1	29.2	12.0	3.3	.4	.1	100.0	3.7
Personal	53.3	32.2	11.1	2.8	.4		99.9	3.3
6								
Phone	43.4	26.0	18.8	8.0	3.2	.6	100.0	11.8
Personal	38.0	28.7	19.5	10.0	3.2	.6	100.0	13.8
Completely satisfied								
Phone	20.3	21.4	20.3	17.5	12.6	8.0	100.1	38.1
Personal	26.3	21.9	18.2	16.5	10.6	6.5	100.0	33.6
No feelings; Never thought								
Phone	97.6	2.2	.2				100.0	—
Personal	99.1	.7	.1				99.9	—
NA								
Phone	95.3	3.0	.6	.5	.6	—[b]	100.0	—
Personal	97.3	2.2	.3	0	.1	—[b]	99.9	—
Total phone								57.9
Total personal								55.2

[a] N for Phone = 843; N for Personal = 760.
[b] Records with NA on all five items deleted from table.

across mode (38.1% on the telephone, 33.6% in person). In total, however, the proportion who choose any answer on three or more items is quite similar in both modes. The smaller method effects for this scale than for the "Delighted–Terrible" scale may again reflect the different methods of adapting the scales to telephone use.

Table 5.3 presents Goodman–Kruskal gamma measures for interassociations among the five life satisfaction items separately for the two different scales utilized. For both scales the two modes of interview produce similar interrelationships; 7 out of 10 pairs of the gammas lie within .10 of each other for the "Delighted–Terrible" scale, and all 10 of the "Satisfied–Dissatisfied" pairs of gammas do so. In almost all

TABLE 5.3
Interitem Association for Life Satisfaction Measures[a] for Phone and Personal Interview Samples

Measure	House	Health	Marriage	Living	Life
		Delighted–Terrible			
House					
Phone		.35	.42	.49	.18
Personal		.19	.42	.49	.29
Health					
Phone			.35	.41	.41
Personal			.27	.23	.33
Marriage					
Phone				.42	.51
Personal				.46	.46
Living					
Phone					.51
Personal					.49
		Satisfied–Dissatisfied			
House					
Phone		.21	.31	.37	.25
Personal		.24	.36	.45	.32
Health					
Phone			.35	.26	.38
Personal			.33	.22	.37
Marriage					
Phone				.36	.58
Personal				.41	.53
Living					
Phone					.45
Personal					.42

[a] Goodman–Kruskal gamma measures; personal data are for households with phones.

cases, however, the relationships between the attitude about "your health" and the other four are stronger in the telephone interview than in the personal interview. Despite this discrepancy the differences in general are very small, probably rarely exceeding sampling error.

Another response card question that was adapted for telephone use by using an unfolding technique asked the respondent to judge the probability that he or she would purchase a car in the next 12 months (Q. A10, V13023). Figure 5.5 presents a plotting of responses in the two modes for this question. In this use of the unfolding technique, the initial responses were "Probably Will," "Even Chance," or "Probably Won't." After any of the three was chosen, a follow-up question probed for a more specific answer. For that reason, it may be useful to compare the results on the middle category ("Even Chance") in this question with the middle category for the "Delighted–Terrible" scale, "Mixed," which was not followed-up with a second question. Figure 5.5 shows that the largest difference in the two distributions is probably due to the responses to the initial question. Among those initially choosing the middle alternative ("Even Chance") on the telephone, the follow-up question forms three equal-sized groups. Conversely, personal interview respondents

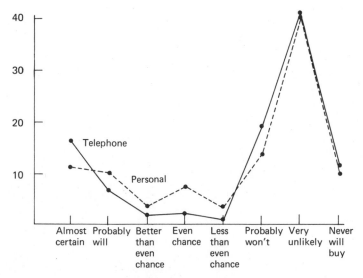

FIGURE 5.5. Response distribution for probability of buying automobile in next 12 months, by mode of interview. Data are weighted by reciprocals of selection probabilities. Personal data are for households with phones.

faced with all eight responses simultaneously tend to choose the middle point ("Even Chance") more than the two adjacent answers. This suggests that asking follow-up questions to unfold initial responses may yield a larger spread across the final response categories.

The final questions we shall examine are spouse's income and total family income. We chose spouse's income because it was the first of a three-question series on income and is subject to the smallest proportion of missing data. Total family income, on the other hand, although the last question in the series, is asked of everyone in the sample and permits analysis on a larger sample size. The reader will recall (Chapter 4) that the income questions utilized an 18-category response card in the personal interview survey; in the telephone survey the respondent was first asked the questions in an open-ended format. These responses were then collapsed into the 18 categories of the response card in Figures 5.6 and 5.7 for comparison with the personal survey results.

Both figures exhibit two differences between modes: (a) larger proportions of telephone respondents give answers from $15,000 to $17,499; and (b) higher proproportions of telephone respondents report incomes $20,000 and over. These results omit 13.5% of the telephone respondents on the spouse's income question and 15.0% on the total family income question. Some of those respondents answered the follow-up question with the trichotomous response scheme used for reluctant responders. Except for the category $17,500–$19,999 all

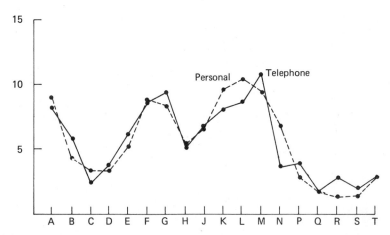

FIGURE 5.6. **Response distribution for spouse's income in 18 categories used in personal interview question, by mode of interview. Data are weighted by reciprocals of selection probabilities. Personal data are for households with phones.**

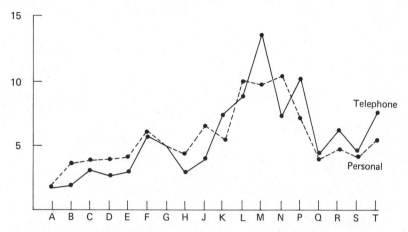

FIGURE 5.7. **Response distribution for total family income in 18 categories used in personal interview question, by mode of interview. Data are weighted by reciprocals of selection probabilities. Personal data are for households with phones.**

categories above $14,999 have proportionately more telephone respondents than personal interview respondents. This result may be influenced by the same phenomenon discovered earlier with the thermometer items. When the questions are asked in an open-ended format, respondents tend to give answers to the nearest thousand dollars; Category 13 contains those answering $18,000 and $19,000 among others, but its neighboring categories each contain *three* different thousands figures.

5.2 AN ANALYSIS OF OVERALL BIAS IN ESTIMATES OF VOTING BEHAVIOR BY SURVEY MODE

Two questions about the 1972 presidential election yield survey estimates for which population parameters are available. Most social science survey data do not permit validity checks with external information and our analysis of these items has few implications for biases in other measures. Indeed, even with these variables some assumptions are required to estimate bias. We examine two different questions, one asking whether the respondent voted in the 1972 presidential election, and another seeking a report of which candidate was chosen by the respondent. Published data on voter turnout and choice of presidential candidate are readily available for the entire United States.

Our survey data are limited to the household population in the coterminous United States. For statistics on the proportion of eligible adults voting in the 1972 election we used data from the Current Population Survey (CPS) (Bureau of the Census, 1973) from the November 1972 survey of the civilian noninstitutionalized population in the 50 states and the District of Columbia. The report on the November survey notes an overestimate of voting by about 9%, using survey data compared to official counts of votes. Instead of relying solely on the CPS data, we have combined data from official statistics[2] and CPS data to form an estimate of the percentage of the United States noninstitutionalized population who voted, and the proportion registered who did not vote. That operation estimates that 57.1% of the eligible adults voted in the 1972 election.

To form analogous estimates from our survey data we performed the following operations: (*a*) eliminated respondents who were not 18 years of age at the time of the election from both survey modes; and (*b*) combined the personal interview estimates of voting among the nonphone household population with those of the telephone survey to produce an estimate for the entire household population. After these operations were performed, the estimated proportion of eligible adults voting is 66.6% for the personal interview survey and 69.1% for the adjusted telephone survey data. Both these estimates are significantly different from the estimated population parameter (57.1%). The error probably arises from tendencies to overreport voting that other surveys have observed (Clausen, 1968–1969), enhanced by the long period of time that had passed since the election of 1972. For our purposes, however, the more important result is that both modes of data collection overestimate the actual vote to about the same degree; the difference between the two surveys is not statistically significant.

The lower panel of Table 5.4 presents similar comparisons for candidate choice from the two surveys and from official statistics. The same adjustments as outlined above were made to the survey data. In addition, only those respondents who reported that they did vote in the election were asked the candidate choice question. The percentage casting votes for Nixon was 60.7 according to published statistics; the personal interview survey estimate is 60.4%, and the telephone survey estimate is 62.3%. Both of these are much closer to the population parameter than was true for the case cited earlier, but once again there is a negligible difference between the two survey modes.

---

[2] U.S. Congress, Clerk of the House, *Statistics of the Presidential and Congressional Election of November 7, 1972* as reported in *Statistical Abstract of the United States 1974*, U.S. Bureau of the Census, Table 683, p. 425.

TABLE 5.4
Comparison of Telephone and Personal Survey Estimates with Official Statistics for Vote and Candidate Choice in 1972 Election[a]

Answer on whether respondent voted in 1972 presidential election

Voted in 1972 election	Sample type				Total household data	
	Phone	Personal with phones	Nonphone personal	Combined personal	Combined phone and nonphone personal[d]	Population statistics[b]
Yes	72.7%	68.7%	28.3%	66.6%	69.1%	57.1%
No—not reg.	9.5	10.7	23.9	11.4	10.7	33.6
No—other	15.4	18.7	44.2	20.0	17.7	9.3[c]
Don't know	2.5	1.9	3.6	2.0	2.6	
Total	100.0%	100.0%	100.0%	100.0%	100.0%	100.0%
Unweighted N	1441	1330	85	1415		

Candidate choice of voters in 1972 presidential election

Candidate choice	Sample type				Total households	
	Phone	Personal with phones	Nonphone personal	Total personal	Combined phone and nonphone personal[d]	Population statistics[e]
Nixon	61.7%	60.2%	68.4%	60.4%	62.3%	60.7%
McGovern	32.6	32.9	21.1	32.7	31.7	37.5
Other	3.8	4.5	7.9	4.6	4.1	1.8
Don't know	1.8	2.3	2.6	2.3	1.9	
Total	100.0%	100.0%	100.0%	100.0%	100.0%	100.0%
Unweighted N	985	890	22	912		

[a] Respondents less than 18 years of age in November, 1972 deleted from table.
[b] From U.S. Bureau of the Census (1973).
[c] Percentage registered who did not vote from U.S. Bureau of Census (1973).
[d] Using estimates of proportion of adults in phone and nonphone households from Klecka (1976), p. 17.
[e] From *Statistical Abstract of U.S.*, U.S. Bureau of the Census (1974), p. 425.

These results resemble those of Rogers (1976), who also compared the two survey modes on voter reports (except that both surveys here yield somewhat better estimates of the actual vote). However, Locander *et al.* (1974) found higher distortion in responses about voting in a primary election among personal interview respondents than among telephone respondents. Our results suggest that the difference between modes on these kinds of measures is probably rather small.

5.3 RESPONSE DIFFERENCES FOR OPEN-ENDED ITEMS

Open-ended measures allow respondents to construct their own answers to questions. The number of different responses that a person gives to open-ended questions in the two modes of data collection may be a useful proxy variable for the amount of effort invested in the task of answering (provided that multiple answers are routinely coded for open-ended items). Table 5.5 presents the percentage of respon-

TABLE 5.5

Percentage of Respondents Answering Open-Ended Questions Who Gave More than One Mention by Mode of Interview[a]

Subject of open-ended item	Telephone interviews	Personal interviews (phone households)	Percentage difference (personal–phone interviews)
1. Reasons for feelings about family's future economic status	27.6 (1316)	34.1 (1132)	6.5
2. Type of economic news recently heard	34.1 (906)	34.2 (728)	.1
3. Reasons for opinions about current conditions for buying a house	27.1 (1463)	35.1 (1252)	8.0
4. Reasons for opinions about conditions for buying a car in the next 12 months	22.9 (1184)	25.7 (1071)	2.8
5. Reasons for opinions about current conditions for buying major items	11.3 (1230)	14.2 (1073)	2.9
6. Type of most important problems facing the country[b]	56.3 (1537)	65.5 (1366)	9.2

[a] Total numbers of respondents giving at least one mention appear in parentheses below percentages. There are a total of 1734 respondents in the telephone sample, and 1440 in phone households with personal interviews. Those respondents absent from the figures had missing data or answered "Don't know" on the open-ended questions.

[b] First of a multiprobe question series.

dents who gave at least two answers among those responding to a given question (i.e., responses of "Don't Know," "INAP" and "Not Ascertained" are excluded). Results for six different open-ended questions show that a consistently smaller proportion of respondents gives multiple mentions on the telephone than in personal interviews. The difference is negligible for some questions (for example, Question 2, about the nature of economic news recently heard), but is rather large for other questions (for example, Question 6 about the most important problems facing the country).

The "most important problems" question was included in the survey as a direct test of the hypothesis that respondents would tend to answer open-ended items more superficially on the telephone than in person. Both telephone and personal interviewers were instructed to use only the probing specifically written into the questionnaire. The question appeared as:

B6. What do you think are the most important problems facing this country?

_____

_____

_____

_____

B6a. What other important problems are there?

_____

_____

B6b. (If problems mentioned in B6a) Are there any other important problems?

_____

_____

As many as two answers were coded for each of the three sections of the question, unless all answers to that section fell into the same one of thirteen response categories. In addition, coders counted the number of different problems mentioned, whether or not they fell into the same category. Figure 5.8 presents a plotting of the distribution of number of answers to the question, for telephone and personal interviews separately. The proportion of respondents giving more than two answers on this question is larger in personal interviews than in telephone interviews. This finding is consistent with the results ex-

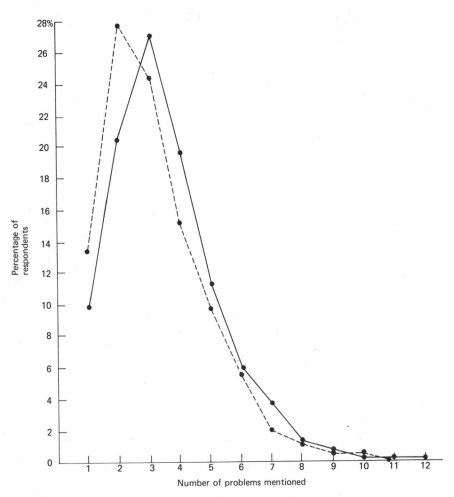

FIGURE 5.8. Percentage distribution of number of problems mentioned on "Most important problems," by mode of interview. Solid line = personal interview; broken line = telephone interview.

hibited in Table 5.5 on five other open-ended questions but is more detailed, since it compares complete counts of answers to each of six open-ended items.

We have shown that the telephone and personal interview samples differ in the number of mentions to the open-ended items and now observe that the number of items mentioned in response to a question is related to the distribution of substantive responses to that question. Table 5.6 presents percentage distributions of problems mentioned for phone and personal interviews separately, for respondents mentioning less than three and for those citing three or more problems. The unit of analysis in this table is not the respondent but rather the response; a respondent who mentions three different problems is counted three times in the table. At the bottom of the table the coefficients of dissimilarity compare the distributions of the telephone and personal interview samples.[3] They show that there are larger method effects ($\Delta = .093$) among those giving few answers than among those giving many answers ($\Delta = .080$).[4] These effects are rather small but in the hypothesized direction. Respondents giving few problems tend to omit mentions of social welfare problems on the phone relative to in-person much more so than respondents who give many answers.[5]

The results observed above include the effects of two different interviewing staffs, one for the telephone survey and another for the personal interview survey. Attempts were made to reduce these effects—similar training procedures, identical wording, and prescribed probing on answers. We cannot separate the method effects

---

[3] Note that the coding instructions for these items specified coding of second mentions for the three parts only if the second mention fell into a different category of problem than that of the first mention. There was no such restriction across the different parts of the question. The result is a coding of three pairs of problems, each pair containing two different types of problems. This coding design forces second mentions in each section into different categories and smooths the distribution of answers somewhat. The fact that the three sections together are not restricted in repeating codes makes the comparison above useful.

[4] $\Delta = \frac{1}{2} \sum_{i=1}^{H} |p_i - p_i'|$ where p_i is the proportion in the ith category for the telephone survey and p_i' is the proportion in the ith category for the personal interview data. The coefficient can be interpreted as the proportion of cases that would have to change categories for the two distributions to be identical.

[5] Data analysts often utilize only the first response to open-ended items with the hope that the first mentioned is the most important to the respondent. The inference is the same, however, if we restrict our comparison to the first mentioned problem—there are larger method effects on first response for those that mention few problems ($\Delta = .150$, $p_{x2} = .0039$) than for those giving many problems ($\Delta = .111$; $p_{x2} = .0016$).

TABLE 5.6
Percentage Distribution of All Answers Given to "Most Important Problems"
Question by Groups Differing on Number of Problems Mentioned

| | Answers of respondents | | | |
| | Giving one or two different problems | | Giving three or more different problems | |
Type of problem mentioned	Telephone interview (%)	Personal interview (phone households) (%)	Telephone interview (%)	Personal interview (phone households) (%)
Social welfare problems	21.5	30.1	24.0	27.3
Agriculture, food supply	.8	.7	.8	.6
Natural resources, ecology	4.2	3.6	5.8	4.7
Labor problems	1.3	.7	1.3	.8
Racial problems	2.8	2.4	3.6	3.5
Public order problems, crime	10.7	10.3	11.4	14.0
Economic, business problems	32.2	31.6	24.5	26.0
Foreign affairs	9.0	6.0	9.4	6.8
National defense	1.5	.9	2.7	3.0
Functioning of government	11.0	9.1	11.1	9.8
Campaign references	.2	.1	.3	.2
Attitudes of people toward life, others	4.1	3.3	3.6	2.2
Need to concentrate on domestic issues	.3	.0	.3	.0
Other problems	.5	1.2	1.1	1.1
Total %	100.1	100.0	99.9	100.0
Total number of answers	1020	671	2753	2918
Coefficient of dissimilarity between telephone and personal interview samples	.093		.080	

here from interviewer effects, but investigate next whether subgroups
of the sample exhibit differential effects.

5.4 CORRELATES OF THE TENDENCY TO TRUNCATE ANSWERS TO OPEN-ENDED ITEMS

The tendency to give shorter responses to open-ended questions on
the telephone deserves further attention because responses to open-
ended measures often enrich the understanding of respondents' feel-

ings and behaviors. Two purposes can be served by examining correlates of the tendency to truncate answers on the telephone. Because many surveys are conducted on subgroups of the population, we first search for differences among demographic subclasses in mode effects on open-ended responses. Such gross differences between groups are useful indicators of the implications of data collection method for surveys of these groups. In searching for explanations for these method differences, however, we also measure the net effects of several characteristics of respondents, in order to identify correlates that maintain their predictive power in the presence of other indicators.

Two types of variables, demographic and attitudinal, will be used. In the set of demographic variables we include age, sex, education, and income. The measures reflecting respondent attitudes about the interview itself include self-perceived uneasiness about answering different kinds of questions, interviewer judgments of the respondent's degree of suspicion toward the interview, and interviewer ratings of the respondent's interest in the interview.[6] Finally, we include the interviewer's judgment of the respondent's ability to articulate his or her thoughts. This second set of variables, labeled "respondent reactions," is included to investigate whether among groups sharing the same demographic characteristics there may be reactions to the interview experience that are related to the tendency toward fewer mentions on the telephone. If these reactions can be observed by the interviewer, then the problem of fewer responses on the phone may yield itself to experimental study of interviewing styles that could reduce its magnitude.

The dependent variable in the analysis is a dichotomy separating those respondents who mentioned one or two problems in total for all sections of the "most important problems" questions from those respondents who mentioned three or more problems. The overall table showing the relationship between mode of administration and number of responses is Table 5.7. This is merely a collapsing of the results presented in Figure 5.8 and shows that a larger proportion of personal interview respondents (69.6%) mention three or more prob-

---

[6] The last series of questions in both the telephone and personal interviews asked the respondent if he or she felt uneasy about answering questions concerning his or her: (a) income, (b) racial attitudes, (c) income tax returns, (d) health, (e) job, (f) voting behavior, and (g) political opinions. A scale was formed by counting the number of question types about which the respondent felt uneasy. The interviewer judgments were made in an "interviewer observation" section after the interview was completed.

TABLE 5.7
Number of Problems Mentioned in "Most Important Problems" Question by Mode
of Administration[a]

Mode of administration	Number of problems mentioned		Total (%)	N	Missing data
	One or two (%)	Three or more (%)			
Telephone	41.3	58.7	100.0	1534	200
Personal	30.4	69.6	100.0	1367	72

[a] Personal data are for households with phones.

lems than do respondents in telephone interviews (58.7%). The multivariate analysis that follows examines whether the relationship between mode of administration and the number of mentions is different
for various demographic and attitudinal subgroups.

Respondent's education (coded less than high school, high school,
more than high school), respondent's age (coded 18–30, 31–50, 51 or
more), and total family income (coded less than $7,500, $7,500–
$15,000, more than $15,000 per year) each singly appear to affect the
relationship between mode and number of mentions. Table 5.8 shows
results that are surprising—it is the better respondents, those that tend
to mention several problems, who exhibit the larger method effects.
For example, the difference between modes in proportions giving
many answers is 10.6% among respondents in the lowest educational
group, but 12.3% for those in the highest educational group. However,
in both modes the highest educational group generally gives larger
numbers of responses than the lowest educational group. Similarly,
the group with the highest total family income tends to mention more
problems in either mode relative to those with lower incomes, but also
exhibits larger differences in that behavior by mode of interview
(13.8%) than does the lowest income group (7.1%).

There were no apparent sex differences in method effects; both men
and women tend to mention fewer problems in the telephone interview. Respondents over 50 years of age show smaller differences
(6.1%) due to mode of interview than younger respondents (14.0% or
more). Two "respondent reaction" variables had no effect on the
relationship between mode of administration and number of problems
mentioned; these were the respondent's self-perceived uneasiness
about answering certain questions and the interviewer's perception of
whether the respondent appeared suspicious about the interview.

TABLE 5.8

Percentage of Those Answering Who Mentioned Three or More Problems by Five Independent Variables by Sample Type

	Percentage		
	Sample type		Difference
Subgroup	Phone	Personal[a]	(personal–phone)
1. Respondent's education			
0–11 years	44.2	54.8	10.6
High school diploma	55.5	68.6	12.1
13 or more years	69.6	81.9	12.3
2. Total family income			
$0–7500	52.1	59.2	7.1
$7500–15,000	59.1	71.3	12.2
$15,000+	64.0	77.8	13.8
3. Respondent's age			
18–30 years	58.0	72.1	14.1
31–50	62.6	76.6	14.0
50 or more	56.4	62.5	6.1
4. Ability to articulate thoughts			
1 on scale—very articulate	72.8	83.3	10.5
2 on scale	58.0	69.4	11.4
3 or 4— limited vocabulary	39.1	56.2	17.1
5. Interest in interview			
Very high	71.8	86.2	14.4
Above average	64.7	76.4	11.7
Average to very low	52.2	60.1	7.9

[a] Personal data are for households with phones.

Those judged most articulate, however, exhibited smaller method effects on number of responses (10.5%) than did those judged to have a "limited vocabulary" (17.1%). Conversely, those judged to have "very high interest" in the interview exhibited larger effects (14.4%) than those judged to have little interest (7.9%). Overall, the results tend to show that the people generally thought to perform best as respondents exhibit the greatest behavior differences in the two modes,[7] with personal interviews evoking consistently larger numbers of problems mentioned.

[7] We should note the possibility of "floor" effects producing these results. If we view the telephone interview as a suppressor of natural tendencies to mention problems in response to the question, then for those that tend to mention few problems naturally,

To construct multivariate models for the contingency tables measuring method effects on number of responses, we first use the demographic variables. Then we add the "respondent reaction" variable to the important demographic predictors. The demographic variables found to be related singly to method effects were included in a multivariate contingency table analysis, and log linear models were constructed to determine the unique effects of these demographic correlates.[8] Table 5.9 presents the results of step-wise model-fitting on the five-way table containing number of problems mentioned (N), mode of administration (M), total family income (I), respondent's age (A), and respondent's education (E). The categories for the five variables are those mentioned above, so the table contains $2 \times 2 \times 3 \times 3 \times 3 = 108$ cells.

In fitting models to this five-way table, we are most interested in terms that specify that the relationship between mode of administration and number of responses is different for different categories of the demographic variables. These terms are the three-way interaction terms denoted by NMI, NMA, and NME. The first model (in Table 5.9) includes all three of these interaction terms, the term measuring interactions among mode of administration and all demographic variables ($MIAE$), and all direct and interaction effects of the demographic variables on the number of responses ($NIAE$). This model fits the data rather poorly ($p = .379$), and later models show that some of the terms included in Model 1 are extraneous to the fit.[9]

Through a series of successful models we learn that education groups show no significant differences in their method effects (i.e., NME is not significant to the fit of the model; compare Models 2 and 1). Categories of age and family income seem to exhibit different method effects (i.e., MNI and MNA are both significant) but models containing both interaction terms do not fit the data significantly

---

the effects of the phone are limited by mentioning at least one problem. This does not appear to be a large problem in these data. The smallest subgroup percentage giving three or more problems in person is 54.8%; there is large opportunity to reduce that before the limiting point of 0% is reached.

   [8] For a description of this analysis technique see L. A. Goodman, "The Multivariate Analysis of Qualitative Data: Interactions among Multiple Classification," *Journal of the American Statistical Association*, 1970, **65**:227–67. The ECTA program was used in these calculations.

   [9] The reader should note that these chi-square and probability levels are calculated under the assumption of simple random sampling and would be somewhat different if all the complexities of the sample design were reflected. We assume that the relative fit across models would be about the same both in the actual sample and in a simple random sample.

TABLE 5.9
Loglinear Models Fit to the Five-Way Contingency Table Including Number of Responses (N), Mode of Administration (M), Family Income (I), Respondent's Age (A), and Respondent's Education (E)[a]

Model	Marginals fit	χ^2	df	p
1	MIAE, NIAE, NMI, NMA, NME	21.31	20	.379
2	MIAE, NIAE, NMI, NMA	21.66	22	.480
3	MIAE, NIAE, NMI, NME	22.21	22	.448
4	MIAE, NIAE, NMA, NME	22.16	22	.451
5	MIAE, NIAE, NMI	22.81	24	.5 < p < .7
6	MIAE, NIAE, NMA	22.97	24	.5 < p < .7
7	MIAE, NIAE, NME	23.53	24	.489
8	MIAE, NIAE, NM	25.01	26	.5 < p < .7
9	MIAE, NMI, NMA, NAE	34.91	38	.5 < p < .75
10	MIAE, NMI, NMA, NE	37.47	42	> .5
11	MIAE, NMI, NAE	36.09	40	.5 < p < .75
12	MIAE, NMI, NA, NE	38.86	44	> .5
13	MIAE, NM, NI, NA, NE	41.82	46	> .5
14	MIAE, NMA, NIE	35.65	40	.5 < p < .75
15	MIAE, NMA, NI, NE	39.31	44	> .5
16	MIAE, NMI, NA	130.29	46	.000
17	MIAE, NMI, NE	44.32	46	> .5
18	MIAE, NMA, NI	131.32	46	.000
19	MIAE, NMA, NE	46.35	46	.458

[a] A total of 2444 cases had no missing data on the five variables, out of a possible 3173. The two largest sources of missing data were income (561 cases) and the 116 cases that broke off interviews before completing all questions. The table contains $2 \times 2 \times 3 \times 3 \times 3 = 108$ cells all of which contained elements. Parameters measuring effects of polytomous variables are differences between the average log frequency over all levels (the so-called "standard effects" in Goodman, 1970).

better than models with each singly. The base model to which we compare models containing method effects for income and age groups is *MIAE, NIAE, NM* (Model 8), which specifies that income, education, and age affect the number of problems mentioned in the same way for both modes, and that the method effects that do exist are the same for all subgroups. This model fits the data well ($\chi^2 = 25.01$, $df = 26$, $p > .5$).

Indeed, comparing Models 5–7 to Model 8 shows that none of the terms, *MNA, NMI,* or *NME* contributes significantly to the fit of the model. For example, once the direct effects of income and education on number of mentions are controlled, age groups do not exhibit significantly different method effects. Similar statements can be made about the other variables, controlling on the remaining two. The percentage differences observed in Table 5.8 disappear when other demographic variables are controlled.

The most attractive model is probably 13 (*MIAE, NM, NI, NA, NE*), incorporating the same method effect for all demographic subgroups, *NM*. Although this model suggests that the subgroup differences in Table 5.8 disappear when proper controls are introduced, the researcher cannot introduce these controls in most work and must deal with the gross effects of the variables. None of the demographic variables usefully predicted method effects in the multivariate analyses. Nevertheless, it is helpful to include a representative of the demographic measures in our analysis of the "respondent reaction" variables and method effects. Either age or income would be appropriate for this purpose; we choose to include age because of a lower missing data rate.

Table 5.10 presents the results of log linear analysis on the five-way table including number of problems mentioned (*N*), mode of administration (*M*), respondent's age (*A*), interviewer judgment of the respondent's ability to articulate his or her thoughts (*T*), and of the respon-

TABLE 5.10
Loglinear Models Fit to the Five-Way Contingency Table Including Number of Problems Mentioned (*N*), Mode of Administration (*M*), Respondent's Age (*A*), Interviewer Judgment of Respondent's Ability to Articulate Thoughts (*T*) and of Respondent's Apparent Interest in the Interview (*R*)[a]

Model	Marginals fit	χ^2	df	p
1	*MATR, NATR, NMA, NMT, NMR*	15.30	20	.7 < p < .8
2	*MATR, NATR, NMA, NMT*	19.78	22	.5 < p < .7
3	*MATR, NATR, NMA, NMR*	17.63	22	.7 < p <.8
4	*MATR, NATR, NMT, NMR*	22.80	22	.41
5	*MATR, NATR, NMA*	20.59	24	.5 < p < .7
6	*MATR, NATR, NM*	27.55	26	.381
7	*MATR, NMA, NTR*	38.19	40	.5 < p < .75
8	*MATR, NMA, NT, NR*	41.13	44	> .5
9	*MATR, NM, NA, NT, NR*	48.52	46	.372
10	*MATR, NMA, NT*	64.59	46	.036
11	*MATR, NMA, NR*	103.94	46	.00002
12	*MATR, NMA*	188.89	48	.0

[a] A total of 2827 cases had no missing data on the five variables out of a possible 3173. The largest sources of missing data were the 116 cases that broke off interviews before completing all questions. The table contains $2 \times 2 \times 3 \times 3 \times 3 = 108$ cells of which 5 contained no elements; .5 cases were added to all cells of the table. Parameters measuring effect of polytomous variables are differences between the average log frequency for each level and the average log frequency over all levels (the so-called "standard effects" in Goodman, 1970).

dent's apparent interest in the interview (R).[10] As before, we are interested in the significance of terms that indicate different method effects across categories of ability to articulate thoughts (T) and interest (R). These terms are NMT and NMR. We want to see if these terms are significant even in the presence of the demographic interaction NMA. Table 5-10 shows that they are not; Model 8, that contains the age interaction NMA, fits the data better ($\chi^2 = 41.13$, $df = 44$) than alternative models including either or both NMR and NMT. A comparison of the fit of Models 8 and 9 tests the significance of age as a predictor of method effects. In the presence of the "respondent reaction" variables, age has significant influence on method effects ($\chi^2 = 7.39$, $df = 2$, $.25 < p < .01$). We have already demonstrated (Table 5.9) that other demographic variables can explain these effects. That is, these particular variables obtained from interviewer judgments do not identify any distinct subgroups susceptible to the method effect that are not also identified by age.[11]

In this section we first learned that phone interviews tended to yield fewer second mentions on open-ended items. Furthermore, discrepancies between the types of problems mentioned on the phone and face-to-face are larger among that group that gives fewer mentions.

Given this evidence, we attempted to identify groups which appeared most susceptible to the tendency to give fewer mentions on the telephone. Both demographic variables and measures of the respondent's reaction to the interview were examined. Gross effects were found for age and income groups. In all cases, those respondents who tend to give many responses in both modes exhibit the larger differences between the two modes of interview. Higher income groups and younger respondents exhibit the greatest tendency to give relatively fewer mentions on the telephone than in person. Method effects were also observed to be larger for those who were judged as having great ability to articulate their thoughts and as being very interested in the interview.

The gross effects associated with demographic variables are important for surveys of subpopulations defined by the various categories,

[10] The respondents' ability to articulate thoughts is employed as a three category variable collapsed from a four category scale, 1 = 1st category on scale—Very Articulate, 2 = 2nd category on scale, 3 = 3rd and 4th categories on scale—Limited Vocabulary). Interest is also a three category collapsing of a four category scale (1 = Very High Interest, 2 = Above Average Interest, 3 = Average to Very Low Interest).

[11] It is useful to note that a similar analysis replacing age by income yields the same conclusion.

even though they diminish when controls are introduced. The method effects associated with the "respondent reaction" variables demonstrate that interviewers can perceive respondent qualities that are associated with the tendency to give fewer responses on the telephone. We were unsuccessful in identifying predictors of method effects that maintain their influence in the presence of control variables. The gross effects are useful for matching mode of interview to subpopulation, but an understanding of the causal structure of method effects was not gained in this work.

5.5 SUMMARY

In this study, comparisons between telephone and personal interview responses are possible for more than 200 questions. With respect to format, three types of measures are noteworthy: (1) questions using visual aids (referred to as show cards or response cards) to help respondents in the personal interview survey; (2) questions for which some external validation of response is feasible; and (3) questions that permit respondents to phrase answers in their own words rather than by selecting among fixed alternatives.

1. Questions for which response cards were used in the personal interview survey usually involved responses along a dimension including many identifiable points, some of which were labeled. The personal interview responses tended to cluster around the labeled points. In the telephone survey, some of these questions were altered to an "unfolding" format, in which the numerous alternatives were presented as a sequence of more limited choices. Responses to such questions did not show the clustering evoked by the visual aids. Other questions with response cards were adapted to the telephone through verbal presentation of all response categories.

In answering questions on life satisfaction, telephone respondents (using an "unfolding" response format) were more likely to choose the "Mixed" alternative than were the personal interview respondents, who were assisted by visual aids showing the full range of responses from "Delighted" to "Terrible." On the positive side of the scale, telephone respondents were more likely to choose the extreme ("Delighted"), and on the negative side less likely to do so ("Terrible"). These differences between telephone and personal interview responses are affected by the specific wording of alternatives. Life-satisfaction questions presented with a response dimension of "Completely satisfied" to "Completely dissatisfied" showed similar distributions for the two modes. Moreover, interrelationships among the five measures of life satisfaction were very similar for the two sets of data—telephone and personal interview.

Response cards were also used in asking questions about personal and family income. Respondents in the personal interview survey were presented with a card showing 18 income categories; in the telephone survey, income questions were asked in open-ended form. The resulting distributions are very similar for the two modes, but the differences that do occur reflect the tendency of people to answer in round numbers—thousands—when the question format is open. There is also some tendency toward higher reported income in the telephone mode; the telephone survey shows slightly larger proportions of the sample in almost all categories of $15,000 or more.

2. A second set of measures for which comparisons are particularly instructive involves voting behavior. Published data on voter turnout and candidate choice provide a validity check on responses in both the telephone and personal interview surveys. According to these external sources, 57.1% of the noninstitutionalized adult civilian population voted in the 1972 presidential election. The corresponding survey estimates were 66.6% for the personal interview mode and 69.1% for the telephone survey. Both overestimated the vote, as retrospective self-reports tend to do, but the difference between the two modes is not statistically significant.

The survey results for candidate choice were more accurate. Official statistics show that Mr. Nixon received 60.7% of the 1972 vote. The estimate from the personal interview survey was 60.4 and from the telephone survey 62.3%. Again, the difference between the two modes was not statistically significant.

3. Open-ended questions constitute the third set of measures for which comparisons between the two modes of data collection were made, and here the differences between the two modes are more complex.

(a) Fewer respondents give answers involving "multiple mentions" on the telephone than in person. Differences were negligible for some questions (e.g., type of economic news recently heard) and large for others (important problems facing the country).

(b) The tendency to give fewer multiple mentions is associated with substantive differences. For example, social welfare problems were mentioned proportionately less often in the telephone survey than in the personal interviews.

(c) Both differences can be seen as part of a more general tendency to give shorter, more truncated answers on the telephone than in person. This tendency occurred in all demographic groups but was, surprisingly, stronger among respondents of higher income. These people tended, on the whole, to give longer and more elaborated responses, but they were more affected by differences in mode. Differences among age groups were small, and there were no differences between male and female response patterns. Differences associated with the telephone or personal mode were smaller among respondents judged highly articulate but larger among those judged highly interested.

Log linear models were constructed in an attempt to illuminate these findings. These models were evaluated in terms of fit to a five-way contingency table including number of responses (multiple mentions), mode of administration, family income, age, and education.

Chapter 6

Measurable Sources of Error in the Survey Data

All survey data are subject to sampling and nonsampling errors which together can create differences between sample estimates and the corresponding population parameters. Sampling errors arise from the fact that only a subset of the population is measured in the survey. When the sample design yields a probability sample (where each member of the population has a known, nonzero chance of selection) the magnitude of those errors can be estimated from the sample itself by calculating the sampling variance. Usually these sampling errors balance out over different samples so that the average of all sample estimates is exactly the population parameter of interest.

Nonsampling errors arise from measurements with poorly formulated questions, from incorrect replies to the questions (response errors), from failure to measure some members of the sample (nonresponse errors), from excluding eligible members of the population (noncoverage errors), and from unintended effects of interviewers on responses. Like sampling errors, some nonsampling errors have no effect on averages over different samples; they merely increase the variation in values obtained across the different sample draws (measured by response variance). Other nonsampling errors create biases in all sample estimates; for example, to the extent that nonrespondents differ from respondents, failure to measure all members of the sample will bias sample values. Not all nonsampling errors can be estimated from the sample itself; some external data are often required. Research designs can be adjusted, however, to estimate some sources of nonsampling errors, notably the effects of different interviewers on responses.

We begin by discussing the undercoverage of the household population by telephone and personal interview surveys. In Section 6.1 we examine the characteristics of households without telephones, those that have no chance of being selected in telephone surveys. We then describe the ways by which households and respondents have larger or smaller chances of being selected into the surveys. Just as excluding some households can affect sample estimates, so too can assigning unequal probabilities to members of the population. In Section 6.2 we estimate some of those effects on the precision of the survey results.

We then examine the sampling errors (Section 6.3) associated with means and proportions from the two telephone samples and from the personal interview sample. We have chosen a set of estimates from those available in the study and have calculated them for the total sample and for different demographic subclasses. Our interest in this analysis is to compare the sampling variance of estimates constructed from the three different designs. In the following chapter we will discuss the cost of implementing the two modes of surveys, and that discussion can be combined with our present analysis to estimate the cost per unit precision purchased in each design. Ignoring differential nonsampling errors, such calculations could guide a researcher in choosing sample designs and mode of interview.

In Section 6.4 we discuss the variance of measures arising from the idiosyncracies of different interviewers who obtain the information from respondents. Although interviewer training attempts to standardize the behavior of interviewers, personality differences among them and interactions between respondent and interviewer traits may result in variations across interviewers in answers obtained from the same respondent. It is the assumption of most survey analysts that these errors across interviewers balance out over the sample and that the unbiased nature of sample estimates is maintained. Variation across interviewers, however, does increase the variance in estimates over different samples and thus is a proper concern of our current discussion.

6.1 COVERAGE OF THE UNITED STATES HOUSEHOLD POPULATION BY THE TWO MODES OF SURVEYS

Areal probability sampling methods used in personal interview surveys give every unit of space throughout the population some nonzero chance of being selected. By sampling physical locations and attempting to assign each member of the population to one housing unit, the method theoretically offers complete coverage of the residential population. When the method is applied, however, errors of field listing occur, and some members of the population are not covered by the resulting frame. Oversights are probably more likely with nontraditional structures (e.g., garage apartments, single family structures divided into several apartments). For the SRC national sample of dwellings, about 95% of all dwellings in the coterminous United States are estimated to be covered by the sampling frame. (See Kish & Hess, 1958, for a more detailed discussion of noncoverage in areal probability samples.)

Sampling for a telephone survey could be performed in the same manner. After a sample household has been identified through areal sampling methods, field workers could determine the best way of contacting the household members by telephone—using the household telephone if present, a telephone at the place of employment, or at a neighbor's residence. The expense of using areal probability sampling methods for telephone surveys makes such a plan less attractive than the use of random-digit generation for sampling telephone numbers. With that technique, sample households are identified only through their telephone numbers. If a household does not subscribe to a telephone service, no members of the household can be selected into the sample. Thus undercoverage in telephone surveys is concentrated in a very well-defined subpopulation.

There are published sources of data on the noncoverage of the household population by telephones. The 1970 census of population included an item asking about the "availability" of a telephone to the household. Such a question would combine into a single category those households that were telephone subscribers and those who could be reached only by a telephone outside the housing unit. Approximately 88% of the households reported having a telephone available. A.T. & T. publishes estimates of the proportion of households with telephones, but notes that their calculation formula produces an overestimate. For 1975 they estimated that 95% of all households

contained a telephone.[1] We prefer a different data source for an estimate of the undercoverage of households by telephones. The Law
Enforcement Assistance Administration's National Crime Survey interviews large samples of households each month. The January 1976
panel of the survey contained about 10,000 households, 90.4% of
which had telephones within the housing unit (Klecka, 1976). We
think that this estimate of telephone coverage more accurately describes the potential coverage of telephone surveys.

The 10% noncoverage of households is double that experienced in
areal probability samples, and the biasing effects of this noncoverage
may be even greater because households without telephones have
very different characteristics from those with telephones. Some information regarding the characteristics of households without telephones is available from personal interview data collected by SRC. In
preparation for this project we inserted a question into the 1975 SRC
Fall Omnibus Survey, a personal interview survey with a sample size
of about 1500 households. The question asked about the presence of a
telephone in the household. We repeated that question in the personal interview survey of this project and have combined the data
from those two surveys to estimate the proportion of households that
are not telephone subscribers. We also used other measures from the
survey to examine the characteristics of households without telephones; the results are presented in Table 6.1.

Combining the data from the two surveys, we find that 7.2% of the
households are not telephone subscribers. We emphasize that this is
7.2% of the *respondent* households; both surveys are subject to about
25% nonresponse. If the nonrespondents are disproportionately nonsubscribers, then our estimate of undercoverage is low. We were
sensitive to this problem and asked interviewers to record on a nonresponse form whether they were able to determine if the household
had a telephone. Many times the interviewers found that this was an
impossible task. Sometimes they made guesses about the existence of
a telephone, and other times they determined this fact with certainty,
either by observation or by asking a household member. If the nonresponse data obtained are added to the results cited, however, the
percentage of households with telephones is largely unchanged. The
lower rate of telephone coverage estimated by the National Crime
Survey data was based on a larger sample of households and a higher

[1] Source: *Statistical Abstract of the United States,* 1976 Bureau of the Census, GPO,
Washington, D.C., Table 877, p. 533.

response rate, and we place greater confidence in that estimate of 90.4% coverage.

The SRC data may be useful nevertheless in measuring the correlates of telephone subscription. The various subtables of Table 6.1 show that nonphone households are disproportionately low-income, rural, rented units, likely to contain only one adult, and more likely occupied by blacks than other racial groups. The most important correlate of telephone ownership appears to be family income; telephone samples will fail to include lower income groups in their proper proportions.

The use of telephone surveys alone for inference to the entire household population is inappropriate to the extent that this undercoverage biases sample statistics. For some studies (e.g., surveys of welfare recipients), low income groups are an important portion of the population of interest, and the bias in sample statistics of a telephone survey would be large. For other purposes, when a large proportion of low income groups is not part of the study population, the bias inherent in studying only telephone households may be smaller. When the entire household population is of interest, telephone surveys will miss about 10% of those eligible. For some measures that are correlated to financial status of respondent or to other attributes related to phone ownership, the bias may be large. For measures unrelated to phone ownership, little bias may be introduced by omitting the nonphone households. The tables in Appendix II can be used to examine the variation in the amount of bias over different kinds of measures.

6.2 CHARACTERISTICS OF RESPONDENT HOUSEHOLDS

The personal interview sample was designed to assure that each occupied housing unit in coterminous United States would have an equal chance of selection. In the telephone sample, since households were sampled by their telephone numbers, each telephone household in coterminous United States had a probability of selection proportional to the number of telephone numbers in the household. If a household had two different telephone numbers, it had twice the probability of selection as had a household with a single number. Table 6.2 illustrates that the problem of unequal probabilities of household selection is a small one in the telephone sample.

From the personal interview results we see that only 3.2% of the

TABLE 6.1
Household Telephone Ownership by Various Household Characteristics in
Combined 1975 Fall and 1976 Spring Omnibus Data

	Percentage		
	Households without telephone	Households with telephone	N
1. Total sample	7.2	92.8	3062[a]
2. Region			
Northeast	5	95	641
North Central	5	95	861
South	13	87	979
West	4	96	581
3. Type of primary area			
Self-representing central cities	9	91	234
Suburbs of self-representing	1	99	477
Non-self-representing SMSAs	6	94	1316
Non-self-representing non-SMSAs	11	89	1035
4. Number of adults in household			
1	12	88	767
2	6	94	1860
3	4	96	312
4 or more	2	98	123
5. Number of children in household			
0 < 18 years	7	93	1687
1 < 18 years	7	93	495
2 < 18 years	7	93	465
3 < 18 years	10	90	234
4 or more < 18 years	10	90	177
Missing data	—	—	4
6. Race			
White	6	94	2662
Black	18	82	303
Other	12	88	86
Missing data	—	—	11
7. 1974 family income			
< $4000	20	80	392
4000–7499	13	87	445
7500–9999	10	90	283
10,000–14,999	4	96	571
15,000–19,999	3	97	437
20,000–24,999	2	98	261
25,000 and over	1	99	297
Missing data	—	—	376

(Continued)

TABLE 6.1 (*Continued*)

	Percentage		
	Households without telephone	Households with telephone	*N*
1975 fall omnibus data only			
8. Housing ownership			
Home owners	4	96	948
Renters	17	83	419
Neither own nor rent	3	97	37
Missing data	—	—	112
9. House value for owners			
< $15,000	16	84	161
15,000–24,999	3	97	185
25,000–34,999	2	98	167
35,000 or more	0	100	318
Missing data; renters	—	—	685
10. Monthly rent			
for renters in dollars			
50 or less	28	72	58
51–100	26	74	119
101–150	16	84	122
151 or more	4	96	126
Missing data; owners	—	—	1091
1976 spring omnibus data only			
11. Type of structure			
Single family house	5	95	1102
Other one-unit structure	0	100	15
2–4 total housing			
units in structure	14	86	157
5–9 total housing			
units in structure	16	84	67
10 or more total			
HUs in structure	6	94	100
Trailer in mobile home			
park	9	91	33
Trailer in other location	20	80	55
Missing data	—	—	17

[a] Five households of the two sample total of 3067 had missing data on the telephone ownership questions.

TABLE 6.2
Number of Different Telephone Numbers in Respondent Telephone Households by Mode of Interview

Number of different numbers	Mode of interview	
	Telephone (%)	Personal in phone households (%)
1	94.7	96.8
2	5.1	3.1
3	.2	.1
4	.1	0
Total	100.1	100.0
N	1638	1435
Missing data	96	4

households with telephones have more than one number. Since these households have multiple chances of being selected into the telephone sample, they represent a larger fraction of that sample, and we see that 5.4% of the interviews taken on the telephone were for households with more than one phone number. To correct for unequal probabilities in estimates of means and proportions, the reciprocals of the number of phone numbers should be used as weights. Therefore, 94.7% of the records should receive a weight of 1.0, 5.1% of a weight of ½; etc. The effect of this weighting is an increase in the sampling variance of the means and proportions calculated; the variance is increased by a factor approximated by

$$\frac{\Sigma p_i w_i^2}{(\Sigma p_i w_i)^2} = 1.013,$$

where p_i proportion of the records receives the weight w_i. The increase in variance due to weighting alone is then approximately 1.3%.

When examining statistics describing households, no selection weights are required for the personal interview sample and only those reflecting the number of telephone numbers are needed for the telephone sample. When examining statistics on respondent characteristics, however, another property of the household is relevant. Since only one adult (18 years or older) was selected in each sample household, the probability of each respondent's being selected is proportional to the total number of adult members of the household. Those respondents living alone in a household have twice the probability of selection of those in households with two adults, three times those in households with three adults, and so on.

Table 6.3 shows that the majority of interviews were taken in households with two adults (57.5% in the phone sample and 60.6% in the personal interview sample). Telephone interview households tend to be larger; proportionately more of them have three or more adults than do personal interview households. The differences are small, however, and a shift of a few cases in either sample would produce identical distributions. The reciprocals of the number of adults are used for selection weights in estimates of means and proportions. The approximate effect of this weighting on the sampling variance of means and proportions is $\sum p_i w_i^2 / (\sum p_i w_i)^2 = 1.179$ for the phone sample and 1.168 for the personal interview sample. This suggests about a 17–18% increase in the sampling variance due to unequal probabilities of selection.

The complete selection weight is the product of the two weights above:[2]

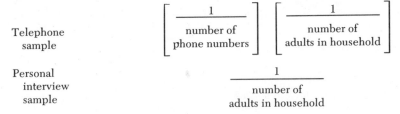

Telephone sample:
$$\left[\frac{1}{\text{number of phone numbers}} \right] \left[\frac{1}{\text{number of adults in household}} \right]$$

Personal interview sample:
$$\frac{1}{\text{number of adults in household}}$$

Sometimes personal interviewers cannot contact respondents because some physical barrier prevents them from doing so; locked apartment buildings, subdivisions with security guards preventing access, some rural areas with locked gates, and other situations generate noninterviews before any interaction with sample households. We began this project with the hypothesis that those types of noninterview in the personal interview survey might become interviews in a telephone survey because the telephone medium circumvents such physical barriers. Table 6.4 shows that every category of multiunit structure has a larger representation among the telephone survey respondents than in the personal mode. The differences are not large; in all, 3.9% more of the telephone respondents live in multiunit structures than do the personal interview respondents. Corre-

---

[2] These weights correct for unequal probabilities of selection *within* the two samples separately. In an analysis combining personal and telephone interview data, other weighting factors would be introduced to adjust for unequal base sampling fractions for the personal and telephone samples.

TABLE 6.3
Total Number of Adults in Respondent's Household by Sample Type

	Percentage	
Number of adults	Telephone interview	Personal interview in phone households
1	23.0	23.5
2	57.5	60.6
3	13.8	10.8
4	4.4	3.9
5	1.0	.8
6	.1	.3
7	.1	.1
8 or more	0	.1
Total	99.9	100.1
N	1619	1439
Missing data		
Terminated	101	
Other	14	0

TABLE 6.4
Type of Structure for Respondents in Telephone Survey and Personal Interview Survey within Telephone Households

Type of structure	Telephone[a] survey (%)	Personal interview (telephone households) (%)
Single family house	71.3	73.8
Other one unit	.5	.7
2–4 housing units	12.1	9.5
5–9 housing units	4.3	3.9
10 or more housing units	7.7	6.8
Mobile home in mobile home park	2.1	2.1
Mobile home in other location	2.1	3.1
	100.1	99.9
Total unweighted N	1600	1442
Missing data	134	17

[a] Weighted by reciprocal of number of different telephone numbers within household.

spondingly, more personal interview respondents live in single family houses (73.9–71.3%).

6.3 SAMPLING ERRORS ON TELEPHONE AND PERSONAL INTERVIEW SAMPLES

Readers who fail to recall the design of the two different telephone samples or of the personal interview sample may wish to review the discussion of Chapter 2. In any case, we begin our presentation of sampling error with a review of properties of a sample that affect the precision of its estimates.[3]

Stratification and clustering are two major dimensions upon which sample designs may vary. In general, stratification can be used to ensure the selection of different kinds of population elements into the sample and increase the precision of sample estimates. In essence, separate samples are drawn from distinct but totally inclusive groupings (strata) within the population. Clustering is generally introduced into a design to reduce the costs of data collection by ensuring that sample households will be on the same block and thereby reduce travel costs. Almost all kinds of clustering in sample design decrease the precision of sample estimates, because people in the same cluster resemble one another to various degrees and less new information about the population is obtained by taking several people from the same cluster than by taking people at random.

One property affecting the precision of sample estimates is relevant only to the telephone samples. Whenever a sample is designed to study only a subset of the population *and* no separate listing of that subset is available, some screening must be done to determine whether each element selected belongs to the desired subset. For example, if one were interested in a sample of elderly people and drew a national household sample as a way of obtaining a sample of this type of person, many selected households would contain no eligible respondent. Just by chance some draws of the sample may contain more elderly people than others. This variation in sample size over different draws decreases the precision of other sample estimates; the smaller the subset of interest, the larger the loss of precision. In the telephone samples, less than one-quarter of all the sample numbers

---

[3] We use the term "precision" to denote the size of variable errors arising from sampling. The higher the precision of an estimate the lower its sampling variance.

are members of our population of interest—working household numbers. For that reason, the sampling variance for the telephone samples is increased over that expected from a sampling of exclusively working household numbers. Some estimates of the size of this effect are presented later in this chapter.

All three samples we are analyzing utilize stratification; in the telephone samples this stratification is possible only through the level of the central office code and does not affect numbers within the same central office code. The stratification is based on geography and size of telephone exchange. The stratification in the personal interview sample is much deeper, through several stages of selection, and includes grouping by size of place, SMSA status, size of largest city in area, rate of population growth, major industry, and, in the South, percentage nonwhite. One telephone sample and the personal interview sample are clustered into the 74 primary areas of the SRC national household sample. In the personal interview sample, further clustering is introduced for sampling within each primary area to reduce travel costs. In the clustered telephone sample, selected telephone numbers are generated at random throughout each entire primary area.

Many data analysis programs assume that the interview records were obtained from a simple random sample. This ignores the stratification and clustering that many designs may have implemented. One often-used measure of sampling error is a multiplicative factor that can be used to correct the simple random sample variance by taking into account the complexities of the design. A design effect or *deff* is defined as

$$Deff = \frac{\text{actual sampling variance}}{\text{simple random sample variance of sample with equal number of elements}}$$

The label *deft* is used to designate the square root of *deff*. If the actual sampling variance is larger than that expected from a simple random sample of the same size, *deft* is greater than 1.0. For the stratified random telephone sample, a *deft* greater than 1.0 or increased variance relative to a simple random sample of the working household numbers arises from the lack of control of sample size. For the clustered telephone sample, a *deft* greater than 1.0 arises from both lack of control on sample size *and* clustering effects. For the personal interview sample, *defts* greater than 1.0 arise from the effects of clustering. We expect the *defts* for the stratified random telephone sample to be lower than those for the clustered telephone sample for the same statistic.

Before describing our expectations for the relative values of *defts* for the personal interview sample we note one complication in the comparison. Design effects can be divided into two components

$$deff = 1 + \rho \, (b - 1)$$
$$deft = \sqrt{deff},$$

where ρ is a measure of intracluster homogeneity and b is the average size of the cluster in number of interviews. (See Hansen, Hurwitz, & Madow, 1953, or Kish, 1965.)

This disaggregation of the design effect reveals the dependence of *deft* on the number of interviews taken from each cluster. For example, ignoring the design differences in the self-representing areas, the primary areas of the clustered telephone sample are the same as those in the personal interview sample. Because the personal interview sample is larger (a larger b in the formula) than the clustered telephone sample, we would expect higher design effects for the personal interview sample. The increase is merely a function of the size of the clusters, not of any differences in the sample design, and for that reason we created *defts* for a reduced personal interview sample. These figures are presented in the fourth column of the *defts* section in Table 6.5. These were calculated using a sample size of 865, the maximum sample size for the clustered telephone sample.

We designed the analysis of sampling errors using the guidelines of Kish, Groves, and Krotki (1976), choosing a wide variety of variables: those that we suspected were sensitive to clustering effects (characteristics related to the socioeconomic status of the respondent) and those that we hypothesized were relatively immune to such effects (demographic characteristics of respondents). We also attempted to represent the various topic areas treated in the questionnaire. Using these criteria we chose 22 variables and computed means or proportions on the total sample and on 11 different demographic subclasses of the samples. These subclasses were defined by categories of age of respondent, total family income, respondent's education, and race.

Table 6.5 presents results for the statistics calculated on the total sample. All statistics are *proportions* of the total sample except for those that are labeled as mean values. We present three separate pieces of information for each sample type: the mean value or proportion of adults having such a characteristic, the unweighted number of observations, and the square root of the design effect (*deft*). All means

TABLE 6.5
Sampling Error Calculations for Stratified Phone, Clustered Phone, and Total Personal Interview Samples

Variable description	Mean value or proportion of adults			Number			Square root of design effect			
	Stratified	Clustered	Personal	Stratified	Clustered	Personal	Stratified	Clustered	Personal	Personal reduced
Reporting that they itemized deductions on 1975 tax return	.53	.53	.47	750	789	1486	1.07	1.11	.95	.97
Feeling satisfied to completely satisfied about life as a whole	.84	.83	.83	402	401	723	1.02	1.56	1.00	1.00
Reporting total family income less than $7500	.19	.20	.26	662	703	1348	1.00	.80	1.05	1.03
Feeling mostly satisfied, pleased, or delighted about life as a whole	.80	.79	.86	393	435	811	1.05	1.20	1.09	1.08
Feeling better off financially now than 1 year ago	.38	.38	.36	837	865	1531	1.07	1.23	1.09	1.05
Reporting that they planned to vote in 1976 presidential election	.85	.86	.78	780	796	1548	1.04	1.28	1.11	1.06
Reporting that they voted in 1972 presidential election	.65	.70	.62	787	814	1507	1.12	1.32	1.18	1.10
Reporting that they were not presently working	.37	.35	.42	799	838	1547	1.07	.97	1.19	1.10
Feeling saving money more important now than usual	.64	.59	.68	800	837	1494	1.05	1.46	1.20	1.11
Feeling "very happy" these days	.34	.30	.30	794	821	1521	1.07	1.41	1.21	1.12
Not obtaining at least a high										

for Gerald Ford	52.90	52.96	54.29	734	769	1485	1.02	1.00	1.22	1.13
Who are 18–29 years old	.31	.30	.28	769	806	1527	1.12	1.06	1.26	1.15
Thinking of themselves as Democrats	.49	.53	.53	759	794	1516	1.08	1.25	1.28	1.16
Feeling whites have right to keep blacks out of their neighborhood	.06	.07	.10	784	812	1525	1.06	1.41	1.34	1.19
Mean feeling thermometer rating for Jimmy Carter	54.57	55.26	57.53	616	630	1290	1.05	1.18	1.46	1.31
Mean number of telephones in home	1.89	1.92	1.73	800	838	1546	.78	1.00	1.54	1.31
Mean number of problems facing the country	3.99	4.02	4.28	775	826	1535	1.06	1.22	1.61	1.35
Who are nonwhite	.13	.13	.14	782	818	1545	1.06	.99	1.62	1.36
Feeling cockroaches are not a problem in their home	.73	.76	.75	798	836	1546	1.07	1.37	1.74	1.44
Mean over 20 variables							1.05	1.21	1.27	1.16

and proportions are calculated using the selection weights detailed previously, in order to adjust for unequal probabilities of selection. The calculation formulas used to estimate the sampling variance for all three designs are described in Appendix IV.

All of the formulas used for the variance were approximations, but the bias of the approximation is negligible with coefficients of variation of cluster size less than .10. All three samples have coefficients of variation safely below that level (ranging from .02 to .05), but there is evidence for increased variability in size within the clustered telephone sample (about a 40% increase in the coefficient of variation over the personal interview design). This probably reflects the variation in proportion of working numbers across the various central office codes sampled.

The *defts* in Table 6.5 are arranged from lowest to highest by their value within the personal interview sample.[4] Using the reduced personal sample, the average over the 22 variables is 1.16. For the clustered telephone sample the order of estimates by the *deft* values is somewhat different, but the mean *deft* is 1.21. The stratified telephone sample in general has the lowest design effects, with a mean *deft* over the 22 proportions of 1.05. These results support our hypothesis that the lack of control on the proportion of working household numbers would produce higher variances for the clustered telephone sample than for the personal interview sample in the same primary areas.[5] Also as expected, the absence of clustering helped to make the sampling variance of the stratified telephone sample the smallest of the three and, on the average, its standard errors are only about 5% higher than those of a simple random sample of the same size.

Another way to summarize the variation of *deft* values across proportions is to classify the statistics into groups; we separated demo-

---

[4] Two estimates, those concerning the respondent's attitude about life as a whole are measured on half samples. This artificially reduces their design effects for the two clustered samples. If they had been measured on full samples, their *defts* would probably be the following

	Clustered	Personal reduced
Feeling satisfied to completely satisfied about life as a whole	1.56	1.00
Feeling mostly satisfied, pleased, or delighted about life as a whole	1.20	1.08

[5] The estimates of *deft* in the table are subject to their own variation over sample draws and we caution against accepting without question individual values of *deft*. It is hoped that mean *defts* of the samples are more stable.

graphic measures (i.e., age, race, education, income, occupation) and factual reports (i.e., itemization of tax deductions, voting reports, and number of telephones) from the attitudinal measures. Table 6.6 presents mean *defts* for the different categories of estimates by the three sample types. Of the 20 variables included in the summarization, 12 are attitudinal measures. In both clustered samples, these variables have the highest average design effects. In the personal interview sample, however, the three groups of variables have *defts* of similar magnitude, and the attitudinal group's average *deft* (1.17) exceeds the smallest average (for the factual measures group) by just .04.

The grouping of variables also distinguishes different design effects only weakly for the stratified telephone sample (a range of .99–1.06). The grouping successfully identifies sets of estimates with different design effects in the clustered telephone sample, with the demographic variables having the smallest design effects (average *deft* of 1.04); next, the factual variables (1.14); and the highest effect for the attitudinal variables (1.30).

We caution that these averages, especially those for the demographic and the factual variables, are based on small numbers and probably subject to large variability over measures chosen. High *deft* values for attitudinal variables were observed in past analyses of this type (Kish *et al.*, 1976). The low design effects for demographic variables in the clustered telephone sample relative to the personal interview sample, if supported with other data, may reflect the secondary clustering within primary areas in the personal sample. Such clustering may produce a larger homogeneity within areas on demographic variables related to residential location (e.g., race, income, education).

Three observations on Table 6.6 summarize our understanding of the qualities of the three designs. First, the variation in design effects

TABLE 6.6
Average *Defts* for Subgroups of Estimates[a]

		Sample type		
Subgroup	N	Stratified	Clustered	Personal reduced
Demographic	5	1.06	1.04	1.15
Factual	3	.99	1.14	1.13
Attitudinal	12	1.05	1.30	1.17
	20			

[a] Means include adjusted *defts* for life satisfaction items.

is much smaller in the stratified element sample because (*a*) the estimates of variance themselves are subject to lower variance because of the large number of independent selections; and (*b*) estimates are not subject to the variable effects of clustering the sample. Lack of control on the proportion of working household numbers tends to increase the design effect, stratification tends to lower it. The variation in *defts* in the sample arises chiefly from varying gains due to stratification. In the two clustered samples, the estimates also suffer differentially from homogeneity within primary areas of the samples. Variables whose values tend to group within the geographical units used as primary selections will show higher design effects than others.

A second observation from the table is that the increase in standard errors for the clustered telephone sample over the personal interview sample is rather small.[6] The larger *defts* arise from the lack of control on the proportion of working household numbers and on the proportion generated within the primary area (from those exchanges only partially serving a primary area). The cost savings from moving to telephone interviews in the clustered sample far exceed any losses of precision relative to the personal interview survey in the same areas. (See the cost analysis, Chapter 7.)

Third, comparing the single-stage and clustered telephone designs, we observe an average 14% increase in the standard error for the clustered sample. That reduced precision, added to the 40–50% increase in sample numbers required in the clustered sample (Chapter 3, tables on proportion of eligible numbers) makes the clustered design more attractive only for studies planning later personal interviews in the same households, or for studies of change from estimates obtained in previous studies in the same primary areas.

Table 6.7 presents a summary of sampling error calculations, using the same estimates as those presented in Table 6.5 but calculated on subclasses of the sample rather than the entire sample. The subclasses used are respondent age, education, race, and total family income. The first three columns of the table present the proportion of the respondents belonging to each subclass. We present this table to demonstrate the operation of $deff = [1 + \rho(b - 1)]$ within subclasses of clustered samples. The reader will recall that b is the average number of respondents in each primary area; the bs for subclasses are smaller than that for the total sample, and with approximately equal ρs we

---

[6] Not all clustered personal samples would yield the same comparison; the SRC design attempts to reduce the clustering effect through design of secondary selections within primary areas.

TABLE 6.7
Summary of Sampling Error Calculations on Subclasses of the Total Sample

Subclass categories	Proportion of sample in subclass category			Mean *deft* over variables			
	Stratified phone	Clustered phone	Personal	Stratified phone	Clustered phone	Personal	Reduced personal
Age of respondent							
18–29 years old	.26	.26	.26	1.04	1.17	1.09	1.03
30–49 years old	.35	.35	.34	1.05	1.06	1.15	1.07
50 years old or more	.31	.32	.39	1.06	1.12	1.16	1.09
Total family income							
Less than $7500	.18	.19	.28	1.11	1.13	1.23	1.11
$7500–$15,000	.24	.25	.27	1.07	1.13	1.11	1.05
More than $15,000	.37	.37	.33	1.05	1.11	1.17	1.08
Respondent's education							
Less than high school diploma	.21	.24	.32	1.06	1.23	1.21	1.11
High school diploma	.33	.33	.34	1.04	1.02	1.13	1.07
More than high school diploma	.39	.39	.34	1.07	1.13	1.13	1.06
Respondent's race							
White	.81	.82	.85	1.05	1.14	1.17	1.11
Nonwhite	.12	.13	.14	1.10	1.09	1.24	1.03

would expect lower design effects for subclasses of the clustered samples. There is no reduction of b for the single-stage sample—it is 1.0 by definition—and we expect no lowering of *defts* for that design. This is precisely what Table 6.7 reveals. Almost all the subclass *defts* for the clustered samples lie below the *average defts* for the same estimates on the total sample. For analyses of subclasses of the sample, the clustered samples thus become relatively more attractive than for analyses on the total sample.

6.4 INTERVIEWER EFFECTS WITHIN THE TELEPHONE SURVEY

Past research has demonstrated that individual interviewers may, because of different styles of asking questions, personality differences, and interactions of respondent and interviewer characteristics, produce different responses from the same respondents (e.g., Hanson & Marks, 1958; Dohrenwend, Colombotos, & Dohrenwend, 1968). These errors are variable over different interviewers, and their values are correlated over the different respondents interviewed by the same interviewer. Hence, interviewer effects are often labeled as "variable, correlated" errors in survey data. Because they are correlated within sets of respondents contacted by the same interviewer, their effects on the variance of sample estimates are not part of variance calculations like those presented in the previous discussion.[7]

The model that we employ in discussing interviewer effects assumes no bias in overall estimates associated with the interviewer characteristics, by positing probability sampling of interviewers from a large population of interviewers. The biasing effects of interviewer errors are eliminated by randomization in selection of interviewers. The departure of this project from the model is not measurable, but is discussed later. In any case, we will not concern ourselves with the measurement of bias attributable to interviewer effects, but rather merely the increase in variance of sample estimates related to these effects.

Following the approach of Hansen *et al.* (1953), we characterize the

[7] In clustered designs where the number of interviewers equals the number of primary areas, and where each interviewer works within only one area, the traditional variance calculations themselves include the effects of interviewer differences. This would also be true for the case of a simple random sample where each interviewer obtained a single interview.

effect of interviewer differences on the variance of a sample mean or proportion as a design effect

$$Deff_{int} = 1 + \rho_{int}(b_{int} - 1),$$

where ρ_{int} is a measure of within-interviewer homogeneity, reflecting the extent to which answers of an interviewer's respondents resemble one another, and where b_{int} is the average number of interviews taken by an interviewer.[8] This design effect measures the change in the variance of sample estimates due to the fact that clusters of respondents were interviewed by the same person instead of by different people. If there are interviewer effects on responses, respondents of the same interviewer will tend to give distinctive answers, ρ will be positive, and the *deff* will be greater than one. Since interviewer effects are a source of variance independent of the sampling variance, these design effects (or their *defts*) should be combined with those of sampling error calculations to determine the overall increase in variance over a simple random sample with each interviewer obtaining responses from only one respondent.

In order to calculate $deff_{int}$, the interviewers must be selected at random from among those available and be assigned sample elements at random to eliminate any covariation of interviewer attributes with respondent attributes. Randomized selection of the 37 interviewers from among those judged eligible did not occur; indeed the selection process attempted to achieve a uniformly high interviewer quality. Homogeneity, rather than heterogeneity, across interviewers would be the expected result of the personnel decisions. The effect of this departure would presumably decrease interviewer variance, and our analysis will probably err on that side. Conversely, in terms of inference to later project experiences, the personnel decisions will probably be repeated, and this project's results are useful guides to later results.

The second requirement for estimating $deff_{int}$, the randomization of assignment of sample elements to interviewers, was painstakingly implemented in the project. As part of the sampling process, equal-sized subgroups of the sample were randomly assigned to interviewers, so that in essence each interviewer was responsible for a small national sample. Since the telephone interviewers worked specific

---

[8] ρ_{int} is a true intraclass correlation coefficient if b_{int} is a constant, or does not vary greatly over interviewers. The coefficient of variation of b_{int} in the telephone survey was about .09, and we view the presented ρ_{int}s as synthetic measures of intracluster homogeneity that also include some effects of varying interviewer load.

hours within each day, however, they could not make calls on numbers at all hours, and periodically sample numbers were randomly reassigned manually to interviewers who worked different shifts. What results from the process is a randomization within interviewer shift. Because of this, the $deff_{int}$ measured will also contain differences between the types of interviewers who work different shifts and respondents reached during different shifts. We suspect that respondent differences across shifts are largest between those reached on weekday mornings and afternoons on one hand, and those reached on weekday evenings and weekends, on the other. An examination of the interviewer staff shows that about two-thirds of the interviewers work in both of these groups, and we have collapsed shifts in the analysis that follows. We ignore this possible source of overestimating interviewer differences in order to achieve adequate numbers of interviewers for obtaining estimates of variance; constructing a within-shift interviewer variance estimate would reduce the numbers on which the estimate is based. Finally, for some sample elements, (e.g., initial refusals converted to interviews) no randomized assignment to interviewer was performed and those interviews are deleted in the calculations below.

To estimate ρ_{int} we calculate

$$Deff_{int} = \frac{\text{clustered variance}_{int}}{\text{simple random sample variance}}$$

using an unstratified clustered variance for the numerator, with clusters defined as groups of respondents questioned by the same interviewer. The denominator is the variance of the sample, treating elements as if they were a simple random sample. Using $deff_{int}$ we calculate

$$\rho_{int} = \frac{deff_{int}-1}{b_{int}-1},$$

where b_{int} is the mean number of interviews taken by each interviewer. We chose 24 estimates, 22 of which were those used in the sampling error calculations (Table 6.5). The two added estimates were the proportion of respondents that did not report their total family income and the proportion that did not mention any important problems facing the country. These two measures were hypothesized to be very sensitive to interviewer effects.

Table 6.8 presents values of ρ_{int} calculated for the 24 estimates; their values range from $-.01$ to $.07$.[9] The highest ρ_{int} (.071) corresponds to the number of problems facing the country mentioned by respondents. This number is probably affected by the quality of probing used by the interviewer. We noted in Chapter 4 that respondent behavior regarding this question seems to differ by mode of interview. The number of problems mentioned is also sensitive to interviewer effects, a fact which is relevant to the analysis in Chapter 5, where we observed that telephone respondents generally cited fewer problems than did personal interview respondents.

Other estimates subject to high interviewer variance are the proportion feeling that it is more important than usual to add to their savings (an open-ended attitudinal measure, $\rho_{int} = .045$), the proportion who report that they are not currently working (a sensitive subject to some respondents, $\rho_{int} = .038$), and the percentage of respondents who did not reveal their total family income (either directly or by responding to the trichotomous categorization of income, $\rho_{int} = .027$). Two other estimates arise from the same questions but have much lower interviewer effects. The proportion of respondents whose total family income was less than \$7500 has a small positive ρ_{int} (.003), and the proportion of respondents who fail to mention any problem facing the country has a small negative ρ_{int} $(-.001)$.

The discrepancies in interviewer effects between the two estimates related to total family income could support the hypothesis that reluctance to provide income to the interviewer may result from interviewer inflection or hesitation in asking the question (a variable over interviewers). The questions asking for a listing of the most important problems facing the country should have a different pattern; we would expect relatively large interviewer effects both for the mean number of problems mentioned and the proportion of respondents who cannot identify any problems. The former is highly variable over interviewers ($\rho_{int} = .071$), but the rate of "don't know" on the item is fairly stable ($\rho_{int} = .001$). Initial delivery style of the question may have little effect on the probability of a respondent's mentioning at least one important problem. In contrast, although the probing was specified in the questionnaire, the *number* of problems mentioned seems to be much more dependent on interviewer style.

These results inform us about interviewer effects in this telephone

[9] These interviewer effects are subject to even greater variation over survey implementations than the defts of sampling discussed earlier. The negative values of ρ_{int} are evidence that we should avoid inference based on small differences between ρ_{int}s.

TABLE 6.8
Interviewer Design Effects ($Deft_{int}$) for Telephone Survey and Intrainterviewer Homogeneity Measures (ρ_{int}) for 24 Sample Estimates

Variable description (mean or proportion)	Mean value or proportion of adults	Square root of design effect	Intrainterviewer homogeneity measure (ρ_{int})	Unweighted N
Mean thermometer rating for Jimmy Carter	54.88	.83	-.011	1114
Who are 18–29 years old	.29	.85	-.008	1399
Feeling satisfied to completely satisfied about life as a whole	.83	.96	-.005	714
Not obtaining at least a high school diploma	.23	.93	-.004	1425
Mean number of telephones in home	1.91	.94	-.003	1452
Reporting they live in or near a city of 50,000 or more	.39	.97	-.002	1316
Feeling better off financially now than 1 year ago	.38	.98	-.001	1504
Not mentioning any problems facing the country	.07	.99	-.001	1529
Feeling cockroaches are not a problem in their home	.74	1.02	.001	1450
Feeling very happy these days	.32	1.02	.001	1436
Reporting that they itemized deductions on 1975 tax return	.51	1.04	.003	1373
Reporting total family income less than $7500	.23	1.04	.003	1223
Who are nonwhite	.13	1.07	.004	1417
Reporting that they planned to vote in 1976 presidential election	.86	1.08	.005	1398
Feeling mostly satisfied, pleased, or				

Mean feeling thermometer rating for Gerald Ford	52.83	1.17	.011	1341
Reporting they live in a rural area	.20	1.23	.014	1437
Reporting that they voted in 1972 presidential election	.70	1.22	.014	1416
Feeling whites have right to keep blacks out of their neighborhood	.07	1.30	.019	1414
Not reporting total family income	.20	1.43	.027	1529
Reporting that they were not presently working	.36	1.54	.038	1451
Feeling saving money more important now than usual	.62	1.62	.045	1446
Mean number of problems facing the country	4.04	1.88	.071	1421

survey, but we cannot present a comparable analysis for the personal interview survey. In some primary areas only one interviewer was used in the study, and comparisons of their respondents' answers would confound interviewer effects with real differences among respondents. In primary areas where several interviewers were used, no randomization of interviewer assignments was implemented. Indeed, interviewers visited segments close to their homes to reduce the field costs of the survey. In the absence of randomization, interviewer effects would be overestimated by calculations like those performed for the telephone survey.

Despite our inability to replicate our analysis on our personal interview data, comparison of telephone interviewer effects with those of previous personal interview surveys may give some insight into the relative magnitudes of interviewer variance in the two modes. For this comparison we utilize three published studies: (a) Hanson and Marks's (1958) analysis of enumerator variance in 21 counties of Ohio and Michigan as part of U.S. Census Population; (b) Kish's (1962) study of interviewer variance in two studies of factory workers; and (c) Freeman and Butler's (1976) study of interviewer effects in a personal interview survey of urban housewives.

We choose these studies because they measure interviewer homogeneity through use of intraclass correlations. The Hanson and Marks results were altered from F-ratios to ρs by Kish (1962). Freeman and Butler used a formula similar to that of Kish's ρ_{int}, which we also utilized. Before we compare the measures of interviewer homogeneity in these studies, we note three complications of our analysis: (a) differences in the populations sampled; (b) differences in the estimates examined; and (c) differences in the interviewing staffs.

The type of variables analyzed in the different studies varies greatly. The census study includes purely demographic measures: some sensitive like income and occupational status; others without any threat to the respondent (sex, residential location); still others measuring missing data on questionnaires returned by the interviewers. The Kish study, yielding the largest range of ρs, asked attitudinal questions about union activities and job satisfaction, in addition to some purely demographic measures. The Freeman and Butler study calculated ρs on all categories of seventeen different variables, some of them attitudinal variables related to the general topic of mental retardation among children, some of them the respondents' reports of their own actions toward their children, and some reports on personal behavior of other kinds.

Interviewers in the census study were paid as enumerators in that census; Kish's study used professional male interviewers employed by the Survey Research Center; and the Freeman and Butler study used schoolteachers, none of whom had interviewing experience, but who participated in a "three-credit-hour university course in interviewing conducted by the project and field directors [p. 84].

Figure 6.1 presents cumulative percentages for values of ρ_{int}s for the four different studies. The results of the telephone study are plotted with the solid black line. The highest ρs are those found by Freeman and Butler's study of housewives. The census study has the smallest ρs, although our telephone survey produces the largest proportion of ρs less than zero. The Freeman and Butler study exhibits interviewer effects much higher than any of the other studies and one wonders whether the use of new, nonprofessional interviewers is associated with that result. Even ignoring that result, however, it appears that the interviewer variance experienced in the telephone survey is often lower than that in the personal interview surveys included in Figure 6.1.

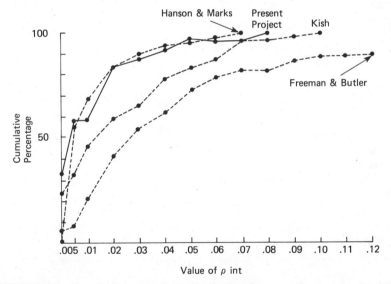

FIGURE 6.1. Cumulative percentage distribution for ρ_{int} values measuring interviewer effects for three personal interview surveys and this telephone survey. [The three personal interview surveys are Hanson and Marks (1958) and Kish (1962), Study 1, distribution taken from Table 2, p. 97 of Kish. Freeman and Butler (1976) distribution taken from their Table 1, pp. 86–87. Telephone survey results in solid line taken from our Table 5.5.]

The census study may have a distribution weighted toward low values of ρs because most items included are demographic items. For example, the proportions of omitted answers in different questions have ρs ranging from .02 to .07, and "difficult" demographic items (e.g., education, income, migration) yield a majority of ρs above .01.

Although inference from Figure 6.1 is complicated by variation in type of measures, interviewers and populations, the data suggest that telephone interviewer effects measured by ρ_{int}s may be somewhat smaller than those in a personal interview survey. The important lesson of Figure 6.1, however, requires additional information. As we noted earlier, the effect on the variance of sample estimates corresponding to interviewer differences can be characterized as

$$deff_{int} = 1 + \rho_{int}(b_{int} - 1),$$

where b is the average number of interviews taken by an interviewer. We have presented ρ_{int}s in order to control differences in the workload of interviewers across the different studies. This is a proper approach when comparing the magnitude of interviewer variation in the two modes, but it ignores possible administrative differences in the modes.

In the telephone survey interviewers each completed an average of 44 interviews; the corresponding number in the personal interview survey is 11. With a ρ_{int} of .04, which is likely in both surveys from an open-ended or sensitive item, the $deff_{int}$ for the telephone survey is 2.72; for the personal survey, 1.40.[10] Simply because the telephone interviewers each take more interviews, the loss of precision arising from interviewer effects is larger. Indeed, the interviewer differences measured by ρ_{int} have to be less than one-quarter the size in the personal interview survey for the design effects due to interviewer differences to be the same. The results in Figure 6.1 suggest that this will not always be the case.

Thus interviewer effects within centralized telephone interviewing facilities may be a larger threat to survey precision than in dispersed personal interviewing situations. The very fact that all telephone interviewers work in the same location and that there are relatively few of them, however, facilitates the study of methods to reduce interviewer variance in ways not possible in personal interviewer studies. The first step of the study requires further measurement of the magnitude of interviewer effects on typical survey questions.

[10] We should note that interviewer effects for subclass statistics will be lower than for statistics on the total sample.

6.5 COMBINING ESTIMATES OF SAMPLING
AND INTERVIEWER ERROR

The information presented in this chapter should be used both to qualify the analyses in other chapters and to guide decisions for other research about sample size and design, and about the desirable workload of interviewers. The coverage by telephone of the household population must be an initial concern of those considering a telephone survey. The absence of about 10% of the households from any telephone survey population must be balanced with the need for precise estimates of parameters for the entire household population, the relative costs of covering that population by other means (i.e., implementing a nonphone household supplement sample), and the likely differences in values for survey estimates between the nonphone population and the covered population.

Data on sampling and interviewer variance should be combined to provide estimates of change in standard errors of the telephone survey as we administered it from one yielding corresponding estimates from a simple random sample interviewed singly by different interviewers.[11] The columns in Table 6.5 and 6.8, listing the square roots of design effects and ρs for sampling and interviewer differences, can be used to provide an overall effect. Table 6.9 presents an ordering of the overall *defts* for the 22 estimates common to the sampling error and interviewer variance analysis, shown separately for the stratified and the clustered telephone samples. The *defts* range from .74 to 1.57 in the stratified sample and from .83 to 1.75 in the clustered sample. This implies a 60–75% increase in the width of confidence intervals for some sample statistics. For those variables sensitive both to clustering and to interviewer effects (e.g., attitudes about the need for saving money), the total design effect is rather large (*deft* = 1.75), but in some cases the interviewer effects actually decrease the overall design effect from that due to sampling alone.

This overall design effect may be a more proper inflation factor for simple random sample standard errors than are produced by most packaged computer programs. It would include both the effects of sampling errors and interviewer effects associated with the particular set of interviewers working on a given study. Only in centralized

[11] The overall design effect including both sampling design and interviewer effects is approximately

$$Deff_{\text{overall}} = Deff_{\text{sampling}} + (b_{\text{int}} - 1)\rho_{\text{int}}$$

following Hansen *et al.*'s model (1953, Vol. 2, pp. 291–293).

TABLE 6.9
Estimated Overall Design Effect Including Sampling and Interviewer Variances for 22 Measures by Telephone Sample Type

| Variable description (mean or proportion) | Square root of design effects | | | | Square root of overall design effect | |
| | Stratified sample | | Clustered sample | | Stratified sample | Clustered sample |
	Sampling	Interviewer[a]	Sampling	Interviewer[a]		
Reporting total family income less than $7500	1.00	1.02	.80	1.03	1.02	.83
Mean number of telephones in home	.78	.97	1.00	.97	.74	.96
Who are 18–29 years old	1.12	.92	1.06	.92	1.06	.98
Who are nonwhite	1.06	1.04	.99	1.04	1.09	1.03
Mean thermometer rating for Gerald Ford	1.02	1.10	1.00	1.11	1.11	1.10
Mean thermometer rating for Jimmy Carter	1.05	.91	1.18	.91	.97	1.11
Reporting they live in or near a city of 50,000 or more	1.07	.98	1.13	.98	1.05	1.12
Reporting that they itemized deductions on 1975 tax return	1.07	1.02	1.11	1.02	1.09	1.13
Feeling mostly satisfied, pleased, or delighted about life as a whole	1.05	1.04	1.09	1.05	1.09	1.14
Feeling better off financially						

pletely satisfied about life as a whole	1.02	.98	1.27	.98	1.00	1.25
Reporting that they planned to vote in 1976 presidential election	1.04	1.04	1.28	1.05	1.08	1.31
Reporting that they were not presently working	1.07	1.32	.97	1.33	1.37	1.32
Reporting they live in a rural area	1.10	1.13	1.20	1.13	1.22	1.32
Thinking of themselves as Democrats	1.08	1.09	1.25	1.10	1.16	1.33
Not obtaining at least a high school diploma	1.07	.97	1.37	.96	1.04	1.34
Feeling cockroaches are not a problem in their home	1.07	1.01	1.37	1.01	1.08	1.37
Feeling "Very Happy" these days	1.07	1.01	1.41	1.01	1.08	1.41
Reporting that they voted in 1972 presidential election	1.12	1.13	1.32	1.13	1.23	1.42
Feeling whites have a right to keep blacks out of their neighborhood	1.06	1.17	1.41	1.18	1.22	1.54
Mean number of problems facing the country	1.06	1.53	1.22	1.56	1.57	1.71
Feeling saving money more important now than usual	1.05	1.37	1.46	1.39	1.41	1.75

[a] Those *defts* were estimated by using the ρ_{int} values presented in Table 5.4 and the number of valid responses in Table 5.2.

telephoning situations can both components of the design effect be measured. Future uses of telephone surveys should implement randomization of sample assignment so that estimates of both errors can be used in analysis of the data.

6.6 SUMMARY

Both sampling and nonsampling errors are present in survey data, and an attempt was made in this study to estimate the magnitudes of some of each type. The sampling frame for the SRC national sample of dwellings is estimated to include about 95% of all dwelling units in the coterminous United States. The proportion of households with telephones has been variously estimated, but the best estimate now available puts it at 90.4%.

As expected, the nonsubscribers were concentrated among people of low income, rural residence, rented rather than owned dwellings, and single person households. They also included disproportionately large numbers of blacks. In sum, noncoverage of the household population is about twice as great for the telephone as for the personal interview survey, other factors aside.

Data from the three samples of the present study—personal interview, clustered telephone, and stratified telephone—were compared for 20 major variables with respect to the design effect and *deft* (defined as the square root of the design effect). Comparisons across the 20 variables show a mean *deft* of 1.05 for the stratified telephone sample, 1.21 for the clustered telephone sample, and 1.16 for the personal interview sample (adjusted for size). Thus, the sampling variance was smallest for the stratified telephone sample; its standard errors were only about 5% greater than a simple random sample of the same size.

Design effects were examined separately for demographic, "factual," and attitudinal items. In the personal interview survey, the magnitudes of these effects were about the same for all three types of questions. The magnitudes for the three types of questions were also of similar (but generally smaller) size in the stratified telephone survey. In the clustered telephone survey, however, the three types of questions showed rather different design effects; the effect was least for the demographic items, somewhat larger for the factual items, and largest for the attitudinal items. There is no apparent reason for these discrepancies other than variation across samples.

In addition to sampling errors and design effects, surveys of all sizes—from samples to censuses—are subject to interviewer effects. These reflect such interviewer characteristics as style of asking questions, personality, and interaction with respondents. Interviewer effects are, of course, variable from one interviewer to another, but they are correlated among the different respondents interviewed by any given interviewer.

Interviewer effects could not be estimated for the personal interview survey, because individual interviewers took interviews only in one primary area. For the telephone samples, interviewer effects varied substantially across questions. The highest interviewer effects appeared for questions suggesting some sensitivity of topic (race relations, income, being unemployed) and for questions that depended on the interviewer's probing to elicit complete responses (number of problems mentioned as facing the country).

Comparison of these findings on interviewer effects with estimates made by other research workers suggests that interviewer variance is often lower in telephone surveys than in those conducted by personal interview—other things being equal. Other things, however, are not equal. Telephone surveys tend to involve fewer interviewers, with larger assignments than those of personal interviewers in a study of the same size. This administrative property creates greater total interviewer variance in the telephone mode, but the closer supervision possible in the telephone mode should work to reduce interviewer effects. The centralized situation of telephone interviewing and the associated differences in supervision and monitoring can also be expected to affect interviewer variance. Future studies will be required to understand the mechanisms of these several factors.

A combination of sampling and interviewer variance shows estimated changes in standard errors of the two telephone surveys (clustered and stratified) as actually conducted, in comparison to the standard errors of a telephone sample of equal size selected on a simple random basis and administered so that each respondent was interviewed by a different interviewer. *Defts* for this comparison, computed for 22 questionnaire items, range from .74 to 1.57 in the stratified sample and from .83 to 1.75 in the clustered sample. Thus, for variables sensitive both to clustering and to interviewer effects, the total design effect is rather large and implies an increase of 60–75% in the width of confidence intervals. For some items, on the other hand, the computed interviewer effects compensate for the sampling effect, and the overall design effect is smaller than that due to sampling alone.

Chapter 7

Sampling and Data Collection Costs for the Surveys

One of the traditional attractions of a telephone survey arises from its presumed lower cost relative to a personal interview survey. By eliminating the need for the interviewer to visit each sample household, telephone surveys avoid both the transportation and salary costs of interviewers en route to and from the sample dwellings. The small literature that exists regarding telephone surveys frequently contains references to the lower costs associated with the method. Coombs and Freedman (1964) estimate that using the telephone wherever possible in a reinterview of respondents "resulted in savings of approximately 60 percent." The field cost per 5-minute telephone interview of the national sample of Kegeles, Fink, and Kirscht (1969) was about $6.00, which they labeled "only a fraction of what a personal interview would cost." Hochstim (1967) incurred telephone interviewing costs which were 50–70% of those for the same interview completed in person.[1] Tuchfarber and Klecka (1976) estimate personal interview costs at five times the costs for a comparable RDD survey of Cincinnati households.

---

[1] The Hochstim results are complicated by the fact that a few sample persons originally designated as personal interview respondents were interviewed on the telephone.

Some of these telephone surveys used randomly generated numbers; others did not. Sometimes the costs compare questionnaires of explicitly equal length; other studies make no mention of possible differences in length. Some of the cost analyses were performed for one-time projects by rather small organizations that may have incurred large initial costs to build a field staff. Much of the analysis compares only gross costs per completed interview; components of the costs are not explicitly stated. Finally, rarely are the person-hours required to accomplish the work noted, and thus the cost differences are confounded with salary and material cost differences over organizations and time. This chapter presents an analysis of costs for this project that attempts to avoid some of the weaknesses of past analyses.

We will present a detailed categorization of costs, and when possible will note the person-hours corresponding to various salary figures and the unit counts for supply and printing costs. The goal in the discussion is to provide information in a form most transferable across research environments. As others have done, we will present per-interview cost comparisons, but for each component of the figures we will specify the nature of the work performed, unique qualities of the project that affected the magnitude of the task, and any other constraints in using these figures for inference to cost comparisons between modes in other contexts.

We begin by describing the methods we used to assemble the cost data (Section 7.1), then present the gross per interview cost comparison (Section 7.2), and finally, using a detailed cost table, describe component cost differences between modes (Sections 7.3–7.12), noting any unique characteristics of these surveys.

7.1 METHODS OF THE COST ANALYSIS

The initial step in preparing for cost comparisons between the two surveys was performed when survey budgets were first established. At that time, several accounts were created for each of the two projects to collect charges separately for sampling, field work, coding, and for costs incurred by the research staff. This facilitated our later cost analysis since some types of charges, such as communications and supplies costs, are incurred across phases of survey work, making them difficult to separate by work area over time. Charges made to each account were routinely monitored by means of monthly accounting statements. At the close of the project, a detailed examination was made of costs accrued in the sampling and field accounts for both the personal interview survey and the telephone survey. We chose to restrict our focus to costs for sampling and field work, since we assumed that differences between the two modes would be most prominent in these two categories. It can be reasonably argued that coding, keypunching, data processing, and analysis activities should be approximately the same regardless of whether or not the completed questionnaires are a result of telephone or personal interviewing.

Two other types of costs were eliminated from the analysis because they vary across organizations and, therefore, might further limit the applicability of these findings to other situations. First, only direct costs were examined; overhead or indirect costs were excluded from consideration. Second, fringe benefits costs, including those for social security, retirement funds, and health and life insurance, were omitted from calculations. Sick and holiday pay *was* included in salary totals, because these items are included as part of the total pay for each salary classification in the accounting system.

In many instances, standard monthly accounting documents provided all the detail necessary to isolate charges. For cases in which additional information was needed, hand examination of specific documents was performed. For example, to identify personnel charges on specific sets of days within pay periods, time sheets were checked. Individual printing, duplicating, and supply requisitions were listed to isolate charges and quantities for specific materials. In a few instances, computer printouts of data processing jobs run on the project were examined to locate particular costs relating to sampling and data collection work.

The combined methods of accessing account statements and reviewing some individual charges identified the proper category for approximately 90% of the charges made for sampling and field work. There were some cases, however, in which estimates of costs or hours had to be made. No separate accounting was kept, for example, on costs or hours devoted to different types of tasks performed within the same work classification. In cases where a person performed different kinds of work within a single pay period, estimates of time devoted to each task were obtained from the relevant person. In a few instances it was necessary to divide charges prior to and after a specific date, such as the beginning of the interviewing period. For the personal interview study this involved cost data on approximately 130 interviewers. To avoid checking each interviewer's time sheets, average hours per day were calculated across all interviewers for the time period in question, and hours before and after the beginning date of interviewing were assigned using this daily average.

7.2 OVERALL COST COMPARISONS

Table 7.1 summarizes the direct costs for sampling and field activities on the two studies. The table is broken into ten categories, representing major divisions of work. Costs for all items, person-hours for salary items, and unit counts for nonsalary items are listed for the components of each category.

Total direct sampling and field costs for the personal interview survey are $84,864. For the telephone survey, the costs total $37,939, about 45% of those on the personal study. Person-hours total 13,523 on the personal mode, 5419 on the telephone mode. For these two studies, therefore, the telephone mode is substantially less expensive, both in terms of direct costs and personnel time required. These results resemble those reported by Hochstim (1967) and Coombs and Freedman (1964).

For the two samples the per-completed-interview cost for sampling and field work is $55 using personal interviews, $23 using telephone interviews. This involves an average of 8.7 person-hours per personal interview, and 3.3 person-hours per telephone interview. Sample sizes were 1548 for the personal interview study, 1618 for the telephone interview study.[2]

While we assume that costs in survey areas other than sampling and field should be unaffected by differences in interviewing method, it would perhaps be helpful to consider our figures in the context of total survey costs. Total costs are subject to wide variation depending on the amount of developmental work and analysis performed. Analysis costs probably have the highest variation of all components but we roughly estimate that other survey activities comprise about 40–50% of total direct costs incurred before analysis for the personal interview survey. Expecting these other activities to cost the same for a telephone survey, we would estimate that 31–40% of total telephone survey costs before analysis are attached to sampling and field work. Using these figures, we would expect that the total telephone survey costs would be 56–87% of total personal interview costs before analysis.

Table 7.1 reveals areas where large portions of sampling and field costs were incurred in each of the two modes and where large cost differences exist *between* the two modes. There are five areas that exhibit the largest differences. Sampling, prestudy, and training costs were markedly different in the two modes. In addition, travel costs

[2] If broken-off interviews are included, the total telephone sample size is 1734.

TABLE 7.1
Direct Costs for Components of Sampling and Data Collection Activities on the Telephone and Personal Interview Surveys

	Telephone survey		Personal interview survey	
	Hours or other units	Costs ($)	Hours or other units	Costs ($)
I. Sampling				
Administrative salaries	86.0[a]	505.27[a]	362.0	3,305.03
Clerical/typing salaries	0	0	186.0	676.12
Chunking and listing		0		4,566.00
Data processing		450.00		0
Category total	86.0 hours	$ 955.27	548.0 hours	$8,547.15
Percentage of total	1.6%	2.5%	4.1%	10.1%
II. Pretest				
Ann Arbor field office salaries	34.0	224.59	32.0[a]	200.08[a]
Clerical/typing salaries	4.0	14.73	17.0	88.65
Supervisors salary	50.5	188.67	25.8	153.30
Interviewers salary	76.4	226.06	125.7	444.13
travel	0	0	(666 mi)	93.32
Duplicating	1688 (pages)	69.40	7370 (pages)	119.62
Postage		0		14.00
Category total	164.9 hours	$ 723.45	200.5 hours	$1,113.10
Percentage of total	3.0%	1.9%	1.5%	1.3%

(*Continued*)

TABLE 7.1 (Continued)

	Telephone survey		Personal interview survey	
	Hours or other units	Costs ($)	Hours or other units	Costs ($)
III. Training and prestudy work				
Interviewing supervisors salaries	37.1	155.57	667.0[a]	3,929.14[a]
Interviewers salaries	314.6	936.58	1,621.3[a]	5,285.51[a]
New interviewer training		660.00	0	0
Duplicating	(524 pp.)	26.95	(6725 pp.)	85.10
Supplies		14.78		223.86
Coding staff salaries	11.0	94.46	0	0
Coding evaluation of questionnaires	40.0	178.00	0	0
Category total	402.7 hours	$2,066.34	2,288.3 hours	$9,523.61
Percentage of total	7.4%	5.4%	16.9%	11.2%
IV. Materials				
Questionnaire	100,800 (pp.)	802.25	224,000 (pp.)	1,466.51
Other data collection instruments		278.70	(24,840 pp.)	704.65
Data collection related materials and reporting forms		274.68	(30,900 pp.)	1,211.24
General supplies		19.33		277.75
Category total		$ 1,374.96		$ 3,660.15

Administrative salaries	156.0	1,222.48	324.0	2,308.29
Clerical/typing salaries	55.0	172.26	392.4	1,651.13
Category total	211.0 hours	$ 1,394.74	716.4 hours	$ 4,159.42
Percentage of total	3.9%	3.7%	5.3%	4.9%
VI. Field salaries				
Supervisor salaries	648.0	2,303.64	988.5[a]	4,956.88[a]
Interviewer salaries	3,442.0	10,181.05	8,389.8[a]	27,321.04[a]
Foreign interviewers salaries	—	60.0	0	0
Category total	4,090.0 hours	$12,544.69	9,378.3 hours	$32,277.92
Percentage of total	75.5%	33.1%	69.4%	38.0%
VII. Field staff travel				
Supervisor travel		0		5,620.35
Interviewer travel		0		10,416.72
Personal auto mileage	0	0	(74,405 mi)	778.04
Other		0		
Category total		0		$16,815.11
Percentage of total		0		19.8%
VIII. Communications				
Postage		0		3,491.03
Telephone				
For data collection		15,793.60		0
For other communications		0		1,756.45
Supplies for mailing		0		732.83
Category total		$15,793.60		$ 5,980.31
Percentage of total		41.6%		7.0%

(Continued)

TABLE 7.1 (*Continued*)

	Telephone survey		Personal interview survey	
	Hours or other units	Costs ($)	Hours or other units	Costs ($)
IX. *Control function*				
Administrative salaries	247.5	830.55	8.0	91.30
Clerical/typing salaries	0	0	188.5	766.93
Printing and duplicating	0	0	(1500 pp.)	24.99
Data processing		372.00[a]		0
Category total	247.5 hours	$ 1,202.55	196.5 hours	$ 883.22
Percentage of total	4.6%	3.2%	1.5%	1.0%
X. *Postinterviewing activities*				
A. Interviewer evaluation/ debriefing				
Supervisor salaries	12.0	44.52	0	0
Interviewer salaries	68.0	199.70	30.2[a]	98.62[a]
Ann Arbor administrative salaries	0	0	16.0	94.87
Ann Arbor clerical/typing salaries	0	0	12.0	37.80
Duplicating	(50 pp.)	2.50	(1200 pp.)	15.55
Postage		0		34.45
Category total	80.0 hours	$ 246.72	58.2 hours	$ 281.29
Percentage of total	1.5%	0.6%	0.4%	0.3%
B. Verification				
Ann Arbor administrative				

Ann Arbor clerical typing

salaries	0	0	9.0	35.13
Duplicating	0	9.30[a]	(1150 pp.)	33.90
Supply		24.79[a]		23.88
Postage		88.66[a]		104.78
Telephone		0		82.25[a]
Category total	100.1 hours	$ 507.53	99.5 hours	$ 876.38
Percentage of total	1.8%	1.3%	0.7%	1.0%
C. Report to respondents				
Ann Arbor administrative				
salaries	3.0	22.63	4.0	28.70
Keypunching	34.2	256.23	32.8	246.00
Data processing		162.32[a]		112.94
Printing	0	555.00[a]	(22,400 pp.)	251.00
Postage		133.76[a]		107.62
Category total	37.2 hours	$1,129.94	36.8 hours	$746.26
Percentage of total	0.7%	3.0%	0.3%	0.9%
OVERALL TOTAL	5,419.4 hours	$37,929.79	13,522.5 hours	$84,863.92
PER-INTERVIEW TOTAL	3.3 hours	23.45	8.7	$ 54.82

[a] Costs based on estimates of those personnel involved in the work, usually necessitated by different categories of work being performed by the same personnel.

accounted for nearly 20% of total personal interview costs but were nonexistent in the telephone survey. Total communication costs (mainly WATS lines charges), on the other hand, formed over a third of all telephone survey charges and were three times as large as those for the personal interview survey. In both modes, interviewer and supervisor salaries accounted for about a third of all sampling and field costs.

There are two design differences in our studies that complicate cost comparisons. First, the fact that the sample sizes on the two studies are not identical makes use of a per-interview cost somewhat difficult. We might wish to estimate costs for a different survey by multiplying the sample size by per-interview cost, assuming constant marginal cost of a single interview across different sample sizes. It is more plausible, however, that the cost of taking one additional interview decreases as the number of interviews increases. Therefore, having a larger telephone sample (N = 1618) probably yields slightly lower per-interview costs than would exist if the telephone sample size were 1548. However, since the difference between the two sample sizes is small (70 cases) relative to total sample sizes (1548 personal, 1618 telephone), the effects of increased size are probably small.

A more serious design difference is the different interview lengths of the two studies. The lengths of the two questionnaires (30-minute telephone and 50-minute personal) make an unadjusted per-interview cost comparison less than satisfying.[3] We can understand this by contrasting two extreme positions; positing that (a) a 30-minute interview in either mode would have the same cost as a 50-minute interview in the same mode—that is, that within this range of times, cost is independent of questionnaire length; or that (b) the most appropriate basis of comparison is the cost per unit of data collected—that these units are the indivisible and equally valued base units of the research. By attempting no adjustment of costs in the table for different length questionnaires, we have, by default, chosen the first argument.

To examine the cost comparison using the second argument, we have counted the number of variables obtained in each mode and formed a weighted sum of data units (variables) collected:

$$V = \Sigma\, n_i,$$

where n_i is the number of respondents asked a particular question, and where i is an index for each variable recorded. This expression is

---

[3] The personal interview questionnaire essentially added questions at the end of the telephone interview questionnaire. See Chapter 2 for a description of the added sections.

simply the sum of data units collected over all individuals in the survey. To obtain V, we counted variables in the data file that were the direct result of answers recorded by the interviewer; we deleted any variables constructed after coding and any variables used to identify the particular respondent. An approximate value of V is 270,000 for the personal interview and 238,000 for the telephone interview survey.[4] Using these calculations, we found the per unit data costs to be about $.31 for the personal and $.16 for the telephone survey (about 51% of the personal interview costs). The limitation of this method of comparison is that total cost is not solely a function of total number of variables collected; the actual relationship lies somewhere between the two extremes mentioned above.

Another approach to calculating per unit costs focuses on time units instead of data units and attempts to simulate equal length interviews in both modes. Reducing the length of the personal interview questionnaire to .6 of its actual size (50–30 minutes) would reduce costs of materials (Ann Arbor field office work, typing, duplicating, printing), interviewer salaries and travel for pretest and final interviewing, and some other costs. But with a 30-minute personal interview it is doubtful that costs in any of these areas would be reduced to 30:50 = .6 of their present size. We would expect that salaries for actual interviewing time would be reduced by 40%, but interviewing time is only a fraction of total interviewer time spent in obtaining interviews. For example, travel costs do not have a direct relationship with interview length; they are more associated with visits to segments than to individual homes. It is likely that opportunities to call on other housing units in the same segment during the same visit *would* increase with an interview 20 minutes shorter than the actual one. This might reduce the total number of trips to a segment. However, these opportunities are related to the time of day in which the interview was taken, at-home patterns of residents, the willingness of the interviewer to remain in the segment to attempt another interview, etc. Travel costs, therefore, are unlikely to be reduced by 40% with such a reduction in interview length. If we merely delete interviewer costs for 20 minutes of questioning, only about $1700 is saved. If all prepa-

[4] These figures were estimated by hand calculation of number of nonmissing data cases in question sets asked only of a subset of the sample and by counts of data fields for sets asked of everyone. Open-ended variables yield two data fields (first and second mentioned answers) and were counted as two variables. The variable counts were multiplied by 1548 for the personal survey and 1676 for the telephone survey. The 1676 figure represents the midpoint between the 1618 complete interviews and the 1734 total data records.

ration, field, and travel costs (Categories II, IV, VI, VII in the table) were reduced by 40%, the cost of the telephone interview survey would be 64% of that of the personal survey.

Instead of simulating a shorter personal interview, we could also artificially expand the size of the telephone interview from 30 to 50 minutes. The issues here are similar to those above; costs for preparation of materials and pretesting would increase, interviewer salaries would rise, and telephone charges would also increase. Increasing the telephone charges by the added numbers of hours spent in interviewing time might add over $2500 to the total telephone survey costs. The interviewer salary increase would be somewhat more than $1600, but we are prevented from placing much faith in this number because it neglects the changes in opportunity costs. The interviewer with 40 minutes left on his or her shift may make more attempts to obtain another 30-minute interview but may balk at doing so for a 50-minute session. As a result, the proportion of interviewers' time spent actually interviewing respondents may decline with a longer interview schedule. Unfortunately, we have little guidance in estimating the effect of increased interview length on interviewer salary and on telephone costs.

We have presented three estimates of the relationship between telephone and personal interview costs. Using unadjusted figures, sampling and field costs of the telephone survey were about 45% of those of the personal; per-unit data costs were 51% of those in person; and per-unit time probably somewhat less than 64% of that in the personal interviews. The sections that follow discuss costs within different categories of Table 7.1 and describe in more detail the sources of differences between the two modes.

7.3 COSTS OF SELECTING THE SAMPLES

Although selection of the sample occurs before the actual interviewing work begins in either mode, it provides an interesting example of cost differences inherent in the two approaches. The figures in Table 7.1 ignore any developmental costs involved in the telephone survey designs or in the SRC national sample of dwellings. Although all projects are usually charged fees to defray development of a master sample, these are probably highly variable across organizations, and the costs in the table reflect only personnel time in drawing the particular samples used for this project. The differences are dramatic; nearly a ninefold increase in costs for the personal survey ($8547) compared to the telephone survey ($955). These large differences result from the personal interview survey requirement to locate new construction and enumerate housing units within newly selected sample areas. The sampling frame for the telephone survey is updated merely by processing central office codes that have been activated or deleted since the last use of the frame. All aspects of the sampling costs are greater in the personal interview survey, but the charges for the total processing of new sample segments ($4566), involving estimating numbers of housing units, subselection of areas, and listing of segments, have no equivalent in the telephone mode and represent about half of total sampling costs.

7.4 PRETEST COSTS

Questionnaires are pretested prior to field administration in order to identify difficulties interviewers encounter in asking questions or problems respondents have in understanding certain questions. In the personal interview survey, seven interviewers from nearby areas (Detroit and Flint, Michigan; and Toledo, Ohio) each conducted five interviews. In the telephone survey, two pretests were conducted using five interviewers, each taking six interviews with respondents throughout the country. In the personal interview pretest, materials were mailed to interviewers; following pretesting they assembled in Ann Arbor to discuss their pretest experiences with the research staff. A similar meeting was held with the telephone interviewers after each pretest. Although the sizes of the pretests are quite small, respondents living in a wider variety of places were contacted in the telephone pretest. The phone pretest, therefore, may have offered a more effective test of the measurement instrument.

The cost of the personal interview pretest ($1113) exceeds that of the telephone survey ($723) mainly because of higher typing costs and interviewer related costs. Typing charges for the telephone pretest are artificially low because essentially the same questionnaire was used in both modes. Since personal interview materials had to be assembled early enough to provide time for mailing to primary areas, the personal interview pretest occurred prior to the telephone pretest, and we were able to "borrow" much of the typed material for use on the telephone pretest. For other telephone surveys, the costs for field office review, formatting, and typing of the pretest would be larger. In all cases, however, costs would probably be somewhat smaller than those for a similar personal interview pretest because much of the

written communication and instruction regarding the questionnaire
can be orally presented in a meeting before the telephone pretest. The
higher pretest costs for personal interviewers probably reflect a
slightly higher pay rate, as well as salary and transportation costs
associated with travel to and from respondents' homes, and with
attending a debriefing session in Ann Arbor.

7.5 TRAINING AND PRESTUDY WORK

As we noted in Chapters 2 and 3, the organizational requirements of
the two survey modes have great effects on the nature of contact of
interviewers with the research staff and the supervisory field staff.
These differences are very clear in the activities that precede the
study period—training new interviewers, taking practice interviews,
and studying the survey instructional materials. In the personal interview survey, field supervisors hire and train new interviewers (approximately ten were hired for this personal interview study), teach-
ing them basic interviewing skills that are useful in the current and all
later studies.[5] Concurrent with this work, field listings of the housing
units in chosen sample segments are completed by the interviewing
staff. As the study period approaches, all interviewing materials
needed are mailed to one interviewer (a "field coordinator") in each
primary area for distribution to individual interviewers working on
the study. After the interviewer receives the survey materials, he or
she studies them, completes a set of problems or exercises prepared
by the Ann Arbor staff to emphasize special study characteristics,
takes a practice interview, and attends a prestudy conference of interviewers (and sometimes supervisors) to discuss problems encountered in the practice interview.

The prestudy period for a telephone survey fulfills the same
functions as that in a personal interview survey, but enjoys greater
efficiencies because of reduced numbers of interviewers and increased ease of communication within a centralized administrative
and interviewing staff. For example, 37 interviewers and supervisors
were used for the telephone mode but 144 for the personal mode. In
the telephone project, the permanent interviewing supervisor
evaluated the availability of interviewers for the coming study, recruited and hired new interviewers (about 12 were hired for this

[5] This training takes 5 days, and is costly because it must be repeated at each site
where interviewers are hired.

project), and trained them in a 4-day training period. There were no sample listings to be completed before the study began and no field coordinators needed to distribute materials to individual interviewers. Materials that were needed were distributed at the beginning of a 2-day training session that provided specific instructions for that study. The project director reviewed the questionnaire with the interviewers item-by-item; the coding supervisor described problems caused by poor recording habits, and Ann Arbor field office personnel administered and discussed a work sheet exhibiting example problems on different sets of questions. On the night of the first training day, practice interviews were taken that were later reviewed by the supervisor.

Despite the somewhat more intensive nature of the prestudy training for the telephone survey, its total cost ($2066) is about one-fifth the cost of the personal interview survey equivalent ($9523). Although all components of personal prestudy costs are higher, the larger number of interviewers and the sample listing work make increased salary costs the primary locus of difference. The per-interviewer prestudy and training costs are about $74 in the personal and $56 in the telephone survey. Although the work in this category represents only about 11% of total sampling and field costs in the personal survey and 5% in the telephone survey, it affects the quality of all phases of the data collection process.

7.6 COST OF PRINTED SURVEY MATERIALS

A striking comparison between the two modes can be seen in the different types of field materials used in the two surveys. These are listed in Table 7.2. At least 20 different types of written field materials were employed in the personal survey as compared with eight on the telephone survey. In addition to questionnaires, the telephone interview mode used computer-generated cards for sample telephone numbers and a respondent selection sheet for data collection. Twenty-three thousand telephone number cards account for most of the $279 in Table 7.1. In the personal survey, sample address "cover sheets" are used instead of the cards. In addition, in the personal interview situation, a noninterview form is used to collect some observational data on nonrespondent households. The personal interview costs for materials ($705) are over twice those of the telephone survey.

The largest difference in types of materials used in the two modes

TABLE 7.2
List of Materials Printed, Duplicated, or Reproduced for Fieldwork

Personal survey	Telephone survey
A. *Data collection instruments*	A. *Data collection instruments*
Coversheet	Computer card for sample number
	Respondent selection sheet
Questionnaire	Questionnaire
Noninterview form	—
Show cards	—
B. *Data collection related materials*	B. *Data collection related materials*
Instruction book	Instruction book
Interviewer worksheet and answer sheet	Interviewer worksheet
"Why we ask you" booklets (English, Spanish)	—
Interviewer calling cards	—
Press release	—
Respondent letters	—
Interviewing progress report forms	—
Interviewer evaluation	—
Respondent verification/evaluation	Respondent verification/evaluation
Correction memos, special memos and letters to interviewers	Correction memos
Persuasion letters	Persuasion letters
C. *Reporting forms*	C. *Reporting forms*
Mileage forms	—
Pay forms	Pay forms
Expense forms	—
Telephone expense forms	—
Miscellaneous reporting forms	—

appears in materials related to data collection. Eleven different types of materials are required on the personal study, and only five for the telephone study. Some of these materials are sent to households prior to interview visits; others, including explanatory folders and calling cards are provided by interviewers when households are contacted. Also, press releases are sent to local papers to publicize the survey. None of these materials can be employed on telephone surveys. Their use in the personal mode increases costs but may have advantages in increasing response rates.

As noted in the previous section, 144 interviewers were employed on the personal survey as compared with 37 on the telephone survey. About five times more materials were needed for the staff in the personal mode than in the telephone mode. General supply costs were $278 for the personal interview mode and $20 for the telephone mode, with the difference due in large part to the size differences in interviewing staffs.

Although the expected number of respondents was larger in the telephone study ($N = 2000$)[6] than in the personal study ($N = 1500$), this difference was offset by the need to mail extra personal interview materials to each of the 74 primary areas in order to accommodate deviation from the number of expected interviews. For example, about 2700 copies of the personal questionnaire versus 2300 copies of the telephone questionnaire were needed for the field staff. Questionnaire printing costs were $1467 for the personal mode and $802 for the telephone mode, but some of this cost difference is attributable to questionnaire length and to extra copies obtained for other purposes.

A number of other materials are required for the personal study to facilitate communication and control over the data collection process (e.g., reporting forms); none of these is needed for telephone interviewing. Over all, materials related to data collection in the personal mode cost $1211, compared to $275 in the telephone survey.

Total costs for all telephone survey materials were $1375 or about 3.6% of total presented costs. Materials costs for the personal interview were $3660, or about 4.3% of the total costs. There are two important sources of difference between modes in this cost category. One is that the difference in interview length between the personal mode (50 minutes) and the telephone mode (30 minutes) has a substantial cost impact. The personal interview questionnaire was 64 pages long, the telephone questionnaire only 42 pages. This difference also affected the length of the instruction books used by interviewers on the two studies and had indirect impact on the length of some other materials. The estimated materials cost arising from the longer personal interview schedule is about $450. A second factor is that substantial quantities of extra Omnibus Survey materials were obtained for teaching and training purposes and for distribution to researchers around the country who might be interested in participating in later Omnibus surveys. Costs for obtaining these extra materials are estimated at about $500. Taking these two factors into account would reduce personal interview survey materials costs to about $2700, or 3.2% of total field and sampling costs, about the same percentage as on the telephone.

---

[6] This sample size was not achieved because of lower response rates due to greater difficulty in making contact with sample households.

7.7 ANN ARBOR FIELD OFFICE COSTS

The primary functions of the Ann Arbor field office are (*a*) scheduling field work and preparing data collection materials; (*b*) serving as an interface between the research staff, the interviewers, and the field supervisors; and (*c*) handling personnel and pay matters for interviewers and supervisors. Costs for Ann Arbor field office (AAFO) work are $4159 on the personal survey, 4.9% of total field and sampling costs.[7] On the telephone survey, AAFO costs are $1395, or 3.7% of total costs.

One reason for lower costs in the telephone mode is that the second function and part of the third function above were not performed by the AAFO for the telephone study. Rather, they were handled by the telephone office supervisor. This was possible because the relatively small interviewer staff was located in one central office, in the same building with the research staff. However, as Section VI of Table 7.1 reveals, the total telephone supervisory costs were also low, $2300 compared with $4957 on the personal study. Thus, even though some AAFO functions were shifted to the telephone supervisor, total phone supervisory costs were not high. This suggests that with a small centralized interviewing staff, AAFO costs diminish.

Clearly the AAFO communications task in a national personal interview survey is a large one, involving interactions with 150 interviewers and supervisors throughout the country. The field office must deal with questions about the interview schedule, problems with specific respondents, assignment loads, procedures, etc. The clerical tasks of simply answering telephones, typing memos, and processing time sheets become large. In addition, the volume of printed materials which must be prepared, assembled, and mailed adds significantly to both AAFO administrative and clerical costs.[8] Most of these tasks are eliminated with random-digit dialed samples and a centralized interviewing staff.

---

[7] Comparing costs from this personal interview survey with other similar personal interview studies indicates that AAFO salary costs were perhaps $1500 lower here than would have been anticipated. This study was conducted at a time when a large number of other studies were being handled by the AAFO.

[8] On the telephone study both administrative and clerical salaries are lower than would normally be expected. Costs for preparing and typing data collection materials were lower because some materials already prepared for the personal mode were used for the telephone mode.

7.8 INTERVIEWER AND SUPERVISOR COSTS DURING THE FIELD PERIOD

Total salary costs for interviewers and supervisors are somewhat more than twice as much for the personal interview survey ($32,278) as for the telephone survey ($12,545). This difference reflects the larger number of person-hours required to administer the personal survey (9378 to 4090 hours). When telephone interviewing was being conducted, one of four different supervisors was always present, but their combined hours (648) were smaller than the part-time work of the 15 personal interview supervisors (989 hours). Interviewer hours show even larger differences—more than twice as many on the personal interview (8390 to 3442 hours). The higher costs for personal interviewing partially result from the longer questionnaire and a slightly higher average salary for personal interviewers. By far the largest differences, however, result from salaries paid during the time required to travel to and from sample households, a cost eliminated in the telephone survey. In addition to the fact that no interviews are being collected while the interviewer travels to the sample segment, even after arrival the interviewer can visit only the few sample households in the segment before returning home or traveling to another segment. In contrast, a telephone interviewer can quickly dial any sample number. The required travel, report writing to inform supervisors of weekly progress, and mailing results back to the central office in Ann Arbor are the major differences between the interviewer's job in a personal interview and a telephone survey.

7.9 COSTS FOR INTERVIEWER AND SUPERVISOR TRAVEL

This cost category is unique to the personal interview method of data collection, in which interviewers must visit sample households personally to obtain interviews, and supervisors must travel to different sample areas to oversee the interviewing staffs.

The organization of telephone interviewing procedures eliminates the need for travel, especially when the survey is conducted from a central facility within offices of the survey organization. In this project, interviewers from the Ann Arbor area were hired and trained at SRC and, like most SRC employees, traveled to and from work at their own expense. All telephone supervisory staff worked in the same offices, and problems that arose during the course of the study were discussed immediately.

Looking at Table 7.1, Section VII, we note that total travel costs in the personal interview survey were $16,815, or about 20% of all field and sampling costs. Since no travel costs were incurred on the telephone study, these costs represent not only a sizable portion of total costs for the personal survey, but also a major portion of the total dollar *difference* in field and sampling costs between the two modes. This difference is $46,925, and travel costs of $16,815 represent 35.8% of the difference. There are, however, telephone charges on the telephone study, which can be considered the analog of travel costs on the personal survey. (See Section 7.10.)

Travel costs cover all travel necessary to the survey, to and from interviewers' homes. This includes travel related to listing housing units, taking practice interviews, attending prestudy conferences, and interviewing itself. During the interviewing period, interviewers make an average of three to four visits to each housing unit to obtain an interview. Distances that interviewers must travel from their homes to a sample cluster vary somewhat, but average distances are approximately 10 miles one way and typically range from the house next door to 45 miles.

Based on data from another 1976 SRC survey, about 93% of interviewer travel costs ($10,417) are mileage charges for driving their own cars; on this study that would imply that interviewers drove over 74,000 miles. This averages 31.4 miles for each of the 2373 sample housing units. The other 7% of costs is made up of parking fees, road tolls, use of public transportation, telephone charges in areas where charges are made for local calls, or tolls for long distance calls when interviewers telephone for appointments with respondents in more rural primary areas.

Mileage charges are a smaller component of supervisor travel costs ($5620).[9] Supervisors often live in one primary area but supervise four or five other areas as well. To hire and train interviewers, monitor field

---

[9] Supervisor travel costs on the personal interview study were higher than normal. Typically, supervisor travel costs at SRC are about 45% of total supervisor salaries for all phases of the survey ($9,039 on this study), which would be about $4100. Actual travel costs were $5620, or about $1500 higher than would be expected. These higher costs resulted partly because of supervisory staff turnover and illness at the time of this study, which required special trips by other supervisors to handle extra supervisory responsibilities, or trips to train new supervisors in the transition period. A very heavy field interviewing load during the spring of 1976 also necessitated some juggling of staff schedules, resulting in more supervisor travel than normal.

progress, and handle problems, they must frequently travel to and stay in a given primary area for several days at a time. Supervisor travel costs are, therefore, composed largely of plane fares, meals and lodging costs, car rentals, and long-distance telephone calls to interviewers. Some costs are, of course, for mileage reimbursement when supervisors take interviews or travel between primary areas in their own cars, but these are minor and are not shown separately in Table 7.1.

7.10 COMMUNICATION COSTS

Communications costs are incurred for two reasons—data collection itself, and the interaction between the data collection staff and supervisory staff during the course of gathering data.

In the telephone survey the only communications charges were telephone costs for data collection itself, totaling $15,794, or 42% of all sampling and field charges on the phone study. A major difference between modes is apparent here, in that costs for the personal study were only $5980, or 7% of all charges, and virtually all of them (phone, postage, supplies) were not for data collection per se, but for communications related to data collection.

Telephone charges for data collection on the phone study—that is, charges for contacting households and taking interviews—were composed of phone installation charges, WATS line fees, and toll call charges. Ten telephone lines were purchased for use on the project— eight WATS lines of varying cost and two regular lines for local calls. Those lines were accessed by one monitoring unit for the interviewing supervisor and 10 separate five-line instruments.

While there are no personal mode costs for data collection per se here, there are complementary nonsalary costs for interviewer travel. Interviewer travel costs total $11,195 or 13% of total charges on the personal study, compared with $15,794 for telephone costs on the phone study, or 42% of total costs. Telephone study costs are clearly more expensive in this area.

However, in the second type of communication costs—those incurred as a result of interactions between supervisory staffs and data collection staffs—the personal interview mode has sizable costs, while there are none on the telephone mode. First, there are postage costs for mailing materials to the 74 primary areas and for returning completed interviews or noninterviews to the Ann Arbor offices ($3491). There are also supply costs for boxes and envelopes ($733). Telephone communication costs for the personal mode do exist (totaling $1756) and result from phone calls between the Ann Arbor field office and interviews or supervisors.

7.11 COSTS OF ADMINISTRATIVE RECORD KEEPING

The control function within a survey includes those activities which record the progress of administering the questionnaires to the sample. The largest component of the work records the results of calls to each sample household (whether they were interviews, refusals, etc.) and summarizes overall progress. In the personal interview survey, listings of each sample address were kept in the Ann Arbor office, and disposition codes were recorded for the materials returned by mail from the interviewers. Identification codes were assigned to each response and nonresponse case processed, and a check was made on the accuracy of respondent selection. A daily plotting of the interviewing progress was kept on a display board in the field office, and a final accounting made of all sample cases into interview and noninterview categories. In the telephone survey, the results were manually entered into a computer data file using a terminal and summarized through machine-generated reports tabulating the disposition of sample numbers. Identification codes for completed questionnaires were assigned by coding section personnel each morning.

This category is one of the few where the telephone survey costs ($1203) are greater than those of the personal interview survey ($883). The fact that over five times as many sample telephone numbers as the desired number of interviews had to be generated created large processing costs. With newer telephone sample designs, the proportion of working household numbers is greater, and the control function constitutes even less than the 3% of total field and sampling costs that was incurred in this project.

7.12 POSTSTUDY ACTIVITIES

7.12.1 Debriefing–Interviewer Evaluation

At the end of the telephone interviewing period, debriefings were held with the field and research staffs to evaluate the questionnaire and data collection activities. Two 2-hour meetings were held with groups of interviewers and their supervisors to review the question-naire and elicit their comments on the procedures used in the survey. These sessions were taped to provide a record of the comments. This required about 80 hours of personnel time at a cost of about $246. In the personal survey, interviewers' evaluations of the survey proce-dures and of the questionnaire were made in writing and returned to the Ann Arbor office. Their comments were tabulated, summarized, and sent to the research staff and to interviewers participating in the Omnibus Survey. Although only 58 personnel hours were required for this task, the added cost of mailing, assembling, and duplicating the interviewers' comments resulted in larger evaluation costs for the personal interview survey ($281) than for the telephone interview survey.

7.12.2 Verification

Verification procedures involve essentially the same activities in both modes. Verification of the personal and telephone interviews was performed by mailing brief questionnaires to one-third of the respon-dents who provided their name and address. These questionnaires asked the respondents about their feelings toward the interviewer as a way both of verifying that the interview actually occurred and also of measuring how respondents judge their treatment by the interviewer. When the return rate among the respondents for any interviewer was very low, some telephone calls were made to those respondents to verify that they, indeed, had been interviewed. Despite the fact that the numbers of respondent verification letters sent on both studies were similar, the costs of the activity for the personal interview survey ($876) are significantly greater than the costs of the telephone survey ($508). The higher costs result partly from higher salaries for staff who performed the personal survey verification and from long-distance phone calls to check on some respondents.

7.12.3 Reports to Respondents

To show appreciation to respondents for giving their time for the interview, respondents to the personal interview were sent three issues of the ISR Newsletter to inform them of the work of the Insti-tute. A similar process occurred in the telephone survey except that four issues of the newsletter were promised. The costs involved in this function are related to adding respondents' names to the computer card file mailing list, and printing and mailing newsletters to the people throughout the year. The four issues for the telephone survey required about $1130 in total costs versus approximately $750 for the three issues sent on the personal interview project.

7.13 APPROPRIATE USES OF THIS COST ANALYSIS

Although we have included this cost analysis to guide the design of later research, we must outline the dangers of inference from the costs of any one project. All of them stem from the fact that each survey has unique characteristics that affect its total costs. One large source of differences is the population studied. Typically, different travel and postage costs are incurred on local metropolitan area surveys than on national surveys; areal household samples result in different costs than list samples; and cross-sectional surveys are generally less expensive than surveys of subpopulations that must be located through screening household samples. Even if we restrict our attention to national surveys of adult residents in housing units, there are cost variations within the same survey organization. The sources of some differences are obvious: the size of the sample, the length and complexity of the questionnaire, and the number of interviewers employed on a particular survey. Others are less well known. The presence of other studies being concurrently administered by the same field staff often implies that interviewers and supervisory staff use their time more efficiently, reducing the cost per interview. Conversely, if a permanent field organization is underutilized, its continuing personnel costs increase the per-interview costs for surveys that do occur. The season of the year in which the study is conducted may also affect costs. Season is often related to the amount of time residents are at home, the number on vacation, and even perhaps the willingness of people to be interviewed once contacted. The turnover of personnel in most interviewing staffs is large relative to other personnel in the survey organization; often interviewers are part-time employees with little long-term commitment to the job. Some projects scheduled when large turnover has been experienced suffer from higher training costs for the newer interviewers. These and other sources of cost differences complicate the use of cost analyses of one project to estimate costs of future studies.

This project itself has some characteristics which may or may not be duplicated in future studies of either mode. This is the first RDD telephone survey ever conducted by the Survey Research Center;

new methods, however pretested, inevitably bring with them difficulties of administration. Since this project we have completed other RDD surveys and are enjoying greater efficiency in some areas than we did earlier. Also, because of the methodological nature of this telephone survey, the research staff had a larger involvement in the interviewing process than in later telephone surveys and its participation no doubt reduced the activities of the field office personnel. A unique characteristic of the personal interview survey was that it consisted of sets of questions from several participants. The organizational structure of SRC Omnibus Survey differed from that of other SRC surveys; the Omnibus secretariat coordinated many of the activities prior to the data collection phase and organized the coding and data processing activities after the field period ended. Although the presence of the Omnibus secretariat probably reduced research staff time spent organizing the data collection phase, it also performed some oversight functions normally carried out by Ann Arbor field staff. Other qualities of the two different surveys, each typical of the particular mode, may complicate the comparison of costs between modes. For example, the average personal interview lasted about 50 minutes, the telephone interview, only 30 minutes. Some salary costs in both modes and travel costs in the personal mode are related to the length of the interview, but adjusting costs to account for differences in length requires assumptions about the use of time by interviewers that cannot be evaluated.

All of these complications limit the utility of our data to other researchers for evaluating the cost of either survey mode. We have chosen not to adjust costs in the two surveys in an attempt to reduce differences; rather we presented costs actually incurred by the two modes. When one mode's work eliminated the need for the same work on the other mode (e.g., typing the questionnaire), we noted this. In most cases, however, any differences or unique characteristics of the two surveys are reflected unaltered in their cost figures. Instead, the sources of differences were documented in order to qualify the cost discrepancies.

We have made some effort in the preceding discussion to note characteristics of this cost comparison that limit its applicability to other environments and even to a replication of the same study. The most valuable contribution of this examination of costs, we believe, is the description of separate sources of survey costs that are unique to each mode of data collection so that researchers contemplating work in a new mode may be aware of the different structures of the survey costs.

We found that the per-interview costs for the personal survey were $55 and for the telephone survey $23. Most important to this cost difference were (a) the reduced needs for the central office field staff in a telephone interview survey; (b) the reduced costs of materials and communication between field office and interviewing personnel; (c) the convenience of research staff interaction with the interviewing staff; and (d) the trade-off between telephone line charges in the telephone survey and travel charges in the personal interview survey. Our comparisons showed that total telephone survey costs were 45% of those in the personal interview survey; we should remember that the phone per-unit data cost was 51% and the per-unit time cost 64% of the corresponding costs for personal interviews. Finally, if *total* survey costs are evaluated, the telephone survey expense might be as much as 87% of the personal interview survey costs before analysis. Perhaps most important, however, we caution the reader that some of the cost comparisons are affected by questionnaires of different length, by the magnitude of work being conducted by the field section at the same time, and by the fact that this telephone survey suffered from the inevitable inefficiencies of being the first of its kind conducted by the organization.

7.14 SUMMARY

The main attractions of the telephone survey, according to its proponents, are its relative speed, its access to some areas where personal interviewing is especially difficult, and its economy. Of these claimed advantages, considerations of costs have dominated the methodological argument, although the magnitude of such savings has been estimated very differently by different investigators. Such differences seem to reflect variations in the studies compared—variations in coverage, content, locale, length of interview, experience, method of cost allocation, and the like.

The present surveys and the comparisons between them reflect their own unique circumstances, including certain factors that would ideally have been held constant between the telephone and personal interview surveys. The random digit dialing survey was the first of its kind conducted by the Survey Research Center, whereas the personal interview survey had some 30 years of experience behind it. The research staff was involved in the process of data collection, especially by telephone, more substantially than would usually be the case. The personal interviews lasted 50 minutes, on the average; the telephone interviews 30 minutes. In the presentation of comparative data on costs, no adjustment has been made for such differences, but they are pointed out whenever relevant.

Total direct costs for sampling and field work were $84,464 for the personal interview survey; for the telephone survey, the costs were $37,939—about 45% as much. Costs per interview were $55 for the personal interview survey and $23 for the telephone survey. Sample size was 1548 for the personal interview survey and 1618 for the telephone survey (stratified and clustered combined), not counting interviews that were broken off before completion.

These overall differences reflect, and occasionally obscure, more specific categorical differences between the two modes. Sampling costs were $955 for the telephone study and $8547 for the personal interview study. Training and prestudy work cost $2066 for the telephone mode and $9524 for the personal interview mode. Interviewer travel costs were nonexistent for the telephone interviews and $16,815 for the personal interviews. Communication costs, on the other hand, were $15,794 for the telephone survey and $5980 for the personal interview survey, the difference being caused by fees for the use of WATS lines for long-distance telephone interviewing. Field salaries, supervisory and interviewer, were $12,545 for the telephone survey and $32,278 for the personal interviews.

Many of these differences seem likely to persist. Differences in sampling costs seem inherent in the two procedures and stem, in large part, from the costs of keeping multistage areal samples up to date by locating new construction and enumerating housing units in newly selected areas. Large differences in costs of training and other prestudy activities are also likely to continue. Prestudy conferences of field interviewers involve travel, and personal interview surveys require more interviewers than telephone studies. Moreover, telephone procedures in some respects require less training; there are no sample listings to be mastered, for example.

Salary costs for personal interview surveys are larger than for equivalent telephone studies, both in their supervisory and their interviewer components. These differences reflect mainly the unavoidable travel time associated with each personal visit to a sample dwelling, whether or not the respondent is at home. Nonsalary travel costs are, of course, unique to the personal interview survey. Interviewer travel in such surveys is almost always by personal automobile. Of total costs of such travel, 93% is for reimbursing interviewers for the use of their cars; 31 miles of such reimbursed travel were required for each respondent in the personal interview survey. These travel costs are somewhat comparable to the costs of WATS lines for long-distance telephone calls, an expense unique to the telephone mode.

On balance, the approximation that personal interviews cost something on the order of twice that of telephone interviews seems justifiable, given the present development of both technologies.

Chapter 8

Summary and Speculation

The theory and practice of sample surveys is in flux today, after years of relative stability. For almost every procedure involved in the workflow of a survey, questions are being raised and methodological alternatives proposed: clustered sampling of dwellings by multistage areal procedures or sampling of telephone numbers by random-digit dialing; interviewing in person or by telephone; coding of responses by the penciled entry of numbers on a coding sheet or the direct entry of numbers at a computer terminal, and more. Many of these alternatives are captured in the comparison of the national telephone and personal interview surveys described in the preceding chapters. The following pages present a summary of the research findings from that comparison, and some speculations about the future of survey methods.

8.1 SAMPLE COVERAGE

The design of this study involves three samples, strictly speaking, one for personal interview and two for interview by telephone. The personal interview survey utilized the SRC national sample of dwelling units, a multistage area probability sample. The telephone interviews followed two sample designs: one a sample of randomly selected numbers within the 74 primary areas (counties and metropolitan areas) of the SRC national sample of dwelling units; the second a stratified random sample of telephone numbers chosen nationwide without restriction as to area.

Among the advantages of the design of this research is the ability to estimate from the personal interview survey the effects on survey results of omitting nonphone households. Failure to include the population without telephone service has been the major obstacle to wider use of the telephone for survey purposes. Indeed, the convenience and economy of telephone sampling made it a tempting alternative to area sampling long before it was a satisfactory one. As the proportion of telephone subscribers has increased in the United States, sampling by telephone numbers has become a more acceptable alternative for national and community populations.

About 9–10% of all households in coterminous United States are without telephones. With 90% of all households thus reachable by telephone, the overall coverage of telephone samples begins to approach the levels typically obtained by area probability samples of households. For the study of some subpopulations, however, the households not covered by telephone are crucial; they are by no means a random subset of the total.

Telephone subscription is lowest among poor households, whose budgets would be noticeably affected by the cost of telephone service. Nonsubscribers also differ from subscribers in other demographic characteristics, which are associated with income but suggest additional reasons for not having telephone service. For example, rural households tend to have lower incomes than urban households, but some rural areas are also relatively inaccessible; telephone service to such areas may be expensive, of poor quality, or lacking entirely. Elderly people tend to be relatively low in the income distribution, but they tend also to have fewer friends and business associates—and more hearing difficulties. All these may be reasons for deciding against telephone subscription. Households consisting of very young adults tend to have less income than those of the middle age range, but they are also more likely to be transient, and they may decide against telephone subscription for the latter reason as well as the former.

In short, the decision to be without telephone service is a self-selective process and it reflects distinctive characteristics. One cannot assume that the nonsubscribers are like the subscribers. On the other hand, the proportion of nonsubscribers has become small and it continues to shrink.

8.2 SAMPLE DESIGN

Sampling strategies for telephone surveys have included direct selection of numbers listed in telephone books; a two-stage variant of that design in which the last digit of each listed number selected at the first stage is replaced with a random number at the second stage; multistage designs where exchanges are sampled in the first stage and prefixes and numbers in later stages (Chilton Research Services, no date); and a two-stage sample where clusters of 100 consecutive numbers are selected in the first stage and specific numbers in the second stage (Waksberg, 1978). Finally, stratified random sampling designs have been implemented through random generation of four-digit random numbers within working central office codes (Glasser & Metzger, 1972).

In this project we utilized two different sampling designs for telephone surveys—one a stratified random design, the other a clustered design not previously documented, which was a selection of numbers from exchanges linked to the primary areas of the SRC national sample of dwellings. The clustered sample design is the more complex of the two, and it is the less efficient. The clustering of telephone numbers within sample areas originally selected for personal interview increases sampling errors and does not offer the compensating economies of operation in telephone interviewing that it does in personal interviewing. Moreover, the boundaries of telephone exchanges do not usually follow county lines, and some numbers generated on a random basis are therefore not eligible for interview. The clustered design used in this project required a sample size about 40% larger than the sample size needed for a stratified random telephone sample.

These characteristics imply rather specialized purposes for telephone samples selected to conform to the areal boundaries of samples originally designed for personal interview. Such clustered telephone samples are useful primarily for mixed-mode surveys, in which some interviewing is to be done by telephone and some (within the same sample) in person. For example, telephone interviews may be used as screening procedures to locate some subpopulation of interest.

8.3 IMPLEMENTING THE DESIGNS

Both telephone designs required interviewers to dial five or more noneligible numbers for every one working household number. We have since implemented an improved sample design that increases the proportion of working household numbers generated from approximately 20% as in this project to over 55%. The improved design is based on a selection of clusters of consecutive numbers and is described more fully in Appendix III. Other designs that are now being used by different survey organizations include sampling of telephone exchanges, the geographical units which contain one or more of the three-digit central office codes. Sampling telephone exchanges often involves attempts to learn blocks of unused numbers within different central office codes, so that the percentage of eligible generated numbers can be increased. An alternative procedure at this final stage is to obtain telephone books for the selected exchanges and choose randomly from the listed numbers.

Through calculation and analysis of sampling errors on random-digit dialed samples of various designs, we have discovered that the loss of precision in sample estimates due to lack of control on sample size (the penalty of not knowing whether generated numbers are working household numbers) was approximately a 5% increase in standard errors for estimates of means and proportions on the total sample. The effect of clustering the sample into the primary areas of the SRC national sample, when added to the effect of loss of control over sample size from random generation of sample numbers, created inflations of standard errors of about 19%.

We had little guidance in designing telephone facilities for interviewers and in developing training techniques for new interviewers. In this project, new telephone interviewers were given initial training similar to that given routinely to personal interviewers. Techniques of introduction, persuasion, question reading, probing, handling respondent questions, and the like were covered in a 4-day seminar. In addition, the study directors and members of the field and coding sections gave the telephone interviewers more complete information about how the collected data were to be used, what interviewing problems were of chief concern to the field staff, common interviewing errors that make coding of responses difficult, and the expectations of the supervisor concerning interview production.

Although no experimentation to test the effects of this closer contact with research staff was conducted in this work, it has been proven over time to be a valuable and flexible tool for quality control. For ongoing studies with experienced interviewers, little seems to be gained by lengthy training sessions on the questionnaire itself, and more emphasis is placed on errors discovered in coding the most recent wave of interviewing for the study. In all telephone studies, however, the continuous contact between the research staff and interviewers has enabled interviewers to understand more fully the purposes of measures in the questionnaire, and has taught research staffs the difficulties that some questions raise during interviews.

One of the greatest advantages of the telephone mode relative to personal interviews is thus experienced after the study has begun, when corrections to errors in the questionnaire, corrections of common interviewer mistakes, or changes in interviewing procedures can be communicated quickly to interviewers. In present SRC telephone interviewing projects, questionnaires are coded soon after they are taken, and interviewer errors discovered during coding are brought immediately to the interviewers' attention by means of notes that the interview supervisor reviews jointly with the interviewer. The feedback loop between the interviewers' behavior and their knowledge of its results and its adequacy is thus very short; the crucial information returns quickly to the interviewers, individually and collectively. Interviewers on a national survey of personal interviews, on the other hand, sometimes get the bulk of their feedback after they have completed their assignments, soon enough for the next study if the information is relevant, but much too late for the study in progress.

8.4 SELECTION OF RESPONDENTS WITHIN HOUSEHOLDS

The selection of respondents within sample households cannot be done in advance, but must be done by the interviewer at the time of interview. The procedures for selection in personal interview surveys use a full listing of household members. In an attempt to simplify this procedure for telephone use, we developed a grid corresponding to different numbers of male and female adults. The telephone interviewer was required only to determine the total number of adults in the household and the number of them who were women. Use of the grid would then indicate the individual selected as respondent. Our analysis of this procedure showed that it yielded an error in selection in about 10% of the sample households.

Since completing this project we have resorted to a complete household listing similar to the procedures used in the personal interview survey. There has not yet been an independent test of the accuracy of such procedures, but information from the 1977 Detroit Area Study suggests that even complete household listing on the telephone may be subject to more errors than in the personal interview case. In that survey the sample was split into telephone and areal probability portions, and households were reinterviewed after a period of weeks. A larger number of discrepant household compositions between original and reinterview listings were noted in the telephone part of the sample than in the personal interview part. Continued work is needed to identify and eliminate sources of error in the selection of telephone respondents. Alternative approaches would (a) routinely verify the household listing once the selected respondent is contacted; (b) introduce questions on the household composition within the questionnaire; or (c) explore different techniques of obtaining household listings from the informant prior to interview.

8.5 DIFFERENCES BETWEEN MODES: RESPONSE AND NONRESPONSE

The large issue confronted by any methodological innovation is whether it equals or exceeds the established way of doing things. For most survey measures, no external standard exists to assist this determination. Perfect validity is an aspiration not expressible by comparison with a platinum cylinder or the wavelength of the cadmium red line. Because personal interview surveys of areal probability samples have become established, it is appropriate to compare the results of telephone surveys to them without suggesting that personal interviews and areal probability samples are without error or bias. Such comparisons can be sharpened by the occasional instances in which external standards of known validity are available, and by the cases in which judgments of quality or desirability are almost beyond argument.

In this section we consider several such comparisons between the telephone and the personal interview mode—their overall rates of response and nonresponse, their relative vulnerability to termination during the interview process, the characteristic completeness or richness of response obtained in the two modes, substantive differences in responses to identical question asked by telephone or in person, and respondent preferences for one mode or the other.

8.5.1 Refusal and Nonresponse

The response rate of national telephone surveys remains at least five percentage points lower than that expected in personal interviews. This has been a rather stable comparison despite changes over time in training of interviewers, monitoring techniques, feedback procedures from monitors, and techniques of introducing the survey to the respondent. Much of the previous literature on introductory techniques (except for Dillman, Gallegos, & Frey, 1976) either does not apply to telephone interviews, cannot be implemented for samples of randomly generated numbers, or shows few differences between techniques.

One promising approach may be to replace the respondent's visual inspection of the interviewer, his or her credentials, and material that occurs in the personal interview, by lengthening the acquaintance procedure on the telephone or even by making separate calls for purposes of introduction (Reingen & Kernan, 1977). An initial telephone call to sample households could be made before the interviewing period begins, requesting no specific information but rather introducing the interviewer to the household, mentioning that the phone number had been selected and explaining that another call would be made later to conduct an interview. The goal of such an initial call would be to establish contact with each sample household through a telephone call that was more social than business-oriented. Especially important would be the fact that during the call no requests would be made of the household. After experiencing such a call and suffering no ill effects from the initial interaction, members of sample households might be more willing to trust the interviewer and grant subsequent requests for the interview.

Whatever the solution turns out to be, the problem of nonresponse in telephone surveys is beyond argument. The exact magnitude of the problem, however, is difficult to determine because of the ambiguous status of unanswered numbers. We have chosen to present a range of possible response rates, depending on what assumptions one makes about numbers not answered after repeated attempts at different times and on different days. Reporting a range of rates is sometimes not satisfactory (e.g., when adjustment for nonresponse must be made), and it is rarely desirable. Although the Bell System maintains capabilities (customer name and address service) to determine the status of all numbers of Bell affiliates, it does not usually make that information accessible to survey organizations. For this project the range of response rates was 11%, 59% if we include all unanswered numbers as households and 70% if we do not. For telephone surveys in nonmetropolitan areas the range may even be greater. The new sample design now used at SRC has reduced the problem of unanswered numbers somewhat, but until a routine method of determining the status of unanswered numbers is developed, they will continue to complicate the computation of response rates.

8.5.2 Partial Interviews

The classification of sample households as either respondents or nonrespondents has always been an oversimplification. Some people begin interviews but do not complete them; they are partial nonrespondents—or partial respondents, to put the case more optimistically. The number of such cases is negligible in a well-administered personal interview survey, perhaps because the norms of politeness make householders reluctant to order the interviewer out, once the request for an interview has been granted and the interview begun. It is much easier to terminate a telephone conversation when it becomes wearisome, and about 5% of all respondents did so.

Premature terminations of telephone interviews come in a variety of forms. Some few people hang up the telephone after the first question; others become fatigued quickly and refuse to continue; still others have appointments to keep, terminate for the time being and are not able to be contacted again. These behaviors pose different problems and will probably require different solutions. The few angry people who hang up quickly perhaps need a description of the survey purposes and procedures to reassure them about the survey itself and to emphasize their own importance to the successful completion of the research. Respondents who break off an interview because of fatigue often give early cues that they are tiring or losing interest, and interviewers can become more sensitive to such cues. One of the advantages of telephone interviewing is the relatively low cost of callbacks, and respondents who do not wish to complete an interview in one conversation can be asked to set a time at which the interview can be resumed. This procedure should increase completion rates among respondents who tire easily and among those who interrupt the initial interview because of other appointments or obligations. For both groups a key requirement for resuming the interview is likely to be the respondents' judgment about its importance or their enjoyment in talking with the interviewer. If the interaction is unpleasant, the likelihood of completing the interview is greatly reduced.

8.5.3 Completeness of Response

Even respondents who answer all questions may differ in the completeness or richness of their answers. When questions are of the open-ended type, such response differences may be very great. Fixed-alternative questions, on the other hand, leave little room for such variations; the respondent either answers the questions "completely" or not at all.

There were consistent differences in interviewing speed between the telephone and personal modes, and that fact raises the question of whether there are associated differences in completeness of response. In a section of the questionnaire that was nearly identical in both modes we discovered that the speed of interview was greater on the telephone than in face-to-face interviews. The effect of pace of interview was an auxiliary concern in research by Cannell, Oksenberg, and Converse (1977), and there is some evidence that the quality of the health status measures collected in that research suffered with faster paced interviews. In this project we saw that there are differences in responses to open-ended items for interviews completed in different amounts of time.

Our work (Chapter 4) suggests that the faster pace of telephone interviews is associated with differences both in the number and type of responses to open-ended items. Moreover, the tendency to give shorter answers in the telephone mode seems most pronounced among those respondents who typically give complete and detailed responses. These people may merely adapt to the faster pace of the interview more quickly; they may alter their behavior to make it more compatible with the speed of interaction suggested by the interviewer's behavior. This result deserves more study, perhaps with some experimentation with different interviewer behavior, different types of probing and feedback on different types of open-ended items.

8.5.4 Optimism, Trust, and Social Desirability

Differences in rates of refusals, partial interviews, and brevity of response raise the question of substantive discrepancies between the two interviewing modes. We found very few such response discrepancies between the two sets of data that were large enough to be considered statistically significant. The differences that did occur included (in addition to the tendency toward more truncated responses to open-ended questions on the telephone) some suggestion of greater optimism among telephone respondents on consumer sentiment and life satisfaction items, and a greater uneasiness among telephone respondents about discussing some subjects.

The optimism we noted on several questions is a small effect generally but it merits future work. If it persists over different surveys, its relationship to interviewer behavior should be explored. The "optimism effect" may be related to the lack of trust that is evident in greater expressed uneasiness and suspicion about the survey among telephone respondents. If there is less trust of telephone interviewers than personal interviewers, respondents may be reticent to reveal uncertainties about their financial status, dissatisfaction with the way their life is arranged, or other sensitive material. This hypothesis contrasts with those offered by Colombotos (1965), which suggest greater validity on the telephone for sensitive questions because the greater social distance between respondent and interviewer may free respondents to answer more honestly.

8.5.5 Respondent Reactions

Nonresponse rates suggest that respondents find the telephone interview to be less a rewarding experience and more of a chore than the personal interview. More direct questions to respondents about their reactions to the interview support this conclusion.

The largest differences between the two modes were on items that measured the respondent's reaction to the interview experience. In each measure, whether a respondent's answer to a question or an observation by the interviewer, the telephone survey respondents gave evidence that they disliked the interaction much more than did the personal interview respondents. Respondents on the telephone showed more suspicion at the start, more frequently asked how much longer the interview would take, often rushed their answers, seemed to show less interest in the interview, more often reported feeling uneasy about discussing certain topics, and more often thought that the interview lasted too long. All these behaviors reflect a lower rapport between interviewers and respondents in the telephone mode. The lack of rapport between interviewer and respondent evident in these results presents a large threat to the long-run utility of telephone surveys. Unless we develop telephone techniques to establish respondent motivation and trust at least equal to that between respondent and interviewer in a face-to-face survey, we will damage our response rates on current studies and produce unpleasant memories of interview experiences among those who do permit the questioning. The long-run effects of such tendencies might severely hamper data collection by telephone.

A first priority for future work, therefore, should be the nature of the respondent–interviewer interaction. We need to experiment with techniques to improve the enjoyment of the interview by the respondent, maximize the overall completion rate, and minimize response error on specific measures. This work might fruitfully begin with efforts at translating into verbal messages the visual cues that fill the interaction in a face-to-face interview: the smiles, frowns, raising of eyebrows, eye contact, etc. All of these cues have informational content and are important parts of the personal interview setting. We can perhaps purposefully choose those cues that are most important to data quality and respondent trust and discard the many that are extraneous to the survey interaction.

8.6 COSTS AND BENEFITS

The direct costs of personal interviews are high, relative to the funds available for social research, and the interest in telephone surveys has had from the beginning a significant fiscal component.

This project was quite successful in assessing comparative costs for the two different survey modes. As reported earlier (Chapter 7), we found that the telephone survey's sampling and data collection costs were 45–64% of those of the personal interviews. Moreover, telephone survey costs have changed since this project. They have decreased through an alteration in the telephone configuration that is used. In this project we purchased WATS lines for the duration of the study; now we are one user of a university-wide WATS system, so that costs are shared with other university users. This new system represents a substantial economy, since there is only a small charge for maintaining an instrument with lines on the University centrex system.

On the other hand, some cost components of telephone surveys have increased, as we have taken advantage of certain potentialities for improved quality control. For example, the monitoring of telephone interviewers is now more routinized. Each interviewer on each study is monitored and scored, by means of techniques for measuring interviewer behavior devised by Cannell, Lawson, and Hausser (1975). This system has clear benefits for data quality through its continued feedback to interviewers on their performance.

The cost advantages of telephone interviewing are likely to persist;

the elimination of interview travel and the administrative economies of training and supervising interviewers in a single location are intrinsic to the method. So is the tendency to use fewer interviewers than are required for a widely scattered operation. For most personal interview studies, the number of interviews taken by individual interviewers is small—too small for economy in training and administration. The telephone mode makes possible a pattern of fewer interviewers and more interviews taken by each of them.

That pattern has administrative and fiscal advantages, but it has disadvantages with respect to interviewer variance—the effects of interviewer differences on the data. The interviewer variance study introduced as part of this project has important implications for telephone survey operations. The issue essentially balances costs and errors. We demonstrated that interviewer effects could significantly increase overall design effects where, as in this project, each interviewer was taking 30–40 interviews. Interviewer effects could be decreased by hiring a larger staff, but that would increase costs. Such error components can be estimated with proper controls over interviewer assignments, and we think designs in which such estimates are made offer great promise for further description of the errors associated with survey data. We are especially enthusiastic about the prospect of using these error estimates in later analysis of the data.

The design of this study permitted the estimation of only gross response differences between modes. The observed differences thus included the effect of nonresponse to both modes, as well as any effects of the medium of data collection on responses. Since the comparison juxtaposed telephone respondents with personal interview respondents from telephone households, it controlled for different rates of coverage as a source of variation between the modes. We did not attempt, however, to determine whether identical inferences would be drawn from an unadjusted telephone survey and a personal interview survey. It is that question that is important to many researchers planning social surveys, and the answer to it depends on the importance of nontelephone households to the issues under investigation.

8.7 FUTURE WORK

We have outlined in our discussion of this project's results several features of telephone survey methodology that need further investigation. We can formally identify three areas of particular concern— nonresponse error, response error, and technological developments.

1. Regarding nonresponse error, the most immediate work should concentrate on techniques to convince selected persons that the purposes of the survey deserve their attention and cooperation. Some of this research can be done on a trial-and-error basis, in which various techniques are tried until something that works is discovered. Variation in the introduction of the interview is probably one of these areas, because alternative approaches to be tested experimentally simply have not been identified at this point. The payoff in this area might come in an evolutionary trend to a desirable approach.

Some work on nonresponse error, however, can only be done with alteration of research designs. For example, the effect of length of interview on response rate could be estimated by comparing response rates on various surveys where interview lengths were different. However, such estimates would contain the confounding effects of different topics discussed in the studies. A formal experimental design with an interview on several different topics might better provide such estimates. Similarly, in an environment where there are several ongoing surveys on a single topic, nonrespondents from previous samples, especially those never previously reached, could be added to a current sample to reduce the effects of nonresponse (Kish & Hess, 1959).

2. We have not yet explored how to minimize response errors once a respondent grants a telephone interview. Research on response error should be conducted jointly with efforts to reduce nonresponse. Such joint investigations are appropriate because changing interviewer behavior to increase respondent cooperation may threaten the quality of responses obtained. Questions of response error will probably not be answered with a single piece of research because different techniques may be required for different types of measures. What may be needed is preliminary work that identifies techniques useful for some measures, followed by continued testing of similar techniques for other measures. Multiple indicators of phenomena and newly developed analytic techniques that permit modeling of error terms should be used in conjunction with interviewer techniques to measure response errors. Experiments on question wording like those we introduced in the project should continue, since they can offer insights into the sources of response error.

We continue to feel the need for a comparison of errors in different data collection modes. It is unlikely that great advances in our understanding can be made merely with replications of this study's design, but a more routine mixing of data collection modes can be useful. Such designs may permit us both to continue investigating response and nonresponse errors in different modes and also to learn which techniques are best used in one medium or the other. They can serve as well to identify which techniques need simultaneous application in multiple modes for high quality data. The matching of data collection mode to populations (e.g., telephone interviews in metropolitan areas, personal interviews in rural areas), simultaneous use of multiple modes to reduce nonresponse bias in the combined data set, the use of telephone interviews to supplement or bring up to date a sample which has already provided longer personal interviews—all of these are possible ways to use both modes in a single study.

3. Some of the most exciting research potentialities for telephone surveys may be created by new technological developments. "Computer-based interviewing" or "computer-assisted telephone interviewing" (CATI) are phrases describing interviewing systems in which the telephone interviewers sit at cathode-ray tube (TV screen) terminals, the questions appear on the screen, and the interviewers enter responses by the keyboard of the terminal. The immediate benefit of such a system is increased efficiency in construction of a machine-readable data base. The coding and data processing work to prepare a data file is greatly reduced. A long-range benefit of such a system, however, arises from the potential it offers for methodological research on telephone surveys.

With such a system, question ordering can be randomized to investigate context effects, and interviewer assignments can be routinely randomized so that interviewer variance estimates can be supplied for each study. Through monitors located at other terminals, duplicate and independent recordings of the respondents' answers can be made and recording variance estimated. With other monitors grading the interviewer behavior, a computer-summarized assessment of the quality of an interview can be given to interviewers immediately following the questioning.

Such immediate feedback can offer valuable incentives to proper interviewing techniques and provide analysts of the survey data with estimates of error rates on the survey. If particular questions are very important to the research purposes, the monitoring system could be focused on those intensively, so that monitors would follow each use of these questions and record objectively the quality of related interviewer behavior. Such records would be stored in a data file that could be accessed anytime during the study. If some questions were found to be yielding unacceptably poor responses or if interviewers were found to make unacceptably high rates of error in recording them, the form of the questions could be changed in the middle of the field period before the entire study is completed.

No doubt systems for interviewing and recording will become increasingly complex and offer even greater research promise over time. Audio units interfaced with machines now have the capability of carrying on understandable speech and recognizing certain phrases. Not too far in the future, telephone interviews may be conducted by machine, with respondents replying either verbally or by pressing certain keys on their own telephones. Indeed, when one assesses the technological capabilities available, the larger question is not whether we can have the machinery to introduce certain efficiencies but whether the researcher, the respondent, and the social milieu will enable their use.

8.8 FUTURE DEVELOPMENTS IN SURVEY RESEARCH

Telephone surveys are only one form of survey research, and developments in other types of surveys and in the society as a whole affect the methodology of surveys. The decades since World War II have seen such a proliferation of surveys and interviewing that they may seem to be a normal and permanent aspect of life. It could be argued, however, that the possibility of collecting valid data on a variety of topics, public and personal, merely by soliciting the cooperation of the potential respondents depends on a number of conditions that have been realized only in a few places and at a few moments in human history.

If the interview content goes beyond simplistic questions of preference or aversion among familiar matters in everyday life, assumptions of certain levels of information, conceptual ability, and verbal expression are clearly involved. If the pledge of confidentiality, which is almost always offered as a condition of the interview, is to be taken seriously, people must believe not only that the survey establishment wishes to keep its word but that it is legally and politically able to do so. To the extent that such pledges are regarded as less than perfect, the validity of survey responses requires the respondents' belief that they can speak their minds without fear of recrimination or disadvantage.

And even if such matters of ability, confidentiality, and safety are taken care of, the success of survey research as a social enterprise requires that respondents consider the game worth the candle. If the norms of openness and courtesy between strangers are not enough to carry the interview, the question of benefits arises. Whose interests does the respondent serve by complying and whose by refusing to comply? To the extent that people consider themselves to be members of a society in which goals are widely shared and well served by corporate, governmental, and academic enterprise, we can expect a generalized readiness to be interviewed. To the extent that there is distrust, fear of recrimination, or the conviction that data collection somehow exploits those who provide the data, refusals will run high.

Finally, the role of the interviewer, no less than that of the respondent, requires certain conditions of social life. In a society of easy conversations, unlocked doors, cordiality between diverse groups, and openness between strangers, interviewing becomes easy. In a society in which people are fearful of strange neighborhoods—or of their own—unwilling to venture out after dark, distrustful of government, and doubtful about the uses to which their responses may be put, interviewing becomes difficult and response validity questionable.

We hope that the quality of survey research in the future will benefit both from methodological innovation and from social conditions of confidence and trust. In such conditions social research can flourish, and to them it can contribute.

Appendix I

Telephone Survey Questionnaire

for office use only

Letter from right-hand corner of Respondent Selection Sheet
☐X ☐Y

P. 462062
April – May 1976

SURVEY RESEARCH CENTER
INSTITUTE FOR SOCIAL RESEARCH
THE UNIVERSITY OF MICHIGAN
ANN ARBOR, MICHIGAN 48106

(Do not write in above space .)

1. Interviewer Number ☐☐

2. Identification Number ☐☐☐☐☐

3. ☐☐☐ / ☐☐☐
   Area Code   Central
                Office Code

4. Date _____

5. Length of Interview _____
                              (Minutes)

Study of
Telephone Survey Methodology

229

time to the nearest minute____

SECTION A

Of course, this interview is completely voluntary. If we should come to
any question you don't want to answer, just let me know and we'll skip over
it.

(IF NOT DETERMINED THAT R LIVES ALONE) Some of the questions I'll ask apply
only to people living together as a family. Do you live alone or do you live
with your family?

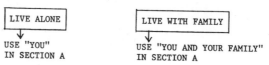

LIVE ALONE	LIVE WITH FAMILY
↓	↓
USE "YOU"	USE "YOU AND YOUR FAMILY"
IN SECTION A	IN SECTION A

A1. We are interested in how people are getting along financially these days.
V13002 Would you say that you (and your family) are <u>better off</u> or <u>worse off</u> financially than you were <u>a year ago</u>?

1. BETTER NOW	3. SAME	5. WORSE NOW	8. DON'T KNOW
↓	↓	↓	↓

A1a. Why do you say so? _____

V23003

V23004 _____

_____

_____

_____

A2. How about compared to three years ago... Would you say that you (and your
V13006 family) are <u>better off</u> financially or <u>worse off</u> now than you were <u>three years</u>
<u>ago</u>?

1. BETTER NOW	3. SAME	5. WORSE NOW	8. DON'T KNOW

A3. Now looking ahead--do you think that <u>a year from now</u> you (and your family)
V13007 will be <u>better off</u> financially, or <u>worse off</u>, or just about the same as now?

1. WILL BE BETTER OFF	3. SAME	5. WILL BE WORSE OFF	8. DON'T KNOW

230

A4.   Now turning to business conditions in the country as a whole--do you think
V13008   that during the next 12 months we'll have <u>good</u> times financially, or <u>bad</u>
times, or what?

| 1. GOOD TIMES | 4. BAD WITH QUALIFICATIONS |

| 2. GOOD WITH QUALIFICATIONS | 5. BAD TIMES |

| 3. PRO-CON | 8. DON'T KNOW |

A5.   Would you say that at <u>the present time</u> business conditions are better or
V13009   worse than they were <u>a year ago</u>?

| 1. BETTER NOW | 3. ABOUT THE SAME | 5. WORSE NOW |

A6.   During the last <u>few months</u>, have you heard of any favorable or unfavorable
V23010   changes in business conditions?
V23011
_____

A6a.   (IF NECESSARY) What did you hear? _____

_____

_____

> IF NOT CLEAR WHETHER A CHANGE R MENTIONS IS FAVORABLE OR UNFAVORABLE
> PROBE: "Would (MENTION CHANGE) be favorable or unfavorable?" AND
> NOTE "favorable" OR "unfavorable."

A7.   How about a year from now--do you expect that in the country as a whole busi-
V13013   ness conditions will be <u>better</u>, or <u>worse</u> than they are at present, or just
about the same?

| 1. BETTER A YEAR FROM NOW | 3. ABOUT THE SAME | 5. WORSE A YEAR FROM NOW |

TURN TO P. 3, A8

A7a.   Do you think that a year from now business conditions will be a lot
V13014   better, or only a little better, or what?

| 1. LOT BETTER | 2. LITTLE BETTER |

A8.
V13015
Generally speaking, do you think now is a good time or a bad time to buy a house?

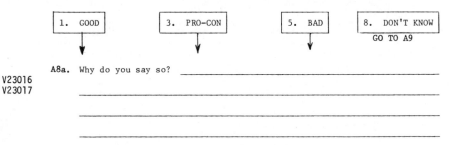

| 1. GOOD | 3. PRO-CON | 5. BAD | 8. DON'T KNOW |

GO TO A9

A8a. Why do you say so? _____

V23016
V23017

_____

_____

_____

A9.
V13019
Speaking now of the automobile market--do you think the next 12 months or so will be a good time or a bad time to buy a car?

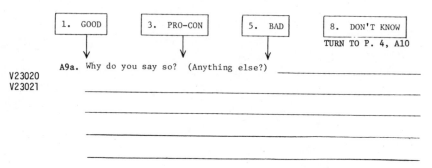

| 1. GOOD | 3. PRO-CON | 5. BAD | 8. DON'T KNOW |

TURN TO P. 4, A10

A9a. Why do you say so? (Anything else?) _____

V23020
V23021

_____

_____

_____

_____

232

A10. How about you (or anyone in your family) -- will you <u>probably</u> buy or
V13023 lease a car in the next 12 months, is there an <u>even chance</u> you will, or
      do you think you <u>probably won't</u> (buy or lease a car in the next 12 months)?

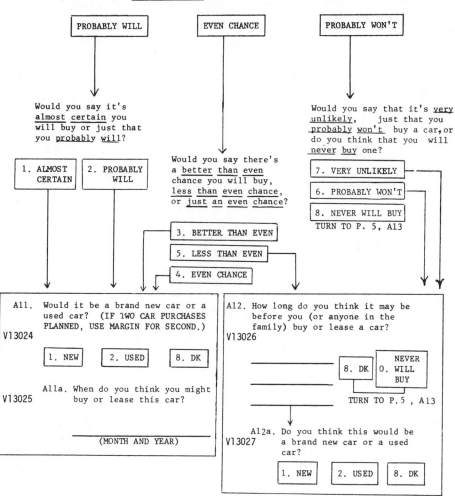

A13.   About the big things people buy for their homes--such as furniture, refrig-
V13028 erator, stove, television, and things like that. Generally speaking, do you
        think now is a good or a bad time for people to buy major household items?

| 1. GOOD | 3. PRO-CON | 5. BAD | 8. DON'T KNOW |

                                                  GO TO A14

A13a.   Why do you say so? _____

V23029
V23030 _____

        _____

A14.   Do you think it is more important now than usual for you to try to add to your
V23032 savings and reserve funds, or are you fairly well satisfied with your savings?

        _____

        _____

        _____

        _____

time to the nearest minute _____

234

B1.   As you may know, there are several ways to learn how people feel about the
V15033   topics we discuss in interviews. We can conduct <u>face-to-face</u> interviews,
we can do interviews on the <u>telephone</u>, or we can <u>mail</u> questionnaires that
people fill out and return. If you had your choice, would you rather answer
these questions...

1.	in a face-to-face interview,	2.	in a telephone interview	or	3.	in a mailed questionnaire?

B1a. Why is that? _____

V25034

_____

_____

_____

_____

_____

B2.   INTERVIEWER CHECKPOINT

☐ 1. RESPONDENT SELECTION SHEET IS MARKED X ⟶ TURN TO P. 7, BX1

☐ 2. RESPONDENT SELECTION SHEET IS MARKED Y ⟶ TURN TO P.11, BY1

BX1. The next questions ask how you feel about different parts of your life. Please take into account the last year and what you expect in the near future. Of course if you don't have any feelings on a question, tell me. If your feelings are on the good side, I'll ask you whether you feel "delighted," "pleased," or just "mostly satisfied." If they are on the bad side, I'll ask whether you feel "terrible," "unhappy" or just "mostly dissatisfied." If your feelings are really mixed, just say so.

Let's start with one about your housing...

     BX1a. How do you feel about your house or apartment? Good, bad, or mixed?
V11039

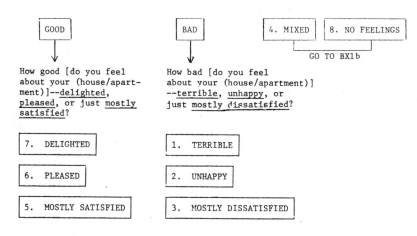

     BX1b. How do you feel about your own health and physical condition? Good,
V11040   bad, or mixed?

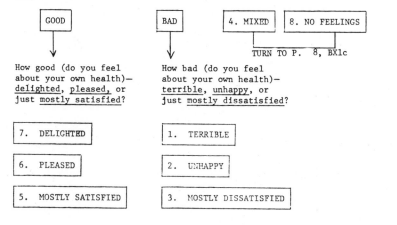

236

BX1c. How do you feel about your marriage? (Good, bad, or mixed?)

V11041

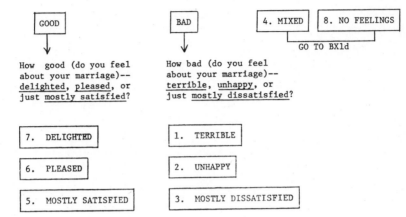

How good (do you feel
about your marriage)--
delighted, pleased, or
just mostly satisfied?

How bad (do you feel
about your marriage)--
terrible, unhappy, or
just mostly dissatisfied?

7. DELIGHTED		1. TERRIBLE
6. PLEASED		2. UNHAPPY
5. MOSTLY SATISFIED		3. MOSTLY DISSATISFIED

BX1d. How about your standard of living--the things you have like housing,
car, furniture, recreation, and the like? (How do you feel--good, bad,
or mixed?)

V11042

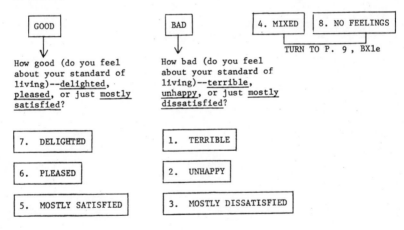

How good (do you feel
about your standard of
living)--delighted,
pleased, or just mostly
satisfied?

How bad (do you feel
about your standard of
living)--terrible,
unhappy, or just mostly
dissatisfied?

7. DELIGHTED		1. TERRIBLE
6. PLEASED		2. UNHAPPY
5. MOSTLY SATISFIED		3. MOSTLY DISSATISFIED

237

BX1e.   Finally, a very general one. How do you feel about your life as
V11043   a whole? Good, bad, or mixed?

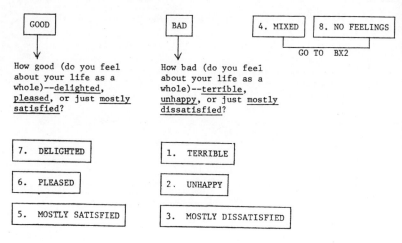

GOOD

How good (do you feel
about your life as a
whole)--delighted,
pleased, or just mostly
satisfied?

7. DELIGHTED

6. PLEASED

5. MOSTLY SATISFIED

BAD

How bad (do you feel
about your life as a
whole)--terrible,
unhappy, or just mostly
dissatisfied?

1. TERRIBLE

2. UNHAPPY

3. MOSTLY DISSATISFIED

4. MIXED   8. NO FEELINGS

                  GO TO BX2

BX2.   Taking all things together, how would you say things are these days--
V11044   would you say you're very happy, pretty happy, or not too happy these
        days?

1. VERY HAPPY   3. PRETTY HAPPY   5. NOT VERY HAPPY

238

BX3. Would you agree or disagree with the following statement... "These days
V12045 it's not safe to open your door to strangers."

| 1. AGREE | | 5. DISAGREE | | 8. DON'T KNOW |

BX4. Not everyone has an opinion on the next question. If you do not have an
V12046 opinion just say so. "The Arab nations are trying to work for a real peace
with Israel." Do you have an opinion on that?

| 8. NO OPINION | | YES, HAVE OPINION |
GO TO BX5

BX4a. Do you agree or disagree? (REPEAT ORIGINAL STATEMENT IF NECESSARY.)

| 1. AGREE | | 5. DISAGREE |

BX5. On most political issues, would you say you are on the liberal side or on
V12047 the conservative side?

| 1. LIBERAL | | 5. CONSERVATIVE | | 3. | (IF VOLUNTEERED) MIDDLE OF ROAD, HALF-WAY BETWEEN |

BX6. Would you say that most men are better suited emotionally for politics than
V12048 are most women, that men and women are equally suited, or that women are
better suited than men in this area?

| 1. MEN BETTER SUITED | | 3. MEN AND WOMEN EQUALLY | | 5. WOMEN BETTER SUITED |

BX7. Do you think the United States should forbid public speeches against democracy?
V12049

| 1. YES, FORBID | | 5. NO, NOT FORBID |
TURN TO P. 13, B3

239

BY1. The next questions ask how you feel about different parts of your life.
Please take into account the last year and what you expect in the near
future. Of course, if you don't have any feelings on a question, tell me.

I'll ask you to give a number from one to seven that describes how you
feel--"one" stands for "completely dissatisfied," and "seven" for
"completely satisfied." If you are neutral, answer "four." So the low
numbers indicate you are dissatisfied; the high numbers, you are satisfied.
(WRITE NUMBER ON LINE TO RIGHT OF QUESTION).

Let's start with one about your housing...

BY1a.   How do you feel about your (house/   a. _____ | 8. NO FEELINGS; NEVER THOUGHT |
V11050   apartment)?

How do you feel about...

BY1b.   Your own health and physical condition? b. _____ | 8. NO FEELINGS; NEVER THOUGHT |
V11051

BY1c.   Your marriage?   c. _____ | 8. NO FEELINGS; NEVER THOUGHT | | 0. INAP |
V11052

BY1d.   Your standard of living--the things
V11053   you have, like housing, car, furni-
         ture, recreation, and the like?   d. _____ | 8. NO FEELINGS; NEVER THOUGHT |

Finally, a very general one...

BY1e.   How do you feel about your life as
V11054   a whole?   e. _____ | 8. NO FEELINGS; NEVER THOUGHT |

BY2.   Taking all things together, how would you say things are these days--would
V11055 you say you're <u>very</u> happy, <u>pretty</u> happy, or <u>not too</u> happy these days?

| 1. VERY HAPPY | | 3. PRETTY HAPPY | | 5. NOT TOO HAPPY |

240

BY3.   Would you agree or disagree with the following statement... "These days
V12056   it's not safe to open your door to strangers."

| 1. AGREE | 5. DISAGREE | 8. DON'T KNOW |

BY4.   "The Arab nations are trying to work for a real peace with Israel." Do you
V12057   agree or disagree?

| 1. AGREE | 5. DISAGREE | 8. (IF VOLUNTEERED) NO OPINION |

BY5.   On most political issues, would you say you are on the <u>liberal</u> side, on the
V12058   <u>conservative</u> side, or <u>middle-of-the-road</u>?

| 1. LIBERAL | 5. CONSERVATIVE | 3. MIDDLE-OF-THE-ROAD |

BY6.   Do you agree or disagree with this statement? "Most men are better suited
V12059   emotionally for politics than are most women."

| 1. AGREE | 5. DISAGREE |

BY7.   Do you think the United States should allow public speeches against democracy?
V12060

| 1. YES, ALLOW | 5. NO, NOT ALLOW |

B3. As you know there will be an election for President in November. These next questions are about people and issues in politics. First a question about the last presidential election. In 1972 Nixon ran on the Republican ticket against McGovern for the Democrats. Do you remember for sure whether or not you voted in that election?

V32061

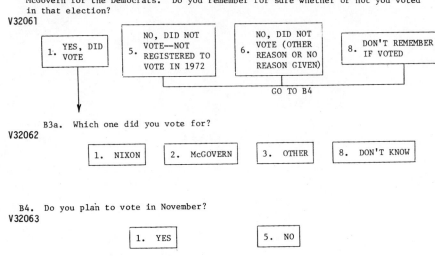

| 1. YES, DID VOTE | 5. NO, DID NOT VOTE--NOT REGISTERED TO VOTE IN 1972 | 6. NO, DID NOT VOTE (OTHER REASON OR NO REASON GIVEN) | 8. DON'T REMEMBER IF VOTED |

GO TO B4

B3a. Which one did you vote for?

V32062

| 1. NIXON | 2. McGOVERN | 3. OTHER | 8. DON'T KNOW |

B4. Do you plan to vote in November?

V32063

| 1. YES | 5. NO |

242

B5. Now I'd like to get your feelings toward some political leaders.

Imagine a thermometer going from 0 to 100 degrees. Give each person I mention a score on the thermometer that shows your feelings toward him -- 0 to 50 degrees if you don't care too much for him; 50 degrees if you don't feel particularly warm or cold toward him; and between 50 and 100 degrees if you have a warm feeling toward him. If you don't know too much about a person, just tell me.

Is it all clear?

1. YES	5. NO
GO TO B5a	

Here is how it works. If you don't feel particularly warm or cold toward a person, then you should place him in the middle of the thermometer, at the 50 degree mark.

If you have a warm feeling toward a person, or feel favorably toward him you would give him a score somewhere between 50° and 100°, depending on how warm your feeling is toward that person.

On the other hand, if you don't feel very favorably toward a person--that is, if you don't care too much for him--then you would place him somewhere between 0 and 50 degrees.

Of course, if you don't know too much about a person, just tell me and we'll go on to the next name.

B5a. Our first person is George Wallace. Where would you put him on the thermometer?

	RATING			RATING		
V12065	_____	B5a. GEORGE WALLACE	V12069	_____	B5e.	Edward "Ted" Kennedy
V12066	_____	B5b. Gerald Ford	V12070	_____	B5f.	Henry "Scoop" Jackson
V12067	_____	B5c. Jimmy Carter	V12071	_____	B5g.	Morris Udall
V12068	_____	B5d. Ronald Reagan	V12072	_____	B5h.	Hubert Humphrey

B6. What do you think are the most important problems facing this country?
V22073
V22074 _____

_____

_____

_____

_____

_____

B6a. What other important problems are there? _____
V22078

_____

_____

B6b. (IF PROBLEMS MENTIONED IN B6a) Are there any other important
V22081 problems?
V22082 _____

_____

_____

Now some questions about relations between the races.

B7. Which of these statements would you agree with:
V12085

| 1. | White people have a right to keep black people out of their neighborhoods if they want to | or | 5. | Black people have a right to live wherever they can afford to, just like anybody else | 8. | DK; DEPENDS; CAN'T DECIDE |

244

V12086 B8. Would you prefer to have a child of yours go to a school with mostly <u>white</u> children, mostly <u>black</u> children, or a school that is mixed half and half?

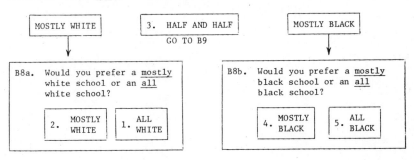

| MOSTLY WHITE | 3. HALF AND HALF
GO TO B9 | MOSTLY BLACK |

B8a. Would you prefer a <u>mostly</u> white school or an <u>all</u> white school?

| 2. MOSTLY WHITE | 1. ALL WHITE |

B8b. Would you prefer a <u>mostly</u> black school or an <u>all</u> black school?

| 4. MOSTLY BLACK | 5. ALL BLACK |

V12087 B9. Do you think it is possible for a white person and a black person to be close friends, or is this just not possible?

| 1. POSSIBLE | | 5. NOT POSSIBLE |

V12088 B10. Would you personally prefer to live in a neighborhood with mostly <u>whites</u>, mostly <u>blacks</u>, or a neighborhood that is mixed half and half?

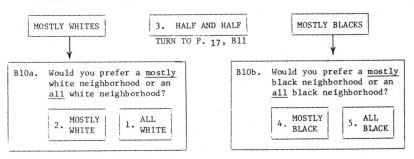

| MOSTLY WHITES | 3. HALF AND HALF
TURN TO P. 17, B11 | MOSTLY BLACKS |

B10a. Would you prefer a <u>mostly</u> white neighborhood or an <u>all</u> white neighborhood?

| 2. MOSTLY WHITE | 1. ALL WHITE |

B10b. Would you prefer a <u>mostly</u> black neighborhood or an <u>all</u> black neighborhood?

| 4. MOSTLY BLACK | 5. ALL BLACK |

B11. I am going to read a list of complaints that people sometimes make about their house or apartment. As I read each one, please tell me whether it is a big problem, a small problem, or not a problem at all in your (house/apartment).

		BIG PROBLEM (1)	SMALL PROBLEM (2)	NOT A PROBLEM (3)
V11089	B11a. Not enough heat during the cold months. Is this a big problem, a small problem, or not a problem at all in your (house/apartment)?			
V11090	B11b. How about the fear of breakins... Is this a big problem, a small problem, or not a problem at all?			
V11091	B11c. How about not enough living space?			
V11092	B11d. How about walls or ceilings cracking or crumbling?			
V11093	B11e. How about cockroaches, ants or other insects?			

B12. Now a different question. How many telephones, counting extensions, do you have
V45094   in your (house/apartment)?

| 0 | 1 | 2 | 3 | 4 | 5 | MORE THAN 5, SPECIFY: ____ |

TURN TO   GO TO B14
P. 19, B16

B13. Do all the telephones have the same number?
V35095

| 1. YES | 5. NO |

GO TO B14

V35096   B13a. How many different numbers are there?

_____(NUMBER)

V35097   B13b. Are any of the numbers for business use only?

| 1. YES | 5. NO | → GO TO B13d

V35098   B13c. How many are used only for business?

_____(NUMBER)

V35099   B13d. Do all the numbers appear in the current telephone book?

| 1. YES | 5. NO | 8. DON'T KNOW |

TURN TO P. 19, B16   GO TO B15

V35100   B13e. How many numbers do appear in the current telephone book?

_____(NUMBER)

GO TO B15

V35101 B14. Does the number appear in the current telephone book?

| 1. YES | 5. NO | 8. DON'T KNOW |

TURN TO P. 19, B16

B15. (Is/Are) the listing(s) too new to appear in the book, did you request an
V35102   unlisted number, or is there some other reason that the number(s) may not
be listed?

| 1. LISTING(S) TOO NEW | 2. R REQUESTED THE UNLISTED NUMBER(S) | 7. OTHER (SPECIFY): |

247

B16. Now, a few questions about filing federal tax returns. Some people use a standard deduction when filing their federal tax return, while others itemize deductible expenses such as property taxes, interest payments, and charitable contributions. When you filed your return for 1975, did you itemize your deductions?

V33103

| 1. YES | 5. NO | 0. DID NOT FILE A RETURN (YET) | 8. DON'T KNOW |

TURN TO P. 20 , SECTION D

B16a. INTERVIEWER OBSERVATION

V33104

DID R CHECK RECORDS OR GET HELP WITH THE ANSWER?

| 1. YES | 5. NO |

B17. Did you (and your husband/wife) find that you were entitled to a refund on your federal tax return, or did you owe the government money, or what?

V33105

| 1. ENTITLED TO REFUND | 2. OWED MONEY | 3. CAME OUT EVEN; NEITHER REFUND NOR OWED MONEY | 8. DON'T KNOW |

GO TO B17c

B17a. About how large is your federal tax refund this year?

V43106

_____(DOLLARS)

B17b. (IF CAN'T SAY) Is it about $50, $100, $200, or what? '

V43107

_____(DOLLARS)

B17c. INTERVIEWER OBSERVATION

V55108

DID R CHECK RECORDS OR GET HELP WITH THE ANSWER?

| 1. YES | 5. NO |

time to the nearest minute_____

D1. We are interested in your present job status. Are you working, retired, temporarily
V44109

1.	WORKING NOW; ON STRIKE; SICK LEAVE

2.	TEMPORARILY LAID-OFF

GO TO D3a

3.	UNEMPLOYED AND LOOKING FOR WORK

D2. About how many hours do you work on
your (main) job in an average week?
V44109
V44110 _____ (HOURS PER WEEK)
V44111

D2a. What is your main occupation?
(What sort of work do you do?)

_____

_____

D2b. Tell me a little more about
what you do.

_____

_____

(IF NOT CLEAR FROM ABOVE ASK):

D2c. What kind of (business/indus-
try) is that in?

_____

D2d. Are you employed by someone
else, are you self-employed
or what?

SOMEONE ELSE	SELF-EMPLOYED

D2e. Have you been unemployed or laid off
for a week or more during the past
12 months?

1. YES	5. NO

TURN TO
PAGE 22,
SECTION E

D2f. For how many weeks or months was this?

_____WEEKS OR _____MONTHS

TURN TO P. 22, SECTION E

D3. Have you ever done any work for pay?
V44114

YES	NO

TURN TO P. 22,
SECTION E

D3a. What was your occupation on your
last regular job? (What sort
of work did you do?)

_____

_____

D3b. Tell me a little more about what
you did.

_____

_____

(IF NOT CLEAR FROM ABOVE ASK):

D3c. What kind of (business/industry)
was that in?

_____

D3d. Were you employed by someone else,
were you self-employed, or what?

SOMEONE ELSE	SELF-EMPLOYED

D3e. How many weeks or months have you
been unemployed or laid off in
the last 12 months?

_____WEEKS OR _____MONTHS

TURN TO P. 22, SECTION E

249

laid off, unemployed, a student, (housewife), or what? (CHECK ALL THAT APPLY)

5. RETIRED OR DISABLED		7. STUDENT	HOUSEWIFE OR OTHER 8. (SPECIFY):

GO TO D6

D4. What was your main occupation before you (retired/became disabled)? (What sort of work did you do?)
V44116

_____

_____

D4a. Tell me a little more about what you did.

_____

_____

(IF NOT CLEAR FROM ABOVE ASK):

D4b. What kind of (business/industry) was that in?

_____

D4c. Were you employed by someone else, were you self-employed, or what?

SOMEONE ELSE	SELF-EMPLOYED

D4d. Are you doing <u>any</u> work for pay at the present time?

YES	NO	TURN TO P. 22, SECTION E

GO BACK TO D2 "WORKING NOW"

D5. Are you a full-time or part-time student?
V44109

FULL-TIME	PART-TIME

D6. Are you doing <u>any</u> work for pay at the present time?

YES	NO
GO BACK TO D2 "WORKING NOW"	TURN TO P. 22, SECTION E

time to the nearest minute _____

SECTION E

Now a few questions about where you live.

(IF COUNTY OF RESIDENCE NOT YET DETERMINED)
E1. Could you tell me what county you live in?

_____COUNTY

E2. Do you live in a city or town, a suburban area, or do you live in a rural area?

| 1. CITY OR TOWN | 2. SUBURBAN AREA | 3. RURAL AREA |

E2a. About how large is your (city/town)—less than 10,000 people, between 10,000 and 50,000, or more than 50,000 people?

| 1. LESS THAN 10,000 |

| 2. 10,000 - 50,000 |

| 3. MORE THAN 50,000 |

| 8. DON'T KNOW |

E2b. About how large is the nearest town—less than 10,000 people, between 10,000 and 50,000, or more than 50,000 people?

| 1. LESS THAN 10,000 |

| 2. 10,000 - 50,000 |

| 3. MORE THAN 50,000 |

| 8. DON'T KNOW |

E2c. About how far away is the town?

_____ MILES | 8. DON'T KNOW |

E3. Could you tell me the name of the (city/town)?

_____ NAME

E4. By any chance is your (house/apartment) located on a military base?

| 1. YES | | 5. NO |

251

E5. How would you describe your housing—as a single family house, a duplex, an apartment building, a mobile home, or something else?

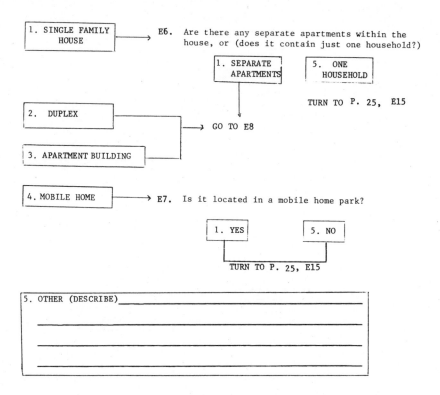

E6. Are there any separate apartments within the house, or (does it contain just one household?)

1. SINGLE FAMILY HOUSE

1. SEPARATE APARTMENTS

5. ONE HOUSEHOLD

TURN TO P. 25, E15

2. DUPLEX

3. APARTMENT BUILDING

GO TO E8

4. MOBILE HOME

E7. Is it located in a mobile home park?

1. YES   5. NO

TURN TO P. 25, E15

5. OTHER (DESCRIBE)_____

E8. How many separate (units/apartments) are there in your building?

1   2   3   4   5   6 or more (SPECIFY)_____

IF NATURE OF BUILDING NOT CLEAR, EXPLAIN SITUATION:

_____

_____

E9. Is your (unit/apartment) rented separately from the other units, is it owned by you (and your family), or is there some other arrangement ?

| 1. RENTED SEPARATELY |
GO TO E10

| 3. OWNED | ⟶ GO TO E11

| 7. OTHER ARRANGEMENT (DESCRIBE)_____
  _____
  _____ |

E10. Are any of the (units/apartments) rented on a short time basis; that is, for less than a month, or on a daily rate?

| 1. YES |

| 5. NO |
GO TO E11

E10a. Are more than half of the (units/apartments) rented on a short time basis?

| 1. YES |

| 5. NO |

E11. Does your (unit/apartment) have its own kitchen facilities separate from the other units?

| 1. YES |
TURN TO P. 25, E14

| 5. NO |

E12. Do you (and your family) prepare your own meals, are the meals part of the rent, or is there some other arrangement?

| 1. PREPARE OWN MEALS | 2. MEALS PART OF RENT | 7. OTHER (SPECIFY)_____
  _____ |

E13. When you enter your (unit/apartment) from the outside, do you have to pass through someone else's living quarters?

| 1. YES |

| 5. NO |

E14. Is this phone number just for your (unit/apartment) or does it also
serve other (units/apartments) in the building?

| 1. | NUMBER FOR R's USE ONLY |

| 5. | NUMBER SERVES OTHER UNITS ALSO |

E14a. How's that? _____

_____

_____

E15. Do you (and your family) live in your (house/apartment) all year long,
or do you have another residence for some part of the year?

| 1. | LIVE HERE ALL YEAR LONG |
TURN TO P. 26, E18

| 5. | HAVE ANOTHER RESIDENCE |

E15a. Could you tell me about it? _____

_____

_____

_____

E16. Is someone at the other residence all year long?

| 1. YES |

| 5. NO |

E17. Is there a telephone that remains in service at the other residence even
when you are not staying there?

| 1. YES |

| 5. NO |

E18. The Survey Research Center sometimes does personal interviewing in
people's homes. We won't come to your home, but we want to see if
some people can be reached by telephone who could not be reached
in person. Is it difficult for someone to come directly to your
door -- for example, is there a (locked gate/locked building entrance)
or something else that might prevent this?

V35138

| 1. YES | | 5. NO |

E18a. How's that? _____

V45139

_____

_____

time to the nearest minute ____

SECTION F

(FOR MULTI-UNIT BUILDINGS)

INTERVIEWER: REMEMBER THAT R'S HOUSEHOLD INCLUDES THOSE PEOPLE WHO —

           1.   LIVE TOGETHER WITH R IN RENTED OR OWNED QUARTERS SEPARATE FROM OTHERS IN THE BUILDING.

    AND   2.   SHARE WITH R THE SAME ENTRANCE FROM OUTSIDE OR SHARE WITH R COMPLETE KITCHEN FACILITIES SEPARATE FROM THE OTHER UNITS.

DEFINE "HOUSEHOLD" TO R IN THESE TERMS WHEN NECESSARY.

F1.   Could you tell me who lives in your household. I don't need their
V44141– names, just their relationship to the head of the household. First,
V44150 there's you....

       (FOR EACH CHILD, LESS THAN 18 YEARS OLD, VERIFY WHETHER OR NOT R IS (HIS/HER) PARENT)

(a) List by Relationship to Head	(b) Sex	(c) Age	(d) Indicate Child of R with
(RESPONDENT)			

256

Now we would like to ask you a few questions about yourself, like your
education , your occupation, your age and race.

F2. What is the highest grade of school or year of college you completed?
V44151
V44152

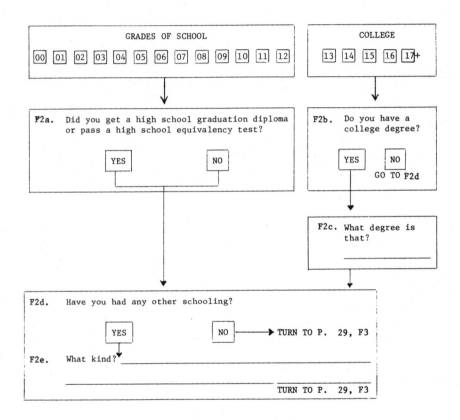

GRADES OF SCHOOL

| 00 | 01 | 02 | 03 | 04 | 05 | 06 | 07 | 08 | 09 | 10 | 11 | 12 |

COLLEGE

| 13 | 14 | 15 | 16 | 17+ |

F2a. Did you get a high school graduation diploma
or pass a high school equivalency test?

YES   NO

F2b. Do you have a
college degree?

YES   NO
        GO TO F2d

F2c. What degree is
that?
_____

F2d. Have you had any other schooling?

YES   NO ——→ TURN TO P. 29, F3

F2e. What kind? _____

_____
                        TURN TO P. 29, F3

257

F3. INTERVIEWER CHECKPOINT

V44153

☐	1. R IS HEAD OF HOUSEHOLD ─────→ **GO TO F5**
☐	5. R IS NOT HEAD OF HOUSEHOLD

F4. What is the highest grade of school or year of college (HEAD OF HOUSEHOLD) completed?

V44154

GRADES OF SCHOOL	COLLEGE
00 01 02 03 04 05 06 07 08 09 10 11 12	13 14 15 16 17+

F5. Would you mind telling me your race?

V44155

1. WHITE	2. BLACK	3. CHICANO; PUERTO-RICAN; MEXICAN- OR SPANISH-AMERICAN	4. AMERICAN INDIAN

5. ORIENTAL	7. OTHER (SPECIFY): _____

(ASK IF NOT KNOWN THAT R IS MARRIED AND LIVING WITH SPOUSE OR VERIFY SITUATION YOU BELIEVE TO EXIST.)

F6. Are you married, separated, divorced, widowed, or have you never been married?

V44156

| 1. | MARRIED, (INCLUDING SPOUSE AWAY IN SERVICE) | 2. SEPARATED | 3. DIVORCED | 4. WIDOWED | 5. NEVER MARRIED |

F7. What is the month and year of your birth? _____ _____

V44157   (MONTH)   (YEAR)

F8. Generally speaking, do you usually think of yourself as a Republican, a Democrat, an Independent, or what?

V44159

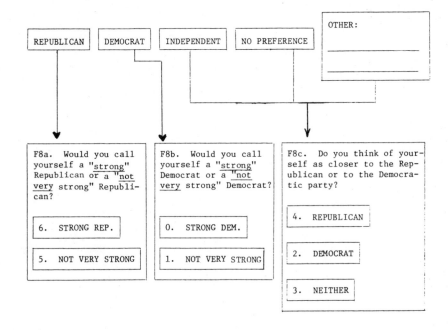

| REPUBLICAN | DEMOCRAT | INDEPENDENT | NO PREFERENCE | OTHER: _____ |

F8a. Would you call yourself a "strong" Republican or a "not very strong" Republican?

6. STRONG REP.

5. NOT VERY STRONG

F8b. Would you call yourself a "strong" Democrat or a "not very strong" Democrat?

0. STRONG DEM.

1. NOT VERY STRONG

F8c. Do you think of yourself as closer to the Republican or to the Democratic party?

4. REPUBLICAN

2. DEMOCRAT

3. NEITHER

259

F9.   INTERVIEWER CHECKPOINT
V44160

[ ]   1.   R IS NOT MARRIED ──────▶ TURN TO P. 34, F17

[ ]   2.   R IS MARRIED

F10. We are interested in your (husband's/wife's) present time job status. Is (he/she) working,
V44161

1.	WORKING NOW; ON STRIKE; SICK LEAVE

2.	TEMPORARILY LAID OFF

(GO TO F12a)

3.	UNEMPLOYED AND LOOKING FOR WORK

F11.   About how many hours does (he/she) work
V44161   on (his/her) (main) job in an average
V44162   week?
V44163

_____HOURS PER WEEK

F11a.   What is your (husband's/wife's)
        main occupation? (What sort of
        work does [he/she] do?)

        _____

        _____

F11b.   Tell me a little more about what
        (he/she) does.

        _____

        _____

        (IF NOT CLEAR FROM ABOVE ASK:)
F11c.   What kind of (business/industry)
        is that in?

        _____

F11d.   Is your (husband/wife) employed
        by someone else, is (he/she) self-
        employed or what?

SOMEONE ELSE	SELF-EMPLOYED

TURN TO P. 34, F16

F12.   Has (he/she) ever done any work for
V44164   pay?

YES		NO	─▶ TURN TO P.34 , F17

F12a.   What was your (husband's/
        wife's) occupation on (his/
        her) last regular job? (What
        sort of work did [he/she] do?)

        _____

        _____

F12b.   Tell me a little more about
        what (he/she) did.

        _____

        _____

        (IF NOT CLEAR FROM ABOVE, ASK:)
F12c.   What kind of (business/indus-
        try) was that in?

        _____

F12d.   Was your (husband/wife) em-
        ployed by someone else, was
        (he/she) self-employed or what?

SOMEONE ELSE	SELF-EMPLOYED

TURN TO P. 34, F16

260

EMPLOYMENT SECTION

retired, temporarily laid-off, unemployed, a student, (housewife), or what? (CHECK ALL THAT APPLY).

5. RETIRED OR DISABLED	7. STUDENT

HOUSEWIFE OR OTHER:
(SPECIFY)

8. _____

GO TO F15

F13. What was your (husband's/wife's) main occupation before (he/she) (retired/ became disabled)? (What sort of work did (he/she) do?)

V44165 _____

_____

F14. Is your (husband/wife) a full-time or part-time student?

FULL-TIME	PART-TIME

F13a. Tell me a little more about what (he/she) did.

_____

_____

F15. Is (he/she) doing any work for pay at the present time?

| YES | NO |→ TURN TO P.34, F16

GO BACK TO F11
"WORKING NOW"

F13b. What kind of (business/industry) was that in?

_____

F13c. Was your (husband/wife) employed by someone else, was (he/she) self-employed or what?

SOMEONE ELSE	SELF-EMPLOYED

F13d. Is (he/she) doing any work for pay at the present time?

| YES | NO |→ TURN TO P. 34, F16

GO BACK TO F11
"WORKING NOW"

F16.   Thinking about <u>last year, 1975</u>, how much did your (husband/wife) earn
V 33166   from (his/her) job, <u>before</u> taxes and other deductions were made? (Just
       tell me the figure to the nearest thousand dollars.)

_____DOLLARS

```
┌─────────────────────────────┐
│ 0.  DIDN'T WORK IN 1975      │
└─────────────────────────────┘
```

(ASK ONLY IF R REFUSES TO GIVE DOLLAR FIGURE)

       F16a. We don't need the exact dollar figure; could you tell me which of
V 33167   these three broad categories it falls in...

```
┌──────────────────┐  ┌──────────────────┐  ┌──────────────────┐
│ 1.  less than    │  │ 2.  between 7,500 │  │ 3.  more than    │
│     7,500 dollars│  │     and 15,000    │  │     15,000?      │
└──────────────────┘  └──────────────────┘  └──────────────────┘
```

F17.   How much did you earn from <u>your</u> job last year, in 1975, before taxes and
V33168   other deductions were made? (Again, just to the nearest thousand dollars.)

_____DOLLARS

```
┌─────────────────────────────┐
│ 0.  DIDN'T WORK IN 1975      │
└─────────────────────────────┘
```

(ASK ONLY IF R REFUSES TO GIVE DOLLAR FIGURE)

       F17a. We don't need the exact dollar figure; could you tell me which of
V13169   these three broad categories in falls in...

```
┌──────────────────┐  ┌──────────────────┐  ┌──────────────────┐
│ 1.  less than    │  │ 2.  between 7,500 │  │ 3.  more than    │
│     7,500 dollars│  │     and 15,000    │  │     15,000 ?     │
└──────────────────┘  └──────────────────┘  └──────────────────┘
```

F18.   Last year, in 1975, did <u>you (and your family living here)</u> receive any income from
       sources <u>other than from wages</u> such as interest on savings, social security, pensions,
V33170   welfare, unemployment compensation, alimony, etc.?

```
┌──────────┐            ┌──────────┐  ┌─────────────────┐
│ 1.  YES  │            │ 5.  NO   │  │ 8.  DON'T KNOW  │
└──────────┘            └──────────┘  └─────────────────┘
      │
      ▼
```
V33171   How much was this? Was it....   TURN TO P. 35, F19

```
┌─────────────────────────────┐   ┌─────────────────────────────┐
│ A.  under $1,000      (1)    │   │ D.  $5,000 - $9,999    (4)   │
└─────────────────────────────┘   └─────────────────────────────┘

┌─────────────────────────────┐   ┌─────────────────────────────┐
│ B.  $1,000 - $2,499   (2)    │   │ E.  $10,000 - $14,999  (5)   │
└─────────────────────────────┘   └─────────────────────────────┘

┌─────────────────────────────┐   ┌─────────────────────────────┐
│ C.  $2,500 - $4,999   (3)    │   │ F.  $15,000 - and over (6)   │
└─────────────────────────────┘   └─────────────────────────────┘
```

F19. Finally, how much income did <u>you (and your family living here)</u> receive in 1975, not just from wages but <u>from all sources</u>, before taxes and other deductions were made? (Just tell me the figure to the nearest thousand dollars.)

V 33172

_____DOLLARS

(ASK ONLY IF R REFUSES TO GIVE DOLLAR FIGURE)

F19a. We don't need the exact dollar figure; could you tell me which of these three broad categories it falls in....

V13173

| 1. less than 7,500 dollars | 2. between 7,500 and 15,000 | 3. more than 15,000? |

SKIP IF R LIVES ALONE

F20. Does that include everyone in your family who lives here?

| YES | | NO |

TURN TO P. 36,

SECTION M

F20a. What should the figure be if you include everyone? _____

(EXPLANATION OF DISCREPANCIES:)_____

_____

time to the nearest minute____

M1. At the beginning of the interview we emphasized that it was voluntary, and we appreciate your cooperation in answering the questions. Sometimes, even though a person answers a question, (he/she) may feel uneasy about discussing the particular subject. I'll mention several types of questions and I would like you to tell me whether or not you felt uneasy about them.

		1. YES	5. NO
V11174	M1a. First of all think about the questions on your income. Did you feel uneasy about them?		
V11175	M1b. How about questions on your racial attitudes?		
V11176	M1c. Your income tax return?		
V11177	M1d. How about questions on your health?		
V11178	M1e. Your job?		
V11179	M1f. Your voting behavior?		
V11180	M1g. Your political opinions?		

M2. How did you feel about the length of the interview? Was it...
V15181

1. Much too long	2. Too long	3. About right	4. Too short	or	5. Much too short?

TURN TO RESPONDENT NAME AND ADDRESS SHEET

time to the nearest minute_____

SECTION T

COMPLETE THE FOLLOWING QUESTIONS AFTER THE INTERVIEW.

T1. SEX OF RESPONDENT:
V54182

| 1. MALE | 5. FEMALE |

T2. WAS THERE A LANGUAGE PROBLEM THAT MADE IT DIFFICULT FOR YOU TO INTERVIEW THIS
V55183 RESPONDENT?

| 1. YES, MAJOR PROBLEM | 3. YES, MINOR PROBLEM | 5. NO, NO PROBLEM |
| | | GO TO T3 |

T2a. (EXPLAIN) _____
V55184
_____

T3. WERE THERE ANY OTHER PROBLEMS THAT MADE IT DIFFICULT FOR YOU TO INTERVIEW THIS
RESPONDENT?
V55185

| 1. YES, MAJOR PROBLEMS | 3. YES, MINOR PROBLEMS | 5. NO, NO PROBLEMS |
| | | GO TO T4 |

T3a. (EXPLAIN) _____
V55186
_____

T4. IN GENERAL, THE RESPONDENT'S UNDERSTANDING OF THE QUESTIONS WAS:
V55187

| 1. EXCELLENT | 2. GOOD | 3. FAIR | 4. POOR |

T5. PLEASE DESCRIBE THE RESPONDENT'S ABILITY TO EXPRESS (HIMSELF/HERSELF) USING
V55188 THE SCALE BELOW.

| 1 |——————| 2 |——————| 3 |——————| 4 |

VERY ARTICULATE;   EXPRESSES SELF WITH
EXCELLENT   GREAT DIFFICULTY;
VOCABULARY   LIMITED VOCABULARY

T6. WAS R SUSPICIOUS ABOUT THE STUDY BEFORE THE INTERVIEW?
V55189

| 1. NO, NOT AT ALL SUSPICIOUS | 3. YES, SOME- WHAT SUSPICIOUS | 5. YES, VERY SUSPICIOUS |

265

T7. OVERALL, HOW GREAT WAS R'S INTEREST IN THE INTERVIEW?
V55190

| 1. VERY HIGH | 2. ABOVE AVERAGE | 3. AVERAGE | 4. BELOW AVERAGE | 5. VERY LOW |

T8. DID R EVER SEEM TO RUSH (HIS/HER) ANSWERS, HURRYING TO GET THE INTERVIEW OVER?
V55191

| 1. YES | 5. NO |

T9. DURING THE INTERVIEW DID R EVER ASK HOW MUCH LONGER THE INTERVIEW WOULD TAKE?
V55192

| 1. YES | 5. NO |

T10. OTHER PERSONS PRESENT AT INTERVIEW WERE: (CHECK MORE THAN ONE BOX IF APPROPRIATE.)
V55193 —
V55198

| 1. NONE | 2. CHILDREN UNDER 6 | 3. OLDER CHILDREN | 4. SPOUSE | 5. OTHER RELATIVES | 6. OTHER ADULTS |

| 8. NO WAY OF KNOWING |

T11. HOW MANY TIMES WAS THE INTERVIEW INTERRUPTED? (ANY TIME THE INTERVIEWER WAS PREVENTED FROM CONTINUING TO ASK QUESTIONS OR R TO RESPOND TO THEM)
V55199

_____TIMES

(IF INTERRUPTIONS)

V55200 | **T11a.** APPROXIMATELY HOW MANY MINUTES WERE TAKEN UP BY INTERRUPTIONS?

_____MINUTES

T11b. WHAT WERE THE CAUSES OF THESE INTERRUPTIONS? (CHECK AS MANY AS APPLY.)

V55201-
V55206

☐ 1. CHILD(REN) FROM THE HOUSEHOLD

☐ 2. OTHER ADULT(S) FROM THE HOUSEHOLD

☐ 3. PHONE CALL(S)

☐ 4. VISITOR(S) TO THE HOUSEHOLD

☐ 7. OTHER (SPECIFY) _____

_____

☐ 8. NO WAY OF KNOWING

266

T12. **NAME AND ADDRESS INFORMATION FROM R:**
V55207

1. R GAVE NAME & ADDRESS	5. R REFUSED NAME AND ADDRESS	8. NAME AND ADDRESS NOT OBTAINED FOR SOME OTHER REASON

T13. <u>THUMBNAIL SKETCH</u>:

Appendix II

Unweighted Responses to Questions by Mode of Interview

The tables in this appendix present unweighted percentage distributions for responses to questions for three groups of respondents: (a) those interviewed in the telephone survey; (b) those interviewed in person who live in households with telephones; and (c) those interviewed in person who live in nontelephone households. All variables that were common to both the telephone and the personal interviews are presented in the tables.

The organization of the appendix was designed to facilitate examination of response differences across mode for similar types of measures. The tables are ordered by the following numbering scheme:

1st digit   *Measurement type*

1. Attitudinal Closed-ended
2. Attitudinal Open-ended
3. Factual Closed-ended
4. Factual Open-ended
5. Interviewer Observation

2nd digit   *Topic area*

1. Life Satisfaction
2. Political and Social Issues
3. Economic
4. Demographic
5. Other

3rd–5th digits   *Variable number in codebook*

Those readers who wish to access the results on a particular question should obtain its variable number from the questionnaire duplicated in Appendix I and then find the table in Appendix II.

269

V 11039 - Form X-Q.BXla.

Feelings Toward House/Apartment

Response Categories	Phone Inter- views	Personal Interviews	
		Phone Households	Non-Phone Households
Terrible	1.0%	1.6%	3.4%
Unhappy	1.7	1.7	8.6
Mostly Dissatisfied	2.7	3.3	15.5
Mixed	15.0	9.7	12.1
Mostly Satisfied	27.4	29.9	19.0
Pleased	29.1	34.2	27.6
Delighted	22.8	19.2	13.8
No Feelings	0.2	0.4	0
TOTAL %	99.9%	100.0%	100.0%
N	838	755	58
MISSING DATA Terminated	51		
Other	3	5	0

V 11050 - Form Y-Q.BYla.

Feelings Toward House/Apartment

Response Categories	Phone Inter- views	Personal Interviews	
		Phone Households	Non-Phone Households
(1) Completely Dissatisfied	3.1%	3.1%	15.7%
(2)	2.3	3.7	3.9
(3)	6.5	4.7	2.0
(4) Neutral	14.1	14.1	19.6
(5)	11.5	15.7	13.7
(6)	19.7	20.6	13.7
(7) Completely Satisfied	42.2	38.0	31.4
No Feelings	0.6	0	0
TOTAL %	100.0%	99.9%	100.0%
N	817	674	51
MISSING DATA Terminated	51		
Other	13	2	0

V 11040 - Form X-Q.BX1b.

Feelings Toward Own Physical Condition

Response Categories	Phone Inter- views	Personal Interviews	
		Phone Households	Non-Phone Households
Terrible	1.4%	2.9%	5.2%
Unhappy	1.4	3.9	8.6
Mostly Dissatisfied	3.0	5.1	10.3
Mixed	18.3	8.4	3.4
Mostly Satisfied	21.3	28.9	17.2
Pleased	26.9	33.2	37.9
Delighted	27.1	17.7	17.2
No Feelings	0.5	0	0
TOTAL %	99.9%	100.0%	99.8%
N	834	752	58
MISSING DATA Terminated	52		
Other	7	8	0

V 11051 - Form Y-Q.BY1b.

Feelings Toward Own Physical Condition

Response Categories	Phone Inter- views	Personal Interviews	
		Phone Households	Non-Phone Households
(1) Completely Dissatisfied	2.6%	5.4%	17.6%
(2)	1.6	3.3	3.9
(3)	6.0	7.3	9.8
(4) Neutral	10.0	14.2	11.8
(5)	14.2	13.0	11.8
(6)	24.2	22.2	9.8
(7) Completely Satisfied	41.0	34.6	35.3
No Feelings	0.4	0.1	0
TOTAL %	100.0%	100.1%	100.0%
N	810	671	51
MISSING DATA Terminated	52		
Other	19	5	0

V 11041 - Form X-Q.BX1c.

Feelings Toward R's Marriage

Response Categories	Phone Interviews	Personal Interviews	
		Phone Households	Non-Phone Households
Terrible	0.4%	1.4%	3.6%
Unhappy	0.7	1.6	3.6
Mostly Dissatisfied	0.7	0.8	
Mixed	6.9	2.1	
Mostly Satisfied	14.2	10.3	10.7
Pleased	23.3	34.4	39.3
Delighted	52.6	49.0	42.9
No Feelings	1.1	0.4	0
TOTAL			
%	99.9%	100.0%	100.1%
N	536	486	28
MISSING DATA			
Terminated	52		
Other	14	10	0
INAP., NOT MARRIED	291	264	30

V 11052 - Form Y-Q.BY1c.

Feelings Toward R's Marriage

Response Categories	Phone Interviews	Personal Interviews	
		Phone Households	Non-Phone Households
(1) Completely Dissatisfied	1.1%	2.0%	13.3%
(2)	0.4	0.5	
(3)	0.7	0.5	
(4) Neutral	5.5	4.5	6.7
(5)	7.3	7.2	3.3
(6)	14.9	18.3	30.0
(7) Completely Satisfied	70.0	67.0	46.7
No Feelings	0.2	0	0
TOTAL			
%	100.1%	100.0%	100.0%
N	550	443	30
MISSING DATA			
Terminated	52		
Other	22	8	0
INAP., NOT MARRIED	257	225	21

V 11042 - Form X-Q.BX1d.

Feelings Toward Standard of Living

Response Categories	Phone Interviews	Personal Interviews	
		Phone Households	Non-Phone Households
Terrible	0.4%	0.7%	1.7%
Unhappy	0.6	1.1	8.6
Mostly Dissatisfied	1.6	4.6	8.6
Mixed	18.0	10.7	15.5
Mostly Satisfied	28.7	29.3	24.1
Pleased	29.3	38.5	32.8
Delighted	21.2	14.8	6.9
No Feelings	0.4	0.3	1.7
TOTAL			
%	100.2%	100.0%	99.9%
N	830	755	58
MISSING DATA			
Terminated	52		
Other	9	5	0

V 11053 - Form Y-Q.BY1d.

Feelings Toward Standard of Living

Response Categories	Phone Interviews	Personal Interviews	
		Phone Households	Non-Phone Households
(1) Completely Dissatisfied	0.9%	2.2%	11.8%
(2)	1.5	2.7	3.9
(3)	3.4	5.4	7.8
(4) Neutral	13.8	12.9	21.6
(5)	20.3	16.7	19.6
(6)	23.6	27.2	13.7
(7) Completely Satisfied	36.0	32.4	21.6
No Feelings	0.5	0.4	0
TOTAL			
%	100.0%	99.9%	100.0%
N	812	669	51
MISSING DATA			
Terminated	52		
Other	17	7	0

V 11043 - Form X-Q.BX1e.

Feelings Toward Life as a Whole

Response Categories	Phone Interviews	Personal Interviews	
		Phone Households	Non-Phone Households
Terrible	0%	0.1%	1.8%
Unhappy	0.5	1.7	
Mostly Dissatisfied	1.2	1.9	3.5
Mixed	18.2	10.8	15.8
Mostly Satisfied	21.6	31.3	19.3
Pleased	31.9	34.4	38.6
Delighted	26.0	19.1	21.1
No Feelings	0.6	0.7	0
TOTAL %	100.0%	100.0%	100.1%
N	828	753	57
MISSING DATA Terminated	54		
Other	11	7	1

V 11054 - Form Y-Q.BY1e.

Feelings Toward Life as a Whole

Response Categories	Phone Interviews	Personal Interviews	
		Phone Households	Non-Phone Households
(1) Completely Dissatisfied	1.0%	0.9%	7.8%
(2)	1.0	1.2	3.9
(3)	1.7	4.0	3.9
(4) Neutral	12.0	11.0	19.6
(5)	14.6	15.7	11.8
(6)	27.3	32.2	19.6
(7) Completely Satisfied	41.3	34.5	33.3
No Feelings	1.1	0.4	0
TOTAL %	100.0%	99.9%	99.9%
N	802	670	51
MISSING DATA Terminated	52		
Other	27	6	0

V 11044 - Form X-Q.BX2.

How Happy is Respondent?

Response Categories	Phone Interviews	Personal Interviews	
		Phone Households	Non-Phone Households
Very Happy	30.5%	28.1%	24.1%
Pretty Happy	55.7	60.0	55.2
Not Too Happy	12.7	11.4	20.7
Don't Know	1.1	0.5	0
TOTAL %	100.0%	99.9%	100.0%
N	822	748	58
MISSING DATA Terminated	54		
Other	17	12	0

V 11055 - Form Y-Q.BY2.

How Happy is Respondent?

Response Categories	Phone Interviews	Personal Interviews	
		Phone Households	Non-Phone Households
Very Happy	33.0%	30.1%	17.6%
Pretty Happy	56.2	60.3	64.7
Not Too Happy	10.4	9.1	17.6
Don't Know	0.4	0.4	0
TOTAL %	100.0%	99.9%	99.9%
N	804	668	51
MISSING DATA Terminated	53		
Other	24	8	0

V 11089 - Q.B11a.

Heat a Problem in R's House/Apartment

Response Categories	Phone Inter-views	Personal Interviews	
		Phone Households	Non-Phone Households
Big Problem	6.7%	7.7%	16.5%
Small Problem	11.9	14.0	18.4
Not a Problem	81.3	77.9	64.2
Don't Know	0.2	0.4	0.9
TOTAL %	100.1%	100.0%	100.0%
N	1637	1435	109
MISSING DATA Terminated	87		
Other	10	4	0

V 11090 - Q.B11b.

How about fear of break-ins?

Response Categories	Phone Inter-views	Personal Interviews	
		Phone Households	Non-Phone Households
Big Problem	13.4%	14.6%	16.5%
Small Problem	30.3	32.4	17.4
Not a Problem	56.1	53.0	66.0
Don't Know	0.1	0.1	0
TOTAL %	99.9%	100.1%	99.9%
N	1636	1437	109
MISSING DATA Terminated	87		
Other	11	2	0

V 11091 - Q.B11c.

How about not enough living space?

Response Categories	Phone Interviews	Personal Interviews	
		Phone Households	Non-Phone Households
Big Problem	7.2%	7.7%	11.1%
Small Problem	14.8	14.5	21.3
Not a Problem	78.0	77.9	67.6
Don't Know	0.1	0	0
TOTAL			
%	100.1%	100.1%	100.0%
N	1635	1436	108
MISSING DATA			
Terminated	87		
Other	12	3	1

V 11092 - Q.B11d.

How about walls or ceilings cracking?

Response Categories	Phone Interviews	Personal Interviews	
		Phone Households	Non-Phone Households
Big Problem	4.8%	4.5%	14.9%
Small Problem	13.2	14.2	23.2
Not a Problem	81.9	81.3	62.1
Don't Know	0.1	0	0
TOTAL			
%	100.0%	100.0%	100.2%
N	1636	1438	108
MISSING DATA			
Terminated	87		
Other	11	1	1

V 11093 - Q.B11e.

How about cockroaches, ants or other insects?

Response Categories	Phone Interviews	Personal Interviews	
		Phone Households	Non-Phone Households
Big Problem	7.0%	5.3%	20.2%
Small Problem	18.8	17.9	29.3
Not a Problem	74.2	76.8	50.5
Don't Know	0.1	0	0
TOTAL			
%	100.0%	100.0%	100.0%
N	1635	1437	109
MISSING DATA			
Terminated	87		
Other	12	2	0

V 11174 - Q.M1-M1a.

Uneasy-Not Uneasy About Questions
Regarding R's Income

Response Categories	Phone Interviews	Personal Interviews	
		Phone Households	Non-Phone Households
Uneasy	27.9%	15.3%	7.3%
Not Uneasy	72.0	84.7	91.8
Don't Know	.1	.1	0.9
TOTAL			
%	100.0%	100.1%	100.0%
N	1605	1426	109
MISSING DATA			
Terminated	115		
Other	14	13	0

V 11175 - Q.M1b.

Uneasy-Not Uneasy About Questions
Regarding R's Racial Attitudes

Response Categories	Phone Interviews	Personal Interviews	
		Phone Households	Non-Phone Households
Uneasy	9.2%	8.8%	4.6%
Not Uneasy	90.8	91.0	95.4
Don't Know	.1	.1	0
TOTAL			
%	100.1%	99.9%	100.0%
N	1606	1428	109
MISSING DATA			
Terminated	116		
Other	12	11	0

V 11176 - Q.M1c.

Uneasy-Not Uneasy About Questions
Regarding R's Income Tax Return

Response Categories	Phone Interviews	Personal Interviews	
		Phone Households	Non-Phone Households
Uneasy	14.1%	8.6%	4.0%
Not Uneasy	85.9	91.4	94.4
Don't Know	.1	0	0.8
TOTAL			
%	100.1%	100.1%	99.2%
N	1591	1403	106
MISSING DATA			
Terminated	116		
Other	27	36	3

V 11177 - Q.M1d.

Uneasy-Not Uneasy About Questions
Regarding R's Health

Response Categories	Phone Interviews	Personal Interviews	
		Phone Households	Non-Phone Households
Uneasy	3.0%	1.6%	1.4%
Not Uneasy	97.0	98.4	98.6
TOTAL			
%	100.0%	100.0%	100.0%
N	1607	933	75
MISSING DATA			
Terminated	116		
Other	11	506	34

V 11178 - Q.Mle.

Uneasy-Not Uneasy About Questions
Regarding R's Job

Response Categories	Phone Interviews	Personal Interviews	
		Phone Households	Non-Phone Households
Uneasy	3.1%	1.9%	1.0%
Not Uneasy	96.9	98.0	99.0
Don't Know	0	.1	0
TOTAL			
%	100.0%	100.0%	100.0%
N	1526	1294	102
MISSING DATA			
Terminated	116		
Other	92	145	7

V 11179 - Q.Mlf.

Uneasy-Not Uneasy About Questions
Regarding R's Voting Behavior

Response Categories	Phone Interviews	Personal Interviews	
		Phone Households	Non-Phone Households
Uneasy	9.1%	8.0%	3.7%
Not Uneasy	90.8	92.0	96.3
Don't Know	.1	.1	0
TOTAL			
%	100.0%	100.1%	100.0%
N	1599	1418	108
MISSING DATA			
Terminated	116		
Other	19	21	1

V 11180 - Q.Mlg.

Uneasy-Not Uneasy About Questions
Regarding R's Political Opinions

Response Categories	Phone Interviews	Personal Interviews	
		Phone Households	Non-Phone Households
Uneasy	12.1%	8.5%	7.4%
Not Uneasy	87.8	91.4	91.7
Don't Know	.1	.1	0.9
TOTAL			
%	100.0%	100.0%	100.0%
N	1596	1427	108
MISSING DATA			
Terminated	116		
Other	22	12	1

V 12045 - Form X-Q.BX3.

Not Safe To Open Your Door To Strangers

Response Categories	Phone Inter- views	Personal Interview	
		Phone Households	Non-Phone Households
Agree	72.9%	76.8%	74.1%
Partially Agree and Disagree	0.4	0.8	
Disagree	22.4	20.7	20.7
Other	0.4	0.3	
Don't Know	4.0	1.4	5.2
TOTAL			
%	100.1%	100.0%	100.0%
N	834	759	58
MISSING DATA			
Terminated	55		
Other	4	1	0

V 12056 - Form Y-Q.BY3.

Not Safe To Open Your Door To Strangers

Response Categories	Phone Inter- views	Personal Interview	
		Phone Households	Non-Phone Households
Agree	75.0%	74.7%	82.4%
Partially Agree and Disagree	0.2	0.9	
Disagree	21.4	22.9	15.7
Other	0.1	0	
Don't Know	3.3	1.5	2.0
TOTAL			
%	100.0%	100.0%	100.1%
N	819	669	51
MISSING DATA			
Terminated	53		
Other	9	7	0

V 12046 - Form X-Q.BX4.

Arab Nations Working For Peace

Response Categories	Phone Inter- views	Personal Interviews	
		Phone Households	Non-Phone Households
Agree	10.8%	12.0%	10.3%
Partially Agree and Disagree	0.1	0.3	
Disagree	21.6	24.8	12.1
Other	0.4	0.7	
No Opinion	67.1	62.3	77.6
TOTAL			
%	100.0%	100.1%	100.0%
N	830	751	58
MISSING DATA			
Terminated	55		
Other	8	9	0

V 12057 - Form Y-Q.BY4.

Arab Nations Working For Peace

Response Categories	Phone Inter- views	Personal Interviews	
		Phone Households	Non-Phone Households
Agree	30.8%	20.2%	18.0%
Partially Agree and Disagree	0.4	0.5	
Disagree	37.1	44.0	32.0
Other	0.5	0.2	
No Opinion	31.2	35.2	50.0
TOTAL			
%	100.0%	100.1%	100.0%
N	808	664	50
MISSING DATA			
Terminated	53		
Other	20	12	1

V 12047 - Form X-Q.BX5.

Respondent Liberal - Conservative

Response Categories	Phone Inter-views	Personal Interviews Phone Households	Non-Phone Households
Liberal	29.5%	28.1%	31.6%
Middle of Road, Half-Way Between	11.5	11.9	17.5
Conservative	50.3	50.9	31.6
Other	1.1	1.1	
Don't Know	7.7	8.0	19.3
TOTAL %	100.1%	100.0%	100.0%
N	784	737	57
MISSING DATA Terminated	55		
Other	54	23	1

V 12058 - Form Y-Q.BY5.

Respondent Liberal - Conservative

Response Categories	Phone Inter-views	Personal Interviews Phone Households	Non-Phone Households
Liberal	17.0%	14.7%	10.0%
Middle of Road	49.1	52.5	36.0
Conservative	28.4	25.0	28.0
Other	0.8	1.8	4.0
Don't Know	4.8	6.0	22.0
TOTAL %	100.1%	100.0%	100.0%
N	790	668	50
MISSING DATA Terminated	55		
Other	36	8	1

V 12048 - Form X-Q.BX6.

R's Feeling Toward Suitability of Men/Women for Politics

Response Categories	Phone Inter-views	Personal Interview Phone Households	Non-Phone Households
Men Better Suited	36.3%	37.4%	40.4%
Men and Women Equally Suited	56.5	56.7	50.9
Women Better Suited	3.0	3.7	1.8
Don't Know	4.3	2.1	7.0
TOTAL %	100.1%	99.9%	100.1%
N	813	748	57
MISSING DATA Terminated	56		
Other	24	12	1

V 12059 - Form Y-Q.BY6.

R's Feeling Toward Suitability of Men/Women for Politics

Response Categories	Phone Inter-views	Personal Interview Phone Households	Non-Phone Households
Agree with - "Men are Better Suited"	44.7%	45.4%	43.1%
Other	0.4	0.8	
Disagree with - "Men are Better Suited"	48.4	48.6	49.0
Don't Know	6.5	5.3	7.8
TOTAL %	100.0%	100.1%	99.9%
N	797	665	51
MISSING DATA Terminated	55		
Other	29	11	0

V 12049 - Form X-Q.BX7.

Should U.S. Forbid Public Speeches
Against Democracy?

Response Categories	Phone Inter-views	Personal Interviews	
		Phone Households	Non-Phone Households
Forbid	19.5%	19.6%	25.9%
Not Forbid	72.7	73.2	63.8
Other	0.1	0.4	
Don't Know	7.6	6.8	10.3
TOTAL			
%	99.9%	99.9%	100.0%
N	798	740	58
MISSING DATA			
Terminated	57		
Other	38	20	0

V 12060 - Form Y-Q.BY7.

Should U.S. Allow Public Speeches
Against Democracy?

Response Categories	Phone Inter-views	Personal Interviews	
		Phone Households	Non-Phone Households
Not Allow	41.2%	47.6%	39.2%
Allow	50.1	45.3	47.1
Other	0.1	0.9	2.0
Don't Know	8.6	6.2	11.8
TOTAL			
%	100.0%	100.0%	100.1%
N	780	664	51
MISSING DATA			
Terminated	56		
Other	45	12	0

V 12065 - Q.B5a.

Where would you put George Wallace
on the scale?

		Personal Interviews	
Response Categories	Phone Inter- views	Phone Households	Non-Phone Households
0-10	23.2%	15.7%	9.3%
11-20	3.6	6.5	8.4
21-30	14.2	8.3	5.6
31-40	7.6	10.5	6.5
41-50	27.8	23.3	17.8
51-60	5.2	11.4	7.5
61-70	2.7	9.5	12.1
71-80	4.6	0.6	1.9
81-90	1.1	6.2	7.5
91-100	2.8	3.2	8.4
Don't Know	7.1	4.8	15.0
TOTAL			
%	99.9%	100.0%	100.0%
N	1571	1424	107
MISSING DATA			
Terminated	70		
Other	93	15	2

V 12066 - Q.B5b.

Where would you put Gerald Ford
on the scale?

		Personal Interviews	
Response Categories	Phone Inter- views	Phone Households	Non-Phone Households
0-10	10.6%	8.5%	10.4%
11-20	2.2	4.2	4.7
21-30	5.6	5.9	4.7
31-40	5.8	8.8	12.3
41-50	28.0	16.9	24.5
51-60	10.9	16.6	13.2
61-70	9.7	18.3	10.4
71-80	14.5	1.7	0.9
81-90	4.4	11.9	9.4
91-100	4.4	4.6	2.8
Don't Know	3.8	2.7	6.6
TOTAL			
%	100.0%	100.1%	99.9%
N	1563	1424	106
MISSING DATA			
Terminated	71		
Other	100	15	3

V 12067 - Q.B5c.

Where would you put Jimmy Carter
on the scale?

		Personal Interviews	
Response Categories	Phone Inter- views	Phone Households	Non-Phone Households
0-10	6.6%	5.8%	1.9%
11-20	1.7	3.1	3.8
21-30	6.2	3.5	1.0
31-40	5.5	6.9	2.9
41-50	22.5	20.5	12.4
51-60	8.5	14.6	9.5
61-70	7.9	14.2	10.5
71-80	13.2	1.0	3.8
81-90	3.4	11.6	10.5
91-100	4.9	4.4	9.5
Don't Know	19.7	14.4	34.3
TOTAL			
%	100.1%	100.0%	100.1%
N	1552	1426	105
MISSING DATA			
Terminated	72		
Other	110	13	4

V 12068 - Q.B5d.

Where would you put Ronald Reagan
on the scale?

		Personal Interviews	
Response Categories	Phone Inter- views	Phone Households	Non-Phone Households
0-10	12.9%	11.1%	7.6%
11-20	2.6	5.3	6.7
21-30	6.6	5.5	2.9
31-40	7.5	8.8	6.7
41-50	23.0	16.1	20.0
51-60	11.4	14.8	9.5
61-70	8.0	13.5	15.2
71-80	11.3	1.3	1.9
81-90	4.5	11.9	10.5
91-100	4.8	5.7	1.9
Don't Know	7.3	6.0	17.1
TOTAL			
%	99.9%	100.0%	100.0%
N	1554	1426	105
MISSING DATA			
Terminated	72		
Other	108	13	4

V 12069 - Q.B5e.

Where would you put Edward "Ted" Kennedy
on the scale?

Response Categories	Phone Inter- views	Personal Interviews	
		Phone Households	Non-Phone Households
0-10	18.0%	13.6%	9.5%
11-20	3.2	4.8	0
21-30	7.2	5.7	1.9
31-40	6.5	6.8	5.7
41-50	18.1	16.6	11.4
51-60	7.6	10.1	7.6
61-70	6.1	13.3	8.6
71-80	11.9	1.2	2.9
81-90	4.2	12.0	21.0
91-100	9.8	11.4	21.9
Don't Know	7.3	4.6	9.5
TOTAL			
%	99.9%	100.1%	100.0%
N	1543	1424	105
MISSING DATA			
Terminated	72		
Other	119	15	4

V 12070 - Q.B5f.

Where would you put Henry "Scoop" Jackson
on the scale?

Response Categories	Phone Inter- views	Personal Interviews	
		Phone Households	Non-Phone Households
0-10	10.5%	8.1%	5.7%
11-20	3.1	4.2	1.9
21-30	7.5	5.3	6.6
31-40	8.1	7.2	1.9
41-50	16.3	26.4	23.6
51-60	7.1	8.1	2.8
61-70	3.1	4.9	2.8
71-80	4.3	0.6	0
81-90	0.8	2.5	2.8
91-100	0.9	1.3	2.8
Don't Know	38.3	31.4	49.1
TOTAL			
%	100.0%	100.0%	100.0%
N	1527	1421	106
MISSING DATA			
Terminated	72		
Other	135	18	3

V 12071 - Q.B5g.

Where would you put Morris Udall
on the scale?

Response Categories	Phone Inter- views	Personal Interviews	
		Phone Households	Non-Phone Households
0-10	9.5%	6.7%	4.8%
11-20	3.1	3.8	3.8
21-30	7.8	4.5	3.8
31-40	7.3	5.1	2.9
41-50	18.0	29.6	20.2
51-60	7.1	8.6	5.8
61-70	4.0	6.8	2.9
71-80	4.7	0.4	0
81-90	1.1	3.8	1.9
91-100	0.7	0.6	0
Don't Know	36.9	30.0	53.8
TOTAL			
%	100.2%	99.9%	99.9%
N	1531	1422	104
MISSING DATA			
Terminated	72		
Other	131	17	5

V 12072 - Q.B5h.

Where would you put Hubert Humphrey
on the scale?

Response Categories	Phone Inter- views	Personal Interviews	
		Phone Households	Non-Phone Households
0-10	14.7%	11.0%	8.5%
11-20	3.6	5.0	2.8
21-30	8.7	7.3	4.7
31-40	8.1	9.5	6.6
41-50	20.2	18.4	23.6
51-60	10.3	14.4	9.4
61-70	7.5	12.7	6.6
71-80	11.9	1.5	3.8
81-90	4.3	9.7	8.5
91-100	5.2	5.6	9.4
Don't Know	5.5	4.9	16.0
TOTAL			
%	100.0%	100.0%	99.9%
N	1547	1426	106
MISSING DATA			
Terminated	72		
Other	115	13	3

V 12085 - Q.B7.

Which of these statements would you agree with?

Response Categories	Phone Inter- views	Personal Interviews	
		Phone Households	Non-Phone Households
White people have a right to keep black people out of their neighborhoods if they want to.	6.4%	10.4%	11.2%
Black People have a right to live wherever they can afford to, just like anybody else.	87.8	82.2	83.2
Other	0.4	0.8	0
Don't Know; Depends; Can't Decide	5.5	6.6	5.6
TOTAL			
%	100.1%	100.0%	100.0%
N	1596	1418	107
MISSING DATA			
Terminated	84		
Other	54	21	2

V 12086 - Q.B8.-B8b.

School Preference for Child

Response Categories	Phone Inter- views	Personal Interviews	
		Phone Households	Non-Phone Households
	6.9%	4.3%	2.8%
All White	11.3	13.6	14.9
Mostly White	19.2	23.8	13.0
Half and Half	54.1	51.4	59.3
Mostly Black	.1	.1	0.9
All Black	.1	.4	1.9
Doesn't Matter	6.3	3.4	4.7
Other	.9	1.2	0.9
Don't Know	1.1	1.9	1.9
TOTAL			
%	100.0%	100.1%	100.3%
N	1586	1404	108
MISSING DATA			
Terminated	84		
Other	64	35	1

V 12087 - Q.B9.

Possible for White and Black to be Friends

Response Categories	Phone Inter-views	Personal Interview	
		Phone Households	Non-Phone Households
Possible	95.8%	94.8%	95.4%
Not Possible	3.4	4.4	4.6
Don't Know	.8	.8	0
TOTAL			
%	100.0%	100.0%	100.0%
N	1626	1428	109
MISSING DATA			
Terminated	84		
Other	24	11	0

V 12088 - Q.B10.-B10b.

Neighborhood Preference

Response Categories	Phone Inter-views	Personal Interviews	
		Phone Households	Non-Phone Households
All White	23.3%	26.1%	24.8%
Mostly White	26.5	29.1	24.7
Half and Half	37.4	34.3	41.0
Mostly Black	0.3	0.7	1.9
All Black	0.4	0.5	4.8
Makes no differ-ence; don't care	9.2	6.3	2.9
Other		0.9	0
Don't Know	2.4	2.3	0
TOTAL			
%	100.1%	100.2%	100.1%
N	1604	1403	105
MISSING DATA			
Terminated	84		
Other	45	36	4

V 13002 - Q.A1.

Better or Worse off Financially

Response Categories	Phone Inter- views	Personal Interviews	
		Phone Households	Non-Phone Households
Better Now	37.2%	34.6%	35.8%
Same	32.2	33.0	22.9
Worse Now	29.4	31.4	40.3
Don't Know	1.2	1.0	.9
TOTAL			
%	100.0%	100.0%	99.9%
N	1723	1438	109
MISSING DATA			
Terminated	0		
Other	11	2	0

V 13006 - Q.A2.

Better-Worse Off Financially Than 3 Years Ago

Response Categories	Phone Inter- views	Personal Interviews	
		Phone Households	Non-Phone Households
Better Now	48.0%	43.6%	42.2%
Same	16.6	23.0	14.7
Worse	32.2	31.3	36.7
Don't Know	3.2	2.1	6.4
TOTAL			
%	100.0%	100.0%	100.0%
N	1711	1427	109
MISSING DATA			
Terminated	7		
Other	16	12	0

V 13007 - Q.A3.

Better-Worse Off Financially in 1 Year

Response Categories	Phone Inter- views	Personal Interviews	
		Phone Households	Non-Phone Households
Will Be Better Off	31.7%	32.4%	32.4%
Same	41.3	43.5	38.0
Will Be Worse Off	14.2	13.5	13.0
Don't Know; uncertain	12.8	10.6	16.6
TOTAL			
%	100.0%	100.0%	100.0%
N	1709	1432	108
MISSING DATA			
Terminated	8		
Other	17	7	1

V 13008 - Q.A4.

Good-Bad Business Times Ahead

Response Categories	Phone Inter-views	Personal Interviews	
		Phone Households	Non-Phone Households
Good Times	37.5%	29.9%	22.4%
Good With Qualifications	12.8	17.2	9.3
Pro-Con	7.6	10 7	15.0
Bad With Qualifications	4.7	6.3	4.7
Bad Times	20.9	19.9	30.8
Don't Know; uncertain	16.5	16.0	17.7
TOTAL			
%	100.0%	100.0%	99.9%
N	1605	1422	107
MISSING DATA			
Terminated	13		
Other	116	17	2

V 13009 - Q.A5.

Business Better-Worse Than 1 Year Ago

Response Categories	Inter-views	Personal Interviews	
		Phone Households	Non-Phone Households
Better Now	59.1%	53.9%	34.9%
About the Same	11.0	14.7	21.1
Worse Now	25.3	25.6	36.7
Don't Know	4.6	5.8	7.4
TOTAL			
%	100.0%	100.0%	100.1%
N	1689	1423	109
MISSING DATA			
Terminated	15		
Other	30	16	0

V 13013 - Q.A7.

Business Better-Worse in 1 Year

Response Categories	Phone Inter-views	Personal Interviews	
		Phone Households	Non-Phone Households
Better a Year From Now	33.7%	31.6%	17.4%
About the Same	44.2	49.0	58.7
Worse a Year From Now	13.3	11.1	17 4
Don't Know; depends	8.8	8.3	6.4
TOTAL			
%	100.0%	100.0%	99.9%
N	1670	1428	109
MISSING DATA			
Terminated	23		
Other	41	11	0

V 13014 - Q.A8.

Business A Lot-A Little Better in 1 Year

Response Categories	Phone Inter-views	Personal Interviews	
		Phone Households	Non-Phone Households
Lot Better	16.3%	11.5%	10.5%
Little Better	80.4	87.6	84.2
Little Better	1.5	0	0
Don't Know	1.8	0.9	·5,3
TOTAL			
%	100.0%	100.0%	100.0%
N	547	445	19
MISSING DATA			
Terminated	23		
Other	14	4	0
INAP., Business not better 1 year from now	1150	990	90

V 13015 - Q.A8.

Good-Bad Time to Buy a House

Response Categories	Phone Interviews	Personal Interviews	
		Phone Households	Non-Phone Households
Good	44.5%	41.3%	35.2%
Pro-Con	6.6	7.3	5.5
Bad	41.0	42.8	41.6
Don't Know	7.9	8.5	17.6
TOTAL			
%	100.0%	99.9%	99.9%
N	1670	1416	108
MISSING DATA			
Terminated	24		
Other	40	23	1

V 13019 - Q.A9.

Good-Bad Time to Buy a Car

Response Categories	Phone Interviews	Personal Interviews	
		Phone Households	Non-Phone Households
Good	38.0%	38.5%	43.0%
Pro-Con	8.1	10.5	6.5
Bad	32.2	31.0	28.1
Depends on Whether New or Used Car	0	.1	0
Don't Know	21.7	20.0	22.4
TOTAL			
%	100.0%	100.1%	100.0%
N	1656	1401	107
MISSING DATA			
Terminated	27		
Other	51	38	2

V 13023 - Q.A10.

Chances of Buying a Car

Response Categories	Phone Inter-views	Personal Interviews Phone Households	Non-Phone Households
Almost Certain	14.6%	10.2%	7.3%
Probably Will	6.1	9.0	13.8
Better Than Even Chance	1.9	2.9	.9
Even Chance; May or May Not	2.4	6.7	3.7
Less Than Even Chance	.8	2.7	4.6
Probably Will Not	19.0	13.4	17.5
Very Unlikely	40.6	40.7	33.0
Never Will Buy	14.6	14.4	19.2
TOTAL			
%	100.0%	100.0%	100.0%
N	1671	1425	109
MISSING DATA			
Terminated	31		
Other	32	14	0

V 13024 - Q.A11.

Buy a New or Used Car?

Response Categories	Phone Inter-views	Personal Interviews Phone Households	Non-Phone Households
New	55.4%	49.1%	14.3%
Used	38.7	46.5	85.7
Don't Know	5.8	4.4	0
TOTAL			
%	99.9%	100.0%	100.0%
N	413	411	28
MISSING DATA			
Terminated	31		
Other	2	0	0
INAP., Car purchase unlikely	1288	1028	81

V 13025 - Q.A11a.

When Buy a Car?

Response Categories	Phone Inter-views	Personal Interviews Phone Households	Non-Phone Households
April-June, 1976	15.6%	19.9%	14.8%
July-Sept. 1976	26.2	23.9	33.3
Oct-Dec. 1976	23.1	27.2	18.5
Jan-March,1976	8.5	6.3	3.7
April-June, 1977	6.2	7.3	11.1
Probably last 3 quarters, 1976	9.5	5.8	3.7
Probably first half of 1977	2.8	1.5	0
Don't Know	8.2	8.1	14.8
TOTAL			
%	100.1%	100.0%	99.9%
N	390	397	27
MISSING DATA			
Terminated	31		
Other	25	14	1
INAP., Car purchase unlikely	1288	1028	81

V 13026 - Q.A12.

How Long Before Buy a Car?

Response Categories	Phone Inter-views	Personal Interviews Phone Households	Non-Phone Households
Last Half 1977	15.3%	10.1%	14.0%
During 1978	30.9	32.7	31.6
During 1979	18.8	18.2	10.5
1980 or Later	19.2	21.3	15.8
Probably Never	0.8	0.5	1.8
When Old Car Falters	1.5	1.2	0
When Necessary	0.4	0.8	5.3
Don't Know	13.0	15.3	21.0
TOTAL			
%	99.9%	100.1%	100.0%
N	974	775	57
MISSING DATA			
Terminated	31		
Other	65	14	0
INAP., Car purchase unlikely	664	650	52

V 13027 - Q.A12a.

Buy New or Used Car?

Response Categories	Phone Inter- views	Personal Interview	
		Phone Households	Non-Phone Households
New	61.1%	60.2%	37.2%
Used	31.9	35.2	58.1
Both (two cars to be bought)	0.7	0	0
Don't Know	6.2	4.6	4.7
TOTAL			
%	99.9%	100.0%	100.0%
N	836	653	43
MISSING DATA			
Terminated	31		
Other	10	3	2
INAP., Car pur- chase unlikely	857	783	64

V 13028 - Q.A13.

Good-Bad Time to Buy Household Items

Response Categories	Phone Inter- views	Personal Interview	
		Phone Households	Non-Phone Households
Good	51.3%	45.9%	46.1%
Pro-Con	12.2	16.9	10.6
Bad	18.0	18.9	21.2
Don't Know	18.5	18.2	22.1
TOTAL			
%	100.0%	99.9%	100.0%
N	1632	1386	104
MISSING DATA			
Terminated	31		
Other	71	53	5

V15033 - Q.B1.

Preferred Method to Answer Questions

Response Categories	Phone Inter- views	Personal Interview	
		Phone Households	Non-Phone Households
Face-to-Face	22.7%	78.3%	70.3%
Telephone	39.4	1.7	0
Mailed Questionnaire	28.1	17.0	21.3
Other	1.8	1.5	0.9
Don't Know	8.0	1.5	7.4
TOTAL			
%	100.0%	100.0%	99.9%
N	1628	1426	108
MISSING DATA			
Terminated	37		
Other	69	13	1

V 33166 - Q.F16.

Spouse's wages in 1975

| | | Personal Interviews | |
Response Categories	Phone Inter-views	Phone Households	Non-Phone Households
Less than $2,000	6.0%	8.4%	21.9%
$2,000 - 2,999	4.1	4.2	9.4
3,000 - 3,999	1.8	3.1	6.3
4,000 - 4,999	2.7	2.8	18.8
5,000 - 5,999	4.6	4.7	12.5
6,000 - 7,499	6.5	8.4	9.4
7,500 - 8,999	6.6	7.7	3.1
9,000 - 9,999	3.6	4.9	0
10,000 - 10,999	4.6	5.9	6.3
11,000 - 12,499	5.8	10.0	3.1
12,500 - 14,999	6.0	9.8	0
15,000 - 17,499	8.0	9.6	0
17,500 - 19,999	2.3	6.6	0
20,000 - 22,499	2.8	2.8	0
22,500 - 24,999	1.3	1.6	0
25,000 - 29,999	1.8	1.4	0
30,000 - 34,999	1.5	1.2	0
35,000 and over	2.2	2.8	0
Refused	8.6	0	0
Don't Know	19.1	4.0	9.4
TOTAL			
%	99.9%	99.9%	100.2%
N	603	572	32
MISSING DATA			
Terminated	107		
Other	94	61	0
INAP., did not work in 1975	930	806	77

V 33168 - Q.F17.

Respondent's wages in 1975

| | | Personal Interviews | |
	Phone Inter-views	Phone Households	Non-Phone Households
Less than $2,000	10.5%	15.5%	30.3%
$2,000 - 2,999	5.0	7.4	14.5
3,000 - 3,999	3.5	6.8	9.2
4,000 - 4,999	4.5	6.5	7.9
5,000 - 5,999	4.8	7.0	5.3
6,000 - 7,499	8.4	8.5	6.6
7,500 - 8,999	6.1	7.6	10.5
9,000 - 9,999	5.4	5.4	1.3
10,000 - 10,999	6.1	4.1	2.6
11,000 - 12,499	5.9	5.3	3.9
12,500 - 14,999	5.3	8.3	5.3
15,000 - 17,499	8.0	4.5	2.6
17,500 - 19,999	3.3	4.0	0
20,000 - 22,499	2.7	2.0	0
22,500 - 24,999	0.9	1.3	0
25,000 - 29,999	2.1	' 2.1	0
30,000 - 34,999	1.6	0.8	0
35,000 and over	1.8	1.9	0
Refused	7.3	0	0
Don't Know	6.7	1.1	0
TOTAL			
%	99.9%	100.1%	100.0%
N	1031	852	76
MISSING DATA			
Terminated	108		
Other	137	67	0
INAP., did not work in 1975	458	520	33

V 33172 - Q.F19, F20-F20a.

Total family income in 1975.

		Personal Interviews	
Response Categories	Phone Inter- views	Phone Households	Non-Phone Households
Less than $2,000	1.7%	2.6%	11.2%
$2,000 - 2,999	2.0	4.6	14.0
3,000 - 3,999	2.9	4.5	14.0
4,000 - 4,999	2.4	4.6	13.1
5,000 - 5,999	2.5	4.7	6.5
6,000 - 7,499	4.6	6.1	8.4
7,500 - 8,999	4.4	5.2	8.4
9,000 - 9,999	2.3	4.1	2.8
10,000 - 10,999	3.3	6.0	1.9
11,000 - 12,499	5.5	5.3	2.8
12,500 - 14,999	6.3	9.1	4.7
15,000 - 17,499	9.7	8.6	3.7
17,500 - 19,999	4.7	8.5	.9
20,000 - 22,499	6.4	5.9	1.9
22,500 - 24,999	3.0	3.6	0
25,000 - 29,999	4.3	4.0	0
30,000 - 34,999	3.0	3.1	0
35,000 and over	5.3	4.5	0
Refused	8.9		0
Don't Know	16.6	5.1	5.6
TOTAL			
%	99.8%	100.1%	99.9%
N	1378	1314	107
MISSING DATA			
Terminated	112		
Other	244	125	2

V 33167 - Q.F16a.

Three category follow-up to spouse's wages question for telephone sample

Response Categories	Phone Interviews
Less than 7,500 dollars	25.6%
Between 7,500 and 15,000 dollars	33.5
More than 15,000 dollars	23.6
Refused	8.9
Don't Know	8.4
TOTAL	
%	100.0%
N	203
MISSING DATA	
Terminated	106
Other	59
INAP., R not married or income ascertained in F16	1366

V 33169 - Q.F17a.

Three category follow-up to Respondent's wages question for telephone sample

Response Categories	Phone Interviews
Less than 7,500 dollars	39.8%
Between 7,500 and 15,000 dollars	28.4
More than 15,000 dollars	16.1
Refused	12.8
Don't Know	2.8
TOTAL	
%	99.9%
N	211
MISSING DATA	
Terminated	109
Other	69
INAP., Ascertained in F17	1345

V 33173 - Q.F19a.

Three category follow-up to total family income question for telephone sample

Response Categories	Phone Interviews
Less than 7,500 dollars	21.5%
Between 7,500 and 15,000 dollars	28.1
More than 15,000 dollars	27.9
Refused	12.8
Don't Know	9.8
TOTAL	
%	100.1%
N	438
MISSING DATA	
Terminated	113
Other	157
INAP., Ascertained in F19	1026

V 15181 - Q.M2.

R's Feelings About the Length of the Interview

Response Categories	Phone Interviews	Personal Interviews	
		Phone Households	Non-Phone Households
Much Too Long	4.6%	1.1%	1.9%
Too Long	31.1	9.0	8.5
About Right	61.9	87.6	84.9
Too Short	1.5	1.3	2.9
Much Too Short	.4	.4	1.0
Don't Know	.4	.7	1.0
TOTAL			
%	99.9%	100.1%	100.2%
N	1574	1413	106
MISSING DATA			
Terminated	116		
Other	44	26	3

V 35095 - Q.B13.

Do all the telephones have the same number?

Response Categories	Phone Inter-views	Personal Interviews	
		Phone Households	Non-Phone Households
Yes	90.5%	94.2%	0
No	9.5	5.8	0
TOTAL			
%	100.0%	100.0%	0
N	927	8.6	0
MISSING DATA			
Terminated	87		
Other	8	3	0
INAP., one number or no phones	712	620	109

V 35096 - B13a.

How many different numbers are there?

Response Categories	Phone Inter-views	Personal Interviews	
		Phone Households	Non-Phone Households
Two	95.4%	95.7%	0
Three	3.4	4.3	0
Four	1.1	0	0
TOTAL			
%	99.9%	100.0%	0
N	87	46	0
MISSING DATA			
Terminated	87		
Other	10	4	0
INAP., one number or no phones	1550	1389	109

V 35099 - Q.B13d.

Do All the Numbers Appear in the Current Telephone Book?

Response Categories	Phone Inter-views	Personal Interviews	
		Phone Households	Non-Phone Households
Yes	70.6%	57.4%	0%
No	29.4	42.6	0
TOTAL			
%	100.0%	100.0%	0
N	85	47	0
MISSING DATA			
Terminated	87		
Other	12	3	0
INAP., one or no phones; or single number	1550	1389	109

V 35101 - Q.B14.

Does the number appear in the current telephone book?

Response Categories	Phone Inter-views	Personal Interviews	
		Phone Households	Non-Phone Households
Yes	78.6%	80.8%	0
No	20.6	18.9	0
Don't Know	0.7	0.3	0
TOTAL			
%	99.9%	100.0%	0
N	1550	1388	0
MISSING DATA			
Terminated	87		
Other	7	5	0
INAP., no phone, more than one number	90	46	109

V 35102 - Q.B15.

Reason why number(s) not listed

		Personal Interviews	
Response Categories	Phone Inter- views	Phone Households	Non-Phone Households
Listings too new	24.7%	25.6%	0
R requested the unlisted number(s)	71.2	70.5	0
Other	4.1	3.2	0
Don't Know	0	0.7	0
TOTAL			
%	100.0%	100.0%	0
N	340	285	0
MISSING DATA			
Terminated	87		
Other	26	6	0
INAP., no phone, number(s) listed	1281	1148	109

V 33103 - Q.B16.

Itemized Deductions in 1975 Federal Tax Returns?

		Personal Interviews	
Response Categories	Phone Inter- views	Phone Households	Non-Phone Households
Yes	48.5%	46.2%	16.7%
No	36.1	33.6	41.7
Did not file a return (yet)	9.6	16.2	37.0
R refused to give answer	0.2	0.3	0
Don't Know	5.6	3.7	4.6
TOTAL			
%	100.0%	100.0%	100.0%
N	1631	1436	108
MISSING DATA			
Terminated	88		
Other	15	3	1

V 33105 - Q.B17.

Tax Refund?

		Personal Interviews	
Response Categories	Phone Inter- views	Phone Households	Non-Phone Households
Entitled to Refund	67.6%	68.4%	79.1%
Owed Money	23.3	23.3	11.9
Came Out Even	5.8	6.6	7.5
R Refused to Give Answer	0.5	0.5	0
Don't Know	2.7	1.3	1.5
TOTAL			
%	99.9%	100.1%	100.0%
N	1457	1198	67
MISSING DATA			
Terminated	89		
Other	32	8	2
INAP., did not file return	156	233	40

V 43106 - Q.B17a.

How large is Federal Tax Refund this year?

Response Categories	Phone Interviews	Personal Interviews	
		Phone Households	Non-Phone Households
$0-$99	9.1%	12.7%	16.0%
$100-$199	14.5	12.2	8.0
$200-$299	13.8	13.5	22.0
$300-$399	12.4	13.1	22.0
$400-$499	5.9	8.9	8.0
$500-$599	7.5	7.6	6.0
$600-$699	3.9	5.3	2.0
$700-$799	3.8	4.0	4.0
$800-$899	4.1	3.0	6.0
$900-$999	2.2	3.0	0
$1000 >	8.9	10.8	2.0
R Refused to Give Answer	5.2	0	0
Don't Know	8.5	5.9	4.0
TOTAL			
%	99.8%	94.1%	100.0%
N	917	777	50
MISSING DATA			
Terminated	90		
Other	99	50	5
INAP., not entitled to refund; refused refund question; or DK-V 33105	628	612	54

V 43107 - Q.B17b.

Is it about $50, $100, $200, or what?

Response Categories	Phone Interviews	Personal Interviews	
		Phone Households	Non-Phone Households
$0-$99	11.5%	13.5%	33.3%
$100-$199	13.5	11.5	0
$200-$299	25.0	28.8	0
$300-$399	3.4	11.5	33.3
$400-$499	0.7	1.9	33.3
$500-$599	2.0	1.9	0
$600-$699	1.4	1.9	0
$700-$799	0	3.8	0
$900-$999	0.7	0	0
$1000 >	6.1	0	0
R Refused to Give Answer	19.6	0	0
Don't Know	16.2	25.0	0
TOTAL			
%	100.1%	99.8%	99.9%
N	148	52	3
MISSING DATA			
Terminated	90		
Other	79	44	4
INAP., not entitled to refund; refused V 33103 question; DK on V 33105; or ascertained in V 43106	1417	1343	102

	V 22073 - Q.B6. Most Important Problems Facing This Country			V 22074 - Q.B6. Most Important Problems Facing This Country		
		Personal Interviews			Personal Interviews	
Response Categories	Phone Inter- views	Phone Households	Non-Phone Households	Phone Inter- views	Phone Households	Non-Phone Households
Social Welfare Problems	19.9%	28.1%	32.1%	27.7%	33.1%	29.8%
Agriculture	0.4	0.4	0.9	0.9	0.3	0
Natural Resources	3.4	3.2	0.9	5.9	4.6	7.0
Labor Problems: Union-Manage- ment Relations	0.6	0.7	0.9	1.8	1.5	1.8
Racial Problems	1.8	1.7	1.8	3.8	2.9	7.0
Public Order Problems	8.3	10.9	6.4	10.8	8.9	5.3
Economic and Business Problems	38.3	33.3	34.0	18.2	28.2	24.6
Foreign Affairs	6.2	5.2	5.5	11.4	6.1	10.5
National Defense	1.4	1.9	1.8	3.2	2.9	1.8
Issues Relating to the Functioning of Government	10.8	7.3	5.5	10.3	8.5	7.0
Campaign/Election References- Not Codable Elsewhere	0.5	0.4	0	0.2	0	3.5
Attitudes of People Toward Life, Work and Others	3.5	2.0	1.8	4.4	1.9	0
Domestic Issues - Take Care of Our Country First	0.2	0	0	0.5	0	0
Other	0.3	0.8	0.9	0.8	1.0	1.8
Don't Know	4.4	4.3	7.3			
TOTAL %	99.7%	100.2%	99.8%	99.9%	100.0%	100.1%
N	1607	1426	109	865	894	57
MISSING DATA Terminated	74			74		
Other	53	13	0	16	3	0
INAP., no second mention	0	0	0	779	542	52

V 22076 - Q.B6. Summary

Different Problems Mentioned

Response Categories	Phone Interviews	Personal Interviews	
		Phone Households	Non-Phone Households
0 Mentions	36.2%	28.4%	34.0%
1 Mention	33.6	32.9	33.0
2 Mentions	18.8	21.3	20.0
3 Mentions	7.2	10.3	10.0
4 Mentions	2.6	4.4	2.0
5 Mentions	1.2	1.5	0
6 Mentions	0.2	1.0	1.0
7 Mentions	0.2	0.1	0
TOTAL			
%	100.0%	99.9%	100.0%
N	1535	1364	100
MISSING DATA			
Terminated	74		
Other	15	4	0
INAP., DON'T KNOW in B6	110	71	9

V 22077 - Q.B6a.

Other Important Problems

Response Categories	Phone Interviews	Personal Interviews	
		Phone Households	Non-Phone Households
Social Welfare Problems	22.1%	21.0%	22.6%
Agriculture	0.8	1.2	1.9
Natural Resources	6.7	4.6	3.8
Labor Problems: Union-Management Relations	1.0	0.9	0
Racial Problems	4.1	5.3	1.9
Public Order Problems	14.0	17.0	13.2
Economic and Business Problems	16.3	17.0	24.5
Foreign Affairs	12.1	7.8	1.9
National Defense	3.3	2.8	0
Issues Relating to the Functioning of Government	10.3	11.4	7.5
Campaign/Election References - Not Codable Elsewhere	0	0.1	0
Attitudes of People Toward Life, Work and Others	3.6	3.1	0
Domestic Issues - Take Care of Our Country First	0.2	0	0
Other	1.2	0.8	5.7
Don't Know	4.3	6.9	17.0
TOTAL			
%	100.0%	99.9%	100.0%
N	860	851	53
MISSING DATA			
Terminated	80		
Other	157	24	2
INAP.	637	564	54

V 22078 - Q.B6a.

What Other Important Problems Are There?

Response Categories	Phone Interviews	Personal Interviews	
		Phone Households	Non-Phone Households
Social Welfare Problems	22.7%	23.2%	60.0%
Agriculture	2.7	0.8	0
Natural Resources	6.0	8.8	0
Labor Problems: Union Management Relations	2.0	0	0
Racial Problems	6.0	1.6	0
Public Order Problems	11.3	16.0	0
Economic and Business Problems	18.0	21.6	20.0
Foreign Affairs	12.7	8.0	0
National Defense	2.7	4.0	0
Issues Relating to the Functioning of Government	11.3	12.8	0
Attitudes of People Toward Life, Work and Others	2.7	1.6	0
Other	2.0	1.6	20.0
TOTAL			
%	100.1%	100.0%	100.0%
N	150	125	5 '
MISSING DATA			
Terminated	80		
Other	13	8	1
INAP., DON'T KNOW in B6; no second mention	1491	1306	103

	V 22081 - Q.B6b.			V 22082 - Q.B6b.		
	Other Important Problems			Other Important Problems		
		Personal Interviews			Personal Interviews	
Response Categories	Phone Inter-views	Phone Households	Non-Phone Households	Phone Inter-views	Phone Households	Non-Phone Households
Social Welfare Problems	24.8%	21.0%	26.7%	18.2%	28.6%	66.7%
Agriculture	1.1	0.8	13.3	3.0	0	0
Natural Resources	7.7	6.2	6.7	4.5	1.8	0
Labor Problems: Union-Management Relations	2.6	0.3	0	3.0	0	0
Racial Problems	4.3	5.4	0	12.1	0	33.3
Public Order Problems	15.1	18.6	13.3	7.6	16.1	0
Economic and Business Problems	14.8	16.7	33.3	21.2	17.9	0
Foreign Affairs	7.7	8.4	0	7.6	5.4	0
National Defense	2.0	2.7	0	0	5.4	0
Issues Relating to the Functioning of Government	11.4	12.1	0	13.6	17.9	0
Campaign/Election References-Not Codable Elsewhere	0	0.3	0	0	0	0
Attitudes of People Toward Life, Work and Others	2.8	2.4	0	4.5	3.6	0
Other	2.0	1.9	0	4.5	3.6	0
Don't Know	3.7	3.2	6.7	0	0	0
TOTAL						
%	100.0%	100.0%	100.0%	99.8%	100.3%	100.0%
N	351	371	15	66	56	3
MISSING DATA						
Terminated	81			81		
Other	156	46	1	12	30	1
INAP., DON'T KNOW in B6 or B6a; no second mention	1146	1022	93	1575	1353	105

	V 23003 - Q.Ala.			V 23004 - Q.Ala.		
	Why Better or Worse off Financially (1st Mention)			Why Better or Worse off Financially (2nd Mention)		
		Personal Interview			Personal Interview	
Reasons Why Better Off	Phone Inter- views	Phone Households	Non-Phone Households	Phone Inter- views	Phone Households	Non-Phone Households
Better Pay, Higher Income	14.5%	17.0%	13.0%	10.2%	7.0%	7.4%
More Work, More Income, Tax Rebate/Refund	20.7	15.0	22.8	6.6	8.3	3.7
Increased Contributions from Outside	1.5	3.1	2.2	0.8	2.1	3.7
Lower Prices, Taxes, Expenses	3.2	2.9	2.2	4.5	7.0	3.7
High Interest Rates, Better Asset Position, Debts Lower	5.0	9.7	4.3	4.2	8.8	7.4
Change in Family Composition	1.0	0.6	1.1	0.3	0	3.7
Other Reasons for Being Better Off	7.3	2.7	3.3	11.0	8.0	0
Reasons Why Worse Off						
Lower Pay, Lower Income	3.7	4.6	3.3	7.4	5.2	7.4
Less Work, Less Income	8.5	11.3	21.7	5.2	5.2	0
Decreased Contributions from Outside	1.1	1.1	1.1	0.8	2.8	3.7
Higher Prices, Taxes, Expenses	24.4	23.0	16.3	40.5	37.7	40.7
High Interest Rates, Worse Asset Position, Debts	1.6	3.2	2.2	1.7	3.1	7.4
Change in Family Composition	1.4	1.8	4.3	0.6	1.6	3.7
Stock Market, Recession, Strikes, Government Policies	1.2	0.3	0	1.1	0.8	0
Other Reasons for Being Worse Off	3.0	2.8	2.2	5.2	2.6	7.4
Don't Know	1.7	1.0	0	0	0	0
TOTAL						
%	99.8%	100.1%	100.0%	100.1%	100.2%	99.9%
N	1339	1143	92	363	386	27
MISSING DATA						
Terminated	4			4		
Other	55	20	3	0	0	0
INAP., No change no reason given; No second mention	336	276	14	1367	1053	82

V 23010 - Q. A6

V 23011 - Q. A6a

| | What Favorable or Unfavorable Changes R Has Heard (1st Mention) | | | What Favorable or Unfavorable Changes R Has Heard (2nd Mention) | | |
| | | Personal Interview | | | Personal Interview | |
Favorable Changes	Phone Interviews	Phone Households	Non-Phone Households	Phone Interviews	Phone Households	Non-Phone Households
Government, Defense	1.4%	2.3%	0.0%	0.3%	1.6%	12.5%
Employment and Purchasing Power	22.0	24.4	18.0	16.6	20.5	0.0
Prices	15.5	10.3	7.6	11.9	10.8	12.5
Miscellaneous	24.1	23.6	15.4	32.6	29.3	25.0
Unfavorable Changes						
Government, Defense	2.9	3.1	5.1	1.0	2.0	0.0
Employment and Purchasing Power	9.7	11.1	20.6	7.6	8.0	25.0
Prices	8.7	8.1	7.7	9.8	9.2	0.0
Miscellaneous	14.3	15.9	23.1	18.7	17.7	25.0
Other Changes, NA whether favorable or unfavorable	1.4	1.0	2.6	1.3	0.8	0.0
TOTAL % N	100.0% 906	99.8% 727	100.1% 39	99.8% 309	99.9% 249	100.0% 8
MISSING DATA Terminated Other	21 61	59	5	21 9	0	0
INAP., Has heard of no changes; No Second Mention	746	653	65	1395	1190	101

	V 23016 - Q.A8a.			V 23017 - Q.A8a.		
	Why Good-Bad Time to Buy House (1st Mention)			Why Good-Bad Time to Buy House (2nd Mention)		
Reasons Why Now is a Good Time	Phone Inter- views	Personal Interview		Phone Inter- views	Personal Interview	
		Phone Households	Non-Phone Households		Phone Households	Non-Phone Households
Good Prices, Credit Easy to Get	33.3%	33.9%	34.2%	26.2%	27.2%	26.7%
High Employment, Good Times	3.6	1.9	4.7	1.5	0.9	0
Good Supply, Good Quality	1.3	1.1	1.2	1.8	0.9	0
Other	13.2	11.5	5.9	10.3	8.3	0
Reasons Why Now is a Bad Time						
High Prices, Credit Tight	36.5	39.7	38.8	42.1	47.5	53.3
Low Employment, Bad Times	7.9	8.9	10.6	10.1	11.2	13.3
Poor Supply, Poor Quality	0.6	0.7	0	1.8	2.0	3.3
Other	2.6	1.5	2.4	6.3	1.8	3.3
Don't Know Any Reasons	0.9	0.8	2.4	0	0	0
TOTAL						
%	99.9%	100.0%	100.2%	100.1%	99.8%	99.9%
N	1477	1262	85	397	439	30
MISSING DATA						
Terminated	25			25		
Other	61	33	4	0	0	0
INAP., Don't know whether Good or Bad Time	171	144	20	1312	1000	79

| | V 23020 - Q.A9a. Why Good-Bad Time to Buy Car (1st Mention) | | | V 23021 - Q.A9a. Why Good-Bad Time to Buy Car (2nd Mention) | | |
| | | Personal Interview | | | Personal Interview | |
Reasons Why Good Time	Phone Interviews	Phone Households	Non-Phone Households	Phone Interviews	Phone Households	Non-Phone Households
Low Prices, Credit Easy to Get	26.2%	36.5%	43.3%	18.5%	20.4%	18.2%
High Employment, Good Times	6.2	3.6	2.5	4.1	3.6	0
Good Supply, Quality	4.9	4.0	4.9	6.3	6.2	9.1
Other	14.5	9.0	8.6	7.7	10.9	0
Reasons Why Bad Time						
High Prices, Tight Credit	27.1	28.7	28.4	18.1	22.5	27.3
Unemployment, Bad Times	6.4	5.7	6.2	11.4	8.7	27.3
Poor Supply, Poor Quality	7.4	7.8	3.7	22.9	20.7	18.2
Other	4.5	3.2	1.3	11.1	6.9	0
Don't Know	2.7	1.7	1.2	0	0	0
TOTAL						
%	99.9%	100.2%	100.0%	100.1%	99.9%	100.1%
N	1217	1089	81	271	275	11
MISSING DATA						
Terminated	27			27		
Other	80	31	2	0	0	0
INAP., Don't know whether Good or Bad Time	410	319	26	1436	1164	98

	V 23029 - Q.Al3a. Why Good-Bad Time to Buy Major Household Items (1st Mention)			V 23030 - Q.Al3a. Why Good-Bad Time to Buy Major Household Items (2nd Mention)		
		Personal Interviews				
Reasons Why Good Time	Phone Inter- views	Phone Households	Non-Phone Households	Phone Inter- views	Phone Households	Non-Phone Households
Low Prices, Credit is easy to get	40.5%	47.6%	38.5%	28.0%	36.2%	50.0%
High Employment, Good Times	6.9	3 0	5.1	5 0	5.9	0
Good Supply, High Quality	1 8	1.3	3.9	13.7	4.7	0
Other	25.3	17.2	23.1	5 8	5.3	0
Reasons Why Bad Time						
High Prices, Credit Tight	15.0	21.2	16.7	24.4	21.7	10.0
Unemployment, Bad Times	5.4	4.7	9.0	7.9	12 5	10.0
Poor Supply, Poor Quality	1.5	2.0	1.3	11.5	11.9	30.0
Other	2.0	1.8	2.6	3.6	2.0	0
Don't Know	1.7	1.3	0	0	0	0
TOTAL % N	 100.1% 1251	 100.1% 1087	 100.2% 78	 99.9% 139	 100.2% 152	 100.0% 10
MISSING DATA Terminated Other	 31 48	 46	 3	 31 0	 0	 0
INAP., Don't know whether Good or Bad Time; no second mention	 404	 306	 28	 1564	 1287	 99

V 23032 - Q.A14.

More Important Than Usual to
Add to Savings

More Important Than Usual, and:	Phone Inter- views	Personal Interviews	
		Phone Households	Non-Phone Households
Satisfied with Savings	2.5%	1.8%	0%
Satisfaction not Mentioned	48.2	48.9	45.7
Dissatisfaction with Savings	10.7	16.2	17.4
Importance not Mentioned, and:			
Satisfied with Savings	17.2	18.8	16.5
Satisfaction not Mentioned	6.0	1.9	4.8
Dissatisfied with Savings	9.2	8.0	12.6
Not More Important Than Usual, and:			
Satisfied with Savings	1.2	0.7	0
Satisfaction not Mentioned	3.7	2.3	2.0
Dissatisfied with Savings	1.2	1.6	1.0
TOTAL			
%	99.9%	100.2%	100.0%
N	1637	1391	103
MISSING DATA			
Terminated	32		
Other	65	48	6

V 25034 - Q.B1a.

Reason for Choice of Mode of Interview

Response Categories	Phone Inter- views	Personal Interviews	
		Phone Households	Non-Phone Households
Favoring Face-to- Face Interview	23.0%	47.0%	55.2%
Against Face-to- Face Interview	6.8	0.8	0
Favoring Telephone	24.1	1.0	0
Against Telephone	2.7	19.9	7.3
Favoring Mailed Questionaire	27.5	15.6	22.9
Against Mailed Questionaire	12.8	14.4	13.5
Other	2.1	0.6	0
Don't Know	1.0	0.7	1.0
TOTAL			
%	100.0%	100.0%	99.9%
N	1434	1386	96
MISSING DATA			
Terminated	39		
Other	19	16	4
INAP., Choice NA or DK	242	37	9

V 32061 - Q.B3.

Do you remember voting in the 1972
presidential election?

Response Categories	Phone Interviews	Personal Interviews	
		Phone Households	Non-Phone Households
Yes, did vote	67.6%	65.0%	22.0%
No, not registered in 1972	13.0	13.1	28.4
No, did not vote (other)	16.8	20.0	45.9
Don't Know	2.6	2.0	3.7
TOTAL			
%	100.0%	100.1%	100.0%
N	1643	1430	109
MISSING DATA			
Terminated	66		
Other	25	9	0

V 32062 - Q.B3a.

Which one did you vote for?

Response Categories	Phone Interviews	Personal Interviews	
		Phone Households	Non-Phone Households
Nixon	59.9%	60.2%	60.9%
McGovern	34.0	33.0	26.1
Other	4.0	4.2	8.7
Don't Know	2.1	2.6	4.3
TOTAL			
%	100.0%	100.0%	100.0%
N	1032	906	23
MISSING DATA			
Terminated	66		
Other	13	23	1
INAP., Did not vote, voting NA or DK	623	510	85

V 32063 - Q.B4.

Do you plan to vote in November (1976)?

Response Categories	Phone Interviews	Phone Households	Non-Phone Households
Yes	82.7%	80.3%	49.5%
No	13.9	16.1	43.1
Other	0.2	0.2	0
Don't Know	3.2	3.4	7.3
TOTAL			
%	100.0%	100.0%	99.9%
N	1628	1423	109
MISSING DATA			
Terminated	67		
Other	39	16	0

V 33170 - Q.F18.

Did R's family receive any income other than wages in 1975?

		Personal Interviews	
Response Categories	Phone Inter- views	Phone Households	Non-Phone Households
Yes	56.0%	66.6%	57.0%
No	42.8	32.2	43.0
Don't Know	1.2	1.2	0
TOTAL			
%	100.0%	100.0%	100.0%
N	1554	1371	107
MISSING DATA			
Terminated	110		
Other	70	68	2

V 33171 - Q.F18a.

How much was this?

		Personal Interviews	
Response Categories	Phone Inter- views	Phone Households	Non-Phone Households
Under $1,000	40.2%	31.4%	30.0%
$1,000-$2,499	19.2	23.8	30.0
$2,500-$4,999	18.2	23.3	30.0
$5,000-$9,999	7.1	10.9	8.3
$10,000-$14,999	2.8	4.0	0
$15,000 and over	2.5	3.4	0
Refused	4.6	0	0
Don't Know	5.3	3.3	1.7
TOTAL			
%	99.9%	100.1%	100.0%
N	845	884	60
MISSING DATA			
Terminated	112		
Other	93	96	3
INAP., No non- wage income or DK if any	684	457	46

V 35097 - Q.B.13b.

Any number for business use only?

Response Categories	Phone Interviews	Personal Interviews	
		Phone Households	Non-Phone Households
Yes	26.4%	34.8%	0
No	73.6	65.2	0
TOTAL			
%	100.0%	100.0%	0
N	87	46	0
MISSING DATA			
Terminated	87		
Other	10	4	0
INAP., one or no phones or single number	1550	1389	109

V 35098 - Q.B13c.

How many are used only for business?

Response Categories	Phone Interviews	Personal Interviews	
		Phone Households	Non-Phone Households
One	91.3%	87.5%	0
Two	0	12.5	0
Three	8.7	0	0
TOTAL			
%	100.0%	100.0%	0
N	23	16	0
MISSING DATA			
Terminated	87		
Other	10	4	0
INAP., one or no phones, single number, or none for business (Q.97)	1614	1420	109

V 35138 - Q.E18.

Is access to R's house restricted?

Response Categories	Phone Interviews	Personal Interviews	
		Phone Households	Non-Phone Households
Yes	11.4%	2.7%	4.6%
No	88.5	97.3	95.4
Don't Know	0.1	0	0
TOTAL			
%	100.0%	100.0%	100.0%
N	1610	1435	109
MISSING DATA			
Terminated	101		
Other	23	4	0

V 44109 - Q.D1., D2., D5.

Present Job Status of Respondent

		Personal Interviews	
Response Categories	Phone Inter-views	Phone Households	Non-Phone Households
Worker-20 or more hours/week	55.6%	49.5%	48.6%
Worker-less than 20 hours/week	3.5	4.0	3.7
Unemployed, Laid Off	5.6	4.0	15.6
Retired/Disabled	13.3	15.6	11.0
Full-Time Student	3.4	3.5	0
Part-Time Student	0.9	0.7	0
Housewife/Other	17.8	22.8	21.1
TOTAL %	100.1%	100.1%	100.0%
N	1636	1438	109
MISSING DATA			
Terminated	91		
Other	7	0	0

V 44110 - Q.D2.

Number of Hours Respondent Works on Main Job in Average Week

		Personal Interviews	
Response Categories	Phone Inter-views	Phone Households	Non-Phone Households
1 - 10 hours	3.9%	3.6%	3.4%
11 - 20 hours	8.0	8.9	3.6
21 - 30 hours	7.1	8.2	0
31 - 40 hours	49.7	48.9	55.2
41 - 50 hours	17.6	19.3	19.0
51 - 60 hours	9.1	8.2	8.6
61 or more	4.3	2.5	5.2
Don't Know	0.3	0.4	0
TOTAL %	100.0%	100.0%	100.0%
N	1035	802	58
MISSING DATA			
Terminated	91		
Other	18	12	0
INAP., not employed	590	626	50

V 44111 - Q.D2a.-D2d.

Main Occupation of Respondent

		Personal Interviews	
	Phone Inter-views	Phone Households	Non-Phone Households
Professional, Technical and Kindred Workers	15.9%	12.5%	2.5%
Managers, Officials and Proprietors	8.7	8.6	0
Clerical and Kindred Workers	15.0	12.3	3.8
Sales Workers	4.8	5.4	2.5
Craftsmen, Foremen, and Kindred Workers	12.0	9.5	10.1
Operatives and Kindred Workers	9.0	8.1	25.3
Laborers	2.4	1.8	7.6
Service Workers	8.8	10.0	17.7
Farmers and Farm Managers	1.9	1.2	2.5
Student, Housewife, never worked	21.6	30.4	27.8
TOTAL %	100.1%	99.8%	99.8%
N	1329	1165	79
MISSING DATA			
Terminated	91		
Other	11	4	2
INAP., Unemployed	303	270	28

V 44114 - Q.D3a.-D3d.

Last Main Job of Unemployed Respondent

		Personal Interviews	
	Phone Inter-views	Phone Households	Non-Phone Households
Professional, Technical and Kindred Workers	11.4%	5.3%	6.3%
Managers, Officials and Proprietors	6.8	8.8	0
Clerical and Kindred Workers	18.2	22.8	18.8
Sales Workers	2.3	5.3	6.3
Craftsmen, Foremen, and Kindred Workers	13.6	22.8	6.3
Operatives and Kindred Workers	26.1	19.3	37.5
Laborers	6.8	7.0	6.3
Service Workers	14.8	8.8	18.7
Farmers and Farm Managers	0	0	0
Student, Housewife, never worked	0	0	0
TOTAL			
%	100.0%	100.1%	100.2%
N	88	57	16
MISSING DATA			
Terminated	92		
Other	6	1	1
INAP., Presently employed	1548	1381	92

V 44116 - Q.D4.,D4a.-D4c.

Retired or Disabled Respondent's Previous Occupation

		Personal Interviews	
Response Categories	Phone Inter-views	Phone Households	Non-Phone Households
Professional, Technical and Kindred Workers	15.1%	14.1%	0
Managers, Officials and Proprietors	11.3	10.3	0
Clerical and Kindred Workers	15.1	13.2	25.0
Sales Workers	7.1	4.3	0
Craftsmen, Foremen, and Kindred Workers	17.9	13.7	0
Operatives and Kindred Workers	11.8	18.4	8.3
Laborers	4.7	5.6	25.0
Service Workers	12.3	13.7	25.0
Farmers and Farm Managers	4.7	6.8	16.7
TOTAL			
%	100.0%	100.1%	100.0%
N	212	234	12
MISSING DATA			
Terminated	93		
Other	7	2	0
INAP., not retired of disabled	1422	1203	97

V 44141 - Q.F1.

Reported Age in Years of Respondent

Response Categories	Phone Interviews	Personal Interviews	
		Phone Households	Non-Phone Households
18 - 20 years	6.0%	4.8%	16.5%
21 - 25 years	11.7	11.0	14.7
26 - 30 years	14.6	12.9	20.1
31 - 35 years	11.2	9.3	11.0
36 - 40 years	9.4	8.5	4.6
41 - 45 years	8.2	7.2	5.5
46 - 50 years	7.2	7.8	8.2
51 - 55 years	7.5	7.4	4.6
56 - 60 years	6.7	6.8	2.8
61 - 65 years	6.1	7.3	7.3
66 - 70 years	4.5	6.3	1.9
71 - 75 years	3.3	5.0	0.9
76 - 80 years	1.8	2.9	0.9
81 - 85 years	1.1	1.8	0
86 or more	0.6	1.0	0.9
TOTAL			
%	99.9%	100.0%	99.9%
N	1580	1432	109
MISSING DATA			
Terminated	101		
Other	53	7	0

V 44142 - Q.F1.

Relationship of Respondent to Head of Household

Response Categories	Phone Interviews	Personal Interviews	
		Phone Households	Non-Phone Households
Male Head of Household	41.0%	36.7%	41.3%
Female Head of Household	19.3	20.6	30.3
Wife of Head of Household	31.5	33.5	24.8
Child, Son-, Daughter-in-law of Head	6.3	6.5	2.8
Parent or In-law of Head	0.3	0.6	0.9
Sibling of Head	0.7	1.0	0
Other Relative	0.1	0.3	0
Roommate	0.6	0.5	0
Roomer	0	0.2	0
Other	0.1	0.2	0
TOTAL			
%	99.9%	100.1%	100.1%
N	1617	1439	109
MISSING DATA			
Terminated	101		
Other	16	0	0

V 44143 - Q.F1.

Total Number of Eligible Respondents in HU

Response Categories	Phone Inter-views	Personal Interviews	
		Phone Households	Non-Phone Households
1 Eligible R	23.0%	23.5%	44.0%
2 Eligible Rs	57.5	60.6	46.8
3 Eligible Rs	13.8	10.8	7.3
4 Eligible Rs	4.4	3.9	0
5 Eligible Rs	1.0	0.8	1.9
6 Eligible Rs	0.1	0.3	0
7 Eligible Rs	0.1	0.1	0
8 Rs or more	0	0.1	0
TOTAL			
%	99.9%	100.1%	100.0%
N	1619	1439	109
MISSING DATA			
Terminated	101		
Other	14	0	0

V 44144 - Q.F1.

Total Number of Persons 18-21 in the HU

Response Categories	Phone Inter-views	Personal Interviews	
		Phone Households	Non-Phone Households
None	81.7%	85.0%	71.6%
1 Person	13.4	11.2	18.3
2 Persons	4.4	3.5	9.2
3 Persons	0.4	0.3	0.9
4 Persons	0.1	0.1	0
TOTAL			
%	100.0%	100.1%	100.0%
N	1598	1437	109
MISSING DATA			
Terminated	101		
Other	25	2	0

V 44145 - Q.F1.

Total Number of Eligible Persons in R's Family Unit

Response Categories	Phone Inter-views	Personal Interviews	
		Phone Households	Non-Phone Households
1 Elig. Person	25.7%	25.8%	48.6%
2 Elig. Persons	56.5	59.0	43.1
3 Elig. Persons	13.0	10.4	7.3
4 Elig. Persons	3.8	3.8	0
5 Elig. Persons	0.9	0.8	0.9
6 Elig. Persons	0.1	0.2	0
7 Elig. Persons	0.1	0.1	0
8 Persons or more	0	0.1	0
TOTAL			
%	100.1%	100.2%	99.9%
N	1613	1439	109
MISSING DATA			
Terminated	101		
Other	20	0	0

V 44146 - Q.Fl. Summary

Number of Persons Under Age 18 Living in HU

Response Categories	Phone Inter- views	Personal Interviews	
		Phone Households	Non-Phone Households
None	53.7%	54.7%	50.0%
1 Person	16.0	16.8	19.4
2 Persons	16.7	16.5	11.1
3 Persons	8.9	7.2	8.3
4 Persons	3.5	3.0	7.4
5 Persons	1.0	1.0	1.9
6 Persons	0.3	0.5	1.9
7 Persons	0.1	0.1	0
8 or more	0.1	0.2	0
TOTAL			
%	100.3%	100.0%	100.0%
N	1615	1436	108
MISSING DATA			
Terminated	101		
Other	15	3	1

V 44147 - Q.Fl. Summary

Number of Persons Age 13-17 Living in HU

Response Categories	Phone Inter- views	Personal Interviews	
		Phone Households	Non-Phone Households
None	78.2%	77.9%	86.1%
1 Person	13.0	13.1	7.4
2 Persons	6.8	7.0	2.8
3 Persons	1.5	1.7	3.7
4 Persons	0.5	0.2	0
5 Persons	0.1	0.1	0
TOTAL			
%	100.1%	100.0%	100.0%
N	1611	1437	108
MISSING DATA			
Terminated	101		
Other	21	2	1

V 44148 - Q.Fl. Summary

Number of People Under Age 18 in R's Family Unit

Response Categories	Phone Inter- views	Personal Interviews	
		Phone Households	Non-Phone Households
None	54.2%	55.2%	50.0%
1 Person	16.1	16.9	19.4
2 Persons	16.5	16.2	11.1
3 Persons	8.6	7.0	8.3
4 Persons	3.6	3.0	7.4
5 Persons	0.9	1.0	1.9
6 Persons	0.3	0.5	1.9
7 Persons	0	0.1	0
8 or more	0.1	0.2	0
TOTAL			
%	100.3%	100.1%	100.0%
N	1613	1435	108
MISSING DATA			
Terminated	101		
Other	17	4	1

V 44149 - Q.Fl. Summary

Number of R's Children Living in HU

Response Categories	Phone Inter- views	Personal Interviews	
		Phone Households	Non-Phone Households
None	57.0%	60.3%	54.6%
1 Child	14.7	15.3	16.6
2 Children	15.8	14.4	9.2
3 Children	8.0	6.2	8.3
4 Children	3.3	2.4	7.4
5 Children	0.8	0.8	1.9
6 Children	0.3	0.3	1.9
7 Children	0	0.1	0
8 or more	0.1	0	0
TOTAL			
%	100.0%	99.8%	99.9%
N	1617	1439	108
MISSING DATA			
Terminated	101		
Other	16	3	1

V 44150 - Q.F1. Summary

Age of R's Youngest Child

Response Categories	Phone Interviews	Personal Interview Phone Households	Non-Phone Households
1 year	14.5%	15.9%	35.4%
2 years	7.2	7.7	8.3
3 years	5.9	7.0	16.7
4 years	6.7	6.9	2.1
5 years	7.1	7.6	10.4
6 years	6.5	7.6	4.2
7 years	5.5	4.2	2.1
8 years	4.8	3.5	0
9 years	3.9	4.4	0
10 years	5.8	6.3	2.1
11 years	5.7	4.2	2.1
12 years	6.2	3.5	4.2
13 years	5.5	4.4	0
14 years	4.3	4.2	4.2
15 years	3.8	5.6	2.1
16 years	4.3	5.1	2.1
17 years	2.2	3.0	2.1
TOTAL %	99.9%	101.1%	98.1%
N	690	569	48
MISSING DATA Terminated	101		
Other	21	0	0
INAP, no children of R	921	869	59

V 44151 - Q.F2.-F2e.

Respondent's Years of Education

Response Categories	Phone Interviews	Personal Interview Phone Households	Non-Phone Households
0 - 7 years	5.0%	7.7%	19.4%
8 years	5.9	8.0	8.3
9 years	3.2	4.3	10.2
10 years	5.2	5.6	12.9
11 years	4.1	5.2	7.4
12 years	36.3	35.7	34.3
13 years	6.8	6.6	1.9
14 years	9.8	6.9	3.7
15 years	3.9	4.6	0
16 years	10.3	8.4	0
17 or more	9.4	7.2	1.9
Don't Know	0.2	0	0
TOTAL %	100.1%	100.2%	100.0%
N	1608	1432	108
MISSING DATA Terminated	103		
Other	23	7	1

V 44152 - Q.F2.-F2e. Summary

Respondent's Education

Response Categories	Phone Interviews	Personal Interviews	
		Phone Households	Non-Phone Households
8 grades or less	9.1%	13.8%	26.2%
8 grades or less, plus non-academic training	1.4	1.5	0.9
9-11 grades, no diploma	9.7	11.1	24.3
9-11 grades, plus non-academic training	3.0	3.5	5.6
High school diploma	20.3	21.1	20.6
High school diploma plus non-academic trng.	14.8	13.1	12.1
Some college - ½ yr. - 3 years	21.4	19.1	5.6
Jr. or Community college degrees	1.8	1.8	2.8
BA level degrees	12.7	11.0	0.9
Advanced degree, including LLB	5.6	3.9	0.9
Don't Know	0.1	0	0
TOTAL			
%	99.9%	99.9%	99.9%
N	1607	1431	107
MISSING DATA			
Terminated	103		
Other	24	8	2

V 44153 - Q.F3

Interviewer Checkpoint

Response Categories	Phone Interviews	Personal Interviews	
		Phone Households	Non-Phone Households
R is head of household	59.7%	57.1%	70.4%
R is not head of household	40.3	42.9	29.6
TOTAL			
%	100.0%	100.0%	100.0%
N	1624	1439	108
MISSING DATA			
Terminated	103		
Other	7	0	1

V 44154 - Q.F4.

Head's Years of Education

Response Categories	Phone Inter-views	Personal Interviews	
		Phone Households	Non-Phone Households
0 - 7 years	5.6%	5.4%	31.3%
8 years	5.6	7.5	12.5
9 years	1.9	2.8	6.3
10 years	4.9	5.7	9.4
11 years	3.1	4.4	6.2
12 years	35.9	36.8	18.7
13 years	5.1	5.2	0
14 years	10.7	8.7	6.2
15 years	2.9	3.1	0
16 years	10.2	10.0	0
17 or more	11.6	9.0	0
Don't Know	3.6	1.3	9.4
TOTAL			
%	100.1%	99.9%	100.0%
N	647	611	32
MISSING DATA			
Terminated	103		
Other	15	6	1
INAP., R is head	969	822	76

V 44156 - Q.F6.

Respondent's Marital Status

Response Categories	Phone Inter-views	Personal Interviews	
		Phone Households	Non-Phone Households
Married (including Spouse away in service)	64.2%	63.1%	45.4
Separated	2.4	2.8	13.9
Divorced	7.4	9.0	12.0
Widowed	10.0	11.5	5.5
Never Married	16.1	13.6	23.2
TOTAL			
%	100.1%	100.0%	100.0%
N	1616	1437	108
MISSING DATA			
Terminated	103		
Other	15	2	1

V 44155 - Q.F5.

Respondent's Race

Response Categories	Phone Inter-views	Personal Interviews	
		Phone Households	Non-Phone Households
White	86.6%	87.0%	67.0%
Black	9.8	10.0	27.5
Chicano;Puerto Rican;Mexican or Spanish American	2.3	2.0	5.5
American Indian	0.2	0.1	0
Oriental	0.4	0.6	0
Other	0.3	0.2	0
TOTAL			
%	99.6%	99.9%	100.0%
N	1600	1436	109
MISSING DATA			
Terminated	103		
Other	31	3	0

V 44157 - Q.F7.

Month and Year of Respondent's Birth

Response Categories	Phone Inter-views	Personal Interviews	
		Phone Households	Non-Phone Households
January	8.1%	8.2%	11.1%
February	7.3	7.0	11.1
March	8.2	8.5	9.2
April	7.6	8.9	8.3
May	7.6	8.5	5.5
June	8.7	7.8	11.1
July	9.4	8.9	7.4
August	8.2	8.7	9.2
September	9.4	9.3	3.7
October	8.9	8.1	5.5
November	8.5	7.7	10.2
December	8.1	8.4	7.4
TOTAL			
%	100.0%	100.0%	99.7%
N	1588	1422	108
MISSING DATA			
Terminated	103		
Other	43	17	1

V 44159 - Q.F8.-F8c.

Respondent's Political Status

Response Categories	Phone Inter- views	Personal Interviews	
		Phone Households	Non-Phone Households
Strong Democrat	14.6%	15.3%	15.7%
Not Very Strong Democrat	22.8	24.3	28.4
Democrat	14.2	12.2	18.6
Neither	14.8	16.9	25.5
Republican	9.2	7.3	0
Not Very Strong Republican	15.6	14.6	5.9
Strong Republican	7.6	8.9	3.9
Other Minor Party	0.1	0.1	1.0
Apolitical	1.1	0.5	1.0
TOTAL %	100.0%	100.1%	100.0%
N	1553	1433	107
MISSING DATA Terminated	104		
Other	77	26	6

V 44160 - Q.F9.

Interviewer Checkpoint - R's Marital Status

Response Categories	Phone Inter- views	Personal Interviews	
		Phone Households	Non-Phone Households
R is not Married	36.8%	37.0%	54.1%
R is Married	63.2	63.0	46.0
TOTAL %	100.0%	100.0%	100.1%
N	1626	1439	109
MISSING DATA Terminated	104		
Other	4	0	0

V 44161 - Q.F10,F11.

Job Status of R's Husband/Wife

Response Categories	Phone Inter- views	Personal Interviews	
		Phone Households	Non-Phone Households
Worker 20 or more hours/week	57.3%	58.5%	56.0%
Worker less than 20 hours/week	2.8	2.2	0
Unemployed, Laid Off	2.4	2.3	4.0
Retired, Disabled	9.2	11.4	8.0
Full Time Student	1.0	0.9	0
Part Time Student	0.2	0.4	0
Housewife/Other	27.1	24.3	32.0
TOTAL			
%	100.0%	100.0%	100.0
N	1023	905	50
MISSING DATA			
Terminated	105		
Other	8	1	0
INAP.,not married	598	533	59

V 44162 - Q.F11.

Average Weekly Work Hours of R's Husband/Wife

Response Categories	Phone Inter- views	Personal Interviews	
		Phone Households	Non-Phone Households
1 - 10 hours	2.9%	1.3%	3.5%
11-20 hours	4.2	5.5	6.9
21-30 hours	5.1	4.7	6.9
31-40 hours	50.3	56.0	55.2
41-50 hours	20.4	19.5	20.7
51-60 hours	9.6	8.2	6.9
61 or more	6.4	4.5	0
TOTAL			
%	99.9%	100.1%	100.1%
N	622	558	29
MISSING DATA			
Terminated	106		
Other	28	12	0
INAP.,not married	978	869	80

Response Categories	V 44163 - Q.F11.-F11d. Main Occupation of Respondent's Husband/Wife			V 44164 - Q.F12a.-F12d. Last Occupation of Respondent's Husband/Wife		
	Phone Inter-views	Personal Interviews		Phone Inter-views	Personal Interviews	
		Phone Households	Non-Phone Households		Phone Households	Non-Phone Households
Professional, Technical and Kindred Workers	15.2%	12.8%	6.8%	8.7%	10.0%	0%
Managers, Officials and Proprietors	12.2	8.9	4.6	8.7	0	0
Clerical and Kindred Workers	9.0	10.6	0	13.0	10.0	0
Sales Workers	4.0	5.6	0	0	10.0	0
Craftsmen, Foremen and Kindred Workers	13.5	12.8	6.8	26.1	25.0	0
Operatives and Kindred Workers	8.1	10.6	18.2	26.0	40.0	100.0
Laborers	2.2	2.3	18.2	0	5.0	0
Service Workers	4.8	6.1	4.5	17.4	0	0
Farmers and Farm Managers	1.3	2.5	6.9	0	0	0
Student, Housewife, never worked	29.7	27.8	34.1	0	0	0
TOTAL						
%	100.0%	100.0%	100.1%	99.9%	100.0%	100.0%
N	900	737	44	23	20	2
MISSING DATA						
Terminated	106			106		
Other	18	2	0	9	2	0
INAP., not married, spouse unemployed	710	650	65	1596	1417	107

V 44165 - Q.F13.-F13c.

Occupation of R's Husband/Wife
Before Retirement/Disablement

| | Phone Inter- views | Personal Interviews | |
Response Categories		Phone Households	Non-Phone Households
Professional, Technical and Kindred Workers	5.3%	12.6%	0%
Managers, Officials and Proprietors	12.6	9.9	0
Clerical and Kindred Workers	9.5	16.2	0
Sales Workers	6.3	3.6	0
Craftsmen, Foremen and Kindred Workers	28.4	25.2	25.0
Operatives and Kindred Workers	21.1	14.4	25.0
Laborers	4.2	5.4	25.0
Service Workers	7.4	5.4	25.0
Farmers and Farm Managers	5.3	7.2	0
Student, Housewife, never worked	0	0	0
TOTAL			
%	100.1%	99.9%	100.0%
N	95	111	4
MISSING DATA			
Terminated	106		
Other	6	1	0
INAP., not married, spouse unemployed	1527	1327	105

V 55193 - Q.T10a.

Other persons present at interview--NONE

Response Categories	Phone Inter-views	Personal Interviews	
		Phone Households	Non-Phone Households
Checked	24.9%	47.4%	32.0%
Not Checked	36.4	52.6	68.0
No way of knowing	38.7	0	0
TOTAL			
%	100.0%	100.0%	100.0%
N	609	750	74
MISSING DATA	57	5	0
INAP., no one present	1068	684	35

V 55194 - Q.T10a.

Other persons present at interview--CHILDREN UNDER 6

Response Categories	Phone Inter-views	Personal Interviews	
		Phone Households	Non-Phone Households
Checked	22.0%	27.8%	41.9%
Not Checked	78.0	72.2	58.1
TOTAL			
%	100.0%	100.0%	100.0%
N	609	750	74
MISSING DATA	57	5	0
INAP., No one present	1068	684	35

V 55195 - Q.T10a.

Other persons present at interview--OLDER CHILDREN

Response Categories	Phone Inter-views	Personal Interviews	
		Phone Households	Non-Phone Households
Checked	18.2%	25.0%	25.6%
Not Checked	81.8	75.0	74.4
TOTAL			
%	100.0%	100.0%	100.0%
N	609	750	74
MISSING DATA	57	5	0
INAP., no one present	1068	684	35

V 55196 - Q.T10a.

Other persons present at interview--SPOUSE

Response Categories	Phone Inter-views	Personal Interviews	
		Phone Households	Non-Phone Households
Checked	55.0%	48.4%	35.1%
Not Checked	45.0	51.6	64.9
TOTAL			
%	100.0%	100.0%	100.0%
N	609	751	74
MISSING DATA	57	4	0
INAP., no one present	1068	684	35

V 55197 - Q.T10a.

Other persons present at interview--OTHER
RELATIVES

Response Categories	Phone Interviews	Personal Interviews	
		Phone Households	Non-Phone Households
Checked	7.2%	13.8%	18.9%
Not Checked	92.8	86.2	81.1
TOTAL			
%	100.0%	100.0%	100.0%
N	609	750	74
MISSING DATA	57	5	0
INAP., no one present	1068	684	35

V 55198 - Q.T10a.

Other persons present at interview--OTHER
ADULTS

Response Categories	Phone Interviews	Personal Interviews	
		Phone Households	Non-Phone Households
Checked	14.4%	17.2%	31.1%
Not Checked	85.6	82.8	68.9
TOTAL			
%	100.0%	100.0%	100.0%
N	609	750	74
MISSING DATA	57	5	0
INAP., no one present	1068	684	35

V 55199 - Q.T11.

Number of Interruptions During Interview

Response Categories	Phone Interviews	Personal Interviews	
		Phone Households	Non-Phone Households
None	77.3%	61.6%	58.4%
One	15.1	16.6	14.0
Two	5.0	10.5	12.0
Three	1.6	5.5	3.7
Four	.5	1.3	0.9
Five or More	.3	4.4	11.1
Don't Know	.1	.1	0
TOTAL			
%	99.9%	100.0%	100.0%
N	1639	1424	108
MISSING DATA	95	15	1

V 45094 - Q.B12.

Number of Telephones in House/Apartment

Response Categories	Phone Inter- views	Personal Interviews Phone Households	Personal Interviews Non-Phone Households
None	0.1%	0%	100.1%
One	43.5	43.1	0
Two	35.3	41.1	0
Three	15.3	11.6	0
Four	3.8	3.1	0
Five	1.4	0.8	0
Six	0.4	0.1	0
Seven	0.1	0.1	0
Eight	0.2	0	0
Nine	0.1	0.1	0
Forty-three	0.1	0	0
TOTAL			
%	100.3%	100.0%	100.1%
N	1638	1437	109
MISSING DATA			
Terminated	87		
Other	9	2	0

V 54182 - Q.T1.

Sex of Respondent

Response Categories	Phone Inter- views	Personal Interviews Phone Households	Personal Interviews Non-Phone Households
Male	43.7%	41.0%	43.1%
Female	56.3	59.0	56.9
TOTAL			
%	100.0%	100.0%	100.0%
N	1706	1439	109
MISSING DATA	28	0	0

V 45100 - Q.B13e.

How many numbers do appear in the current telephone book?

Response Categories	Phone Inter- views	Personal Interviews Phone Households	Personal Interviews Non-Phone Households
One	85.0%	92.9%	0%
Two	10.0	7.1	0
Three	4.0	0	0
TOTAL			
%	99.9%	100.0%	0%
N	20	14	0
MISSING DATA			
Terminated	87		
Other	14	3	0
INAP., none; one or no phones; single number; all listed; or DK (V 35099)	1613	1422	109

V 55104 - Q.B16a.

Interviewer Observation: Did R Check Records or Get Help with the Answer?

Response Categories	Phone Inter- views	Personal Interviews Phone Households	Personal Interviews Non-Phone Households
Yes	3.9%	2.0%	1.5%
No	96.1	98.0	98.5
TOTAL			
%	100.0%	100.0%	100.0%
N	1424	1182	67
MISSING DATA			
Terminated	88		
Other	66	24	2
INAP., Did not file	156	233	40

V 55108 - Q.B17c.

Interviewer Observation: Did R Check Records or Get Help with the Answer?

Response Categories	Phone Inter- views	Personal Interviews Phone Households	Personal Interviews Non-Phone Households
Yes	4.4%	2.3%	3.1%
No	95.6	97.7	96.9
TOTAL			
%	100.0%	100.0%	100.0%
N	1238	1110	64
MISSING DATA			
Terminated	90		
Other	243	90	5
INAP., did not file; or refused V 33103 question	163	239	40

V 55183 - Q.T2.

Language Problem

Response Categories	Phone Inter-views	Personal Interview Phone Households	Non-Phone Households
Major Problem	1.1%	1.1%	2.8%
Minor Problem	3.5	2.4	1.9
No Problem	95.4	96.5	95.3
TOTAL			
%	100.0%	100.0%	100.0%
N	1690	1434	108
MISSING DATA	44	5	1

V 55184 - Q.T2a.

Explanation of Language Problem

Response Categories	Phone Inter-views	Personal Interviews Phone Households	Non-Phone Households
English not R's first language	37.5%	54.9%	50.0%
English R's first language-R spoke/ understood poorly	3.8	11.8	0
Physical Speech Impairment	3.8	15.7	50.0
R mumbled	3.8	7.8	0
R's accent-No mention foreign language	42.5	0	0
Other	7.5	9.8	0
TOTAL			
%	98.9%	100.0%	100.0%
N	80	51	6
MISSING DATA	42	4	0
INAP., No language problem	1612	1384	103

V 55185 - Q.T3.

Any other Problems with Interview

Response Categories	Phone Inter-views	Personal Interviews Phone Households	Non-Phone Households
Major Problems	5.4%	5.3%	6.4%
Minor Problems	16.6	17.6	25.7
No Problems	77.9	77.1	67.9
Don't Know	.1	0	0
TOTAL			
%	100.0%	100.0%	100.0%
N	1686	1429	109
MISSING DATA	48	10	0

V 55186 - Q.T3a.

Explanation of Other Problems with Interview

Response Categories	Phone Inter-views	Personal Interviews	
		Phone Households	Non-Phone Households
R did not answer question	10.4%	10.3%	2.9%
R mentally slow	14.1	7.9	17.1
R hostile	28.5	16.9	5.7
Interference-Other People/Pets	6.6	34.1	51.4
R was sick; hard of hearing	13.3	14.2	2.9
Noises in or near i'ew location	1.3	5.7	8.6
R hard to hear; bad connection	15.2	0	0
Other	10.6	10.9	11.4
TOTAL %	100.0%	100.0%	100.0%
N	376	331	35
MISSING DATA	43	6	0
INAP., No other problems	1315	1102	74

V 55187 - Q.T4.

Respondent's General Understanding of Question

Response Categories	Phone Inter-views	Personal Interviews	
		Phone Households	Non-Phone Households
Excellent	35.6%	30.6%	7.3%
Good	47.0	51.9	49.6
Fair	14.0	15.2	31.2
Poor	3.1	2.3	11.9
Don't Know	.2	0	0
TOTAL %	99.9%	100.0%	100.0%
N	1694	1429	109
MISSING DATA	40	10	0

V 55188 - Q.T5.

Respondent's Ability To Express Him/Herself

Response Categories	Phone Inter-views	Personal Interviews	
		Phone Households	Non-Phone Households
(1) Very Articulate; Excellent Vocab.	26.1%	23.0%	2.8%
(2)	52.7	51.9	52.3
(3)	18.1	22.1	26.6
(4) Poor Self-Expression; Limited Vocab.	3.0	3.0	18.3
Don't Know	.1	.1	0
TOTAL %	100.0%	100.1%	100.0%
N	1690	1406	109
MISSING DATA	44	33	0

V 55189 - **Q.T6.**

R Suspicious About Study Before Interview?

Response Categories	Phone Inter-views	Personal Interviews	
		Phone Households	Non-Phone Households
Not at all Suspicious	73.5%	75.9%	76.1%
Somewhat Suspicious	21.1	20.8	22.0
Very Suspicious	5.4	3.3	1.9
TOTAL			
%	100.0%	100.0%	100.0%
N	1694	1433	109
MISSING DATA	40	6	0

V 55190 - **Q.T7.**

R's Overall Interest in the Interview

Response Categories	Phone Inter-views	Personal Interviews	
		Phone Households	Non-Phone Households
Very High	10.8%	13.7%	9.2%
Above Average	30.8	35.7	24.8
Average	44.8	37.9	40.4
Below Average	10.1	10.5	19.2
Very Low	3.4	2.2	6.4
Don't Know	.1	0	0
TOTAL			
%	100.0%	100.0%	100.0%
N	1688	1430	109
MISSING DATA	46	9	0

V 55191 - **Q.T8.**

Did R Seem to Rush Answers?

Response Categories	Phone Inter-views	Personal Interviews	
		Phone Households	Non-Phone Households
Yes	10.5%	9.2%	9.2%
No	89.4	90.7	90.8
Don't Know	.1	.1	0
TOTAL			
%	100.0%	100.0%	100.0%
N	1679	1433	109
MISSING DATA	55	6	0

V 55192 - **Q.T9.**

Did R Ask How Much Longer the I'ew Would Take?

Response Categories	Phone Inter-views	Personal Interviews	
		Phone Households	Non-Phone Households
Yes	14.7%	5.8%	3.7%
No	85.3	94.2	96.3
TOTAL			
%	100.0%	100.0%	100.0%
N	1687	1432	109
MISSING DATA	47	7	0

V 55200 - Q.T11a.

How many minutes of interruptions
during interview?

Response Categories	Phone Inter-views	Personal Interviews Phone Households	Non-Phone Households
None	80.4%	62.5%	59.8%
1 minute	13.4	8.6	12.1
2 minutes	3.4	8.3	7.4
3 minutes	.8	4.7	3.8
4 minutes	.3	1.5	0.9
5 minutes	.6	6.5	8.3
6-10 minutes	.3	2.3	4.7
11-20 minutes	.2	4.5	2.8
21-30 minutes	.1	.8	0
31 or more	.4	.4	0
Don't Know	.1	.1	0
TOTAL %	100.0%	100.2%	99.8%
N	1700	1424	107
MISSING DATA	34	15	2

V 55201 - Q.T11b.

Interruptions by Children from the
Household

Response Categories	Phone Inter-views	Personal Interviews Phone Households	Non-Phone Households
Checked	26.3%	30.8%	54.6%
Not Checked	64.7	69.2	45.4
No way of knowing	9.1	0	0
TOTAL %	100.1%	100.0%	100.0%
N	320	551	44
MISSING DATA	46	0	1
INAP., no interruptions	1368	888	64

V 55202 - Q.T11b.

Interruptions by Other Adults from the
Household

Response Categories	Phone Inter-views	Personal Interviews Phone Households	Non-Phone Households
Checked	20.6%	19.2%	31.9%
Not Checked	79.4	80.8	68.1
TOTAL %	100.0%	100.0%	100.0%
N	291	551	44
MISSING DATA	45	0	1
INAP.,no interruptions, no way of knowing cause of interruption	1398	888	64

V 55203 - Q.T11b.

Interruptions by Phone Calls to the Household

Response Categories	Phone Inter-views	Personal Interviews Phone Households	Non-Phone Households
Checked	2.4%	36.8%	4.6%
Not Checked	97.6	63.2	95.4
TOTAL			
%	100.0%	100.0%	100.0%
N	291	551	44
MISSING DATA	44	0	1
INAP., no inter-ruptions, no way of knowing cause of interruption	1398	888	64

V 55204 - Q.T11b.

Interruptions by Visitor(s) to the Household

Response Categories	Phone Inter-views	Personal Interviews Phone Households	Non-Phone Households
Checked	15.5%	22.5%	36.4%
Not Checked	84.5	77.5	63.6
TOTAL			
%	100.0%	100.0%	100.0%
N	291	551	44
MISSING DATA	45	0	1
INAP., no inter-ruptions, no way of knowing cause of interruption	1398	888	64

V 55205 - Q.T11b.

Other Interruptions

Response Categories	Phone Inter-views	Personal Interviews Phone Households	Non-Phone Households
Checked	42.5%	22.5%	13.7%
Not Checked	57.5	77.5	86.3
TOTAL			
%	100.0%	100.0%	100.0%
N	292	551	44
MISSING DATA	44	0	1
INAP., no inter-ruptions, no way of knowing cause of interruption	1398	888	64

V 55206 - Q.T11b.

What other interruptions?

Response Categories	Phone Inter-views	Personal Interviews Phone Households	Non-Phone Households
R him/herself did something to interrupt interview	60.7%	61.5%	50.0%
Interruption by pet/animal	5.7	23.0	16.7
Stopped for explanation	6.6	0	0
Connection Broken	12.3	0	0
Party Line Interference	2.5	0	0
I'er stopped for mechanical adjustment or sup-ervisory help	4.1	0	0
Other	8.2	15.6	33.3
MISSING DATA	39	1	0
INAP., no other source of inter.	1573	1317	102

V 55207 - Q.T12.

R's Name and Address Information

Response Categories	Phone Interviews	Personal Interviews	
		Phone Households	Non-Phone Households
R gave name and address	78.6%	97.1%	96.2%
R refused name and address	16.4	2.7	3.8
R gave address but not name	.2	0	0
Name and address not obtained for some other reason	4.8	.1	0
R gave name but not address	.1	0	0
TOTAL			
%	100.1%	99.9%	100.0%
N	1670	1423	107
MISSING DATA	64	16	2

Appendix III

A Comparison of Two Telephone Sample Designs

This appendix compares two different random-digit dialed samples of the coterminous United States household population with respect to the proportion of working household numbers generated and the sampling variance of various estimates. One design is the stratified random design we used in this project; the other is a clustered design suggested by Waksberg (1978). Both of the designs utilized the A.T. & T. listing of central office codes. The data record of the A.T. & T. tape is an area code–central office code combination (e.g., 313-764); thus each record represents 10,000 distinct telephone numbers (e.g., 313-764-0000 through 313-764-9999). Stratification of the frame, therefore, cannot be accomplished below the level of the central office code, and the variables available for stratification are few. Since systematic samples were to be drawn, the stratification implicit in the design is specified by the ordering of the central office code records. The following was performed:

1. Group together all central office codes in the same telephone exchange.
2. Group together exchanges within the same area code.
3. Form size categories of exchanges using number of central office codes in an exchange. These categories are proxy categories for levels of population density within the exchanges.
4. Within each area code and each exchange size grouping, order exchanges using the geographical coordinates provided on the tape; within area codes rotate the geographical order across size groups (this results in a serpentine geographical ordering across exchange size groups—Northwest to Southeast, Southeast to Northwest, Northwest to Southeast, etc.).
5. Order area codes geographically, keeping states and major census regions intact.

331

Given this ordering of the frame for the first design, each replicate group was drawn by taking a random start between 1 and the selection interval specified by the desired sample size. When a central office code designated for a selection was determined by application of the selection interval and random start, a four-digit random number was machine generated (e.g., 4424) and appended to the AC–COC combination, yielding the ten-digit sample telephone number (e.g., 313-764-4424).[1]

The second sample, described in Waksberg (1978), is a stratified clustered design where primary selections are groups of 100 consecutive telephone numbers; there are 100 such clusters in every central office code (0000–0099, 0100–0199, etc.). This design is similar to the Lahiri method (1951) of selecting primary units with probabilities proportional to a size measure; in this case, clusters of 100 consecutive numbers are selected with probabilities proportional to the number of working household numbers in the cluster.

The second design used the same stratification order of the A.T. & T. tape, and primary selections were taken in nine replicate groups each of which was a systematic sample of clusters. When a selection was indicated from a specific central office code, one of the 100 clusters was tentatively designated for selection by randomly generating a single four-digit number. For example, if 4424 is generated, the cluster containing numbers 4400–4499 is tentatively designated for selection. At this point all clusters are given equal probabilities since all have exactly 100 numbers. These initial numbers could be termed "primary numbers." These primary numbers are called; if they are not working household numbers, the clusters in which they fall are not selected. If they are working household numbers, their clusters are selected into the sample and a specified number of additional four-digit numbers ("secondary numbers") within the same cluster is generated. For example, if the desired cluster size is nine, eight more four-digit numbers within the same hundred series would be generated. Each of these eight would also be called, and if any yielded a nonresidential or nonworking number, it would be replaced by a newly generated four-digit number in the same hundred series, until ultimately eight more working household numbers were generated.

Let us now examine the probabilities of each number being selected into the clustered sample. In the first stage, we sample individual clusters of 100 telephone numbers; since we discard those primary numbers that are not working household numbers, the probability of each cluster being selected is proportional to the number of working household numbers in the hundred series (see below). In the second stage, a fixed number of working household numbers is sampled from among all working household numbers in the hundred series, so the probability of a number in a chosen cluster being selected is inversely proportional to the number of working household numbers in the hundred series. The product of the probabilities of the two stages is a constant for all numbers in working area code–central office code combinations; the sample yields an epsem design:[2]

$$\frac{\text{No. working households Nos.}}{k} \cdot \frac{b}{\text{No. working household Nos.}} = \frac{b}{k}$$

where b, the desired cluster size, and k, a sampling constant, are chosen to fit the needs of the particular study.

[1] This design could be viewed as a two-stage sample, first selecting area code–central office code combinations systematically and then randomly sampling one secondary selection, a single telephone number in each first stage unit.

[2] Epsem samples are those giving each population element an equal chance of selection.

Several properties of this second design are important for our consideration:

1. The design will always eliminate clusters that have no working numbers in them, and thus increase the proportion of working household numbers generated in each sample. In other words, the proportion of working household numbers is increased because the probability that the number is working given that another number in the same hundred series is a working household number is greater than the unconditional probability that a generated number is a working household number. The design takes advantage of the fact that as the central office code fills up with working numbers, numbers are generally assigned into the same hundred and thousand series (e.g., the company may begin assigning the 2000 series first, filling that up before going to the next thousand series). The smaller the portion of active hundred series in a central office code, the greater the advantage of the clustered design.

2. Departures from an epsem design can occur for two different reasons; some clusters may not contain the desired number of working household numbers (in the example above there may be a cluster of 100 numbers with only 1–8 working household numbers); second, a small percentage of nonworking numbers give a ringing tone whenever dialed, thus the investigator will not know whether or not to replace the number by a new sample from the same hundred series.

3. The sample is clustered into groups of hundred series of single central office codes, and a loss of precision due to clustering will occur. There is little documentation on the causes of numbers sharing the same hundred series; they may have come into service at about the same time,[3] or they may share the same type of service (touch-tone telephones, party lines). In any case, the sources of homogeneity among numbers in the same hundred series seem smaller than those for clusters in most areal probability samples.

Having described the nature of the two designs, we will now examine the results of implementing them. The stratified random sample was used in a study conducted by the Survey Research Center in April–May, 1976. The clustered design was constructed for a study in November–December, 1976. The population of each study included all currently working AC–COC combinations serving the coterminous United States. First, we will examine the efficiency of the two designs in terms of the proportion of working household numbers each yielded. Then we will present estimates of design effects for the two samples on a variety of measures common to both studies, and examine a variance-cost model for the two designs.

A.III.1. DISPOSITION OF SAMPLE NUMBERS IN THE TWO DESIGNS

Table A.III.1 presents the status of all sample numbers in the two designs. Only about one-fifth (21.6%) of the numbers in the stratified element sample were confirmed working household numbers. Another 2.9% gave a ringing tone whenever dialed, but were never answered.[4] For primary selections in the clustered sample, the experience was very similar; 24.5% of all primary numbers generated were working household numbers. The figures in Table A.III.1 for the clustered sample present the results for

---

[3] However, it is the practice of some companies to recycle disconnected numbers so that hundred series experiencing some out-mobility would receive new residents.

[4] Examination of the location of the "ring, no answer" numbers shows that they are concentrated in rural areas where the nonworking numbers are less likely to be connected to a recording or an operator intercept.

TABLE A.III.1
Final Disposition of Sample Numbers and Type of Nonworking Number by Sample Type

	All sample numbers		Nonworking numbers	
Disposition of sample number	Spring, 1976 Stratified element sample (%)	Fall, 1976 Stratified cluster sample (%)	Spring, 1976 Stratified element sample (%)	Fall, 1976 Stratified cluster sample (%)
Working household numbers (answered)	21.6	65.8		
Ring, no answer numbers (confirmed household)[a]	0	.7		
Ring, no answer numbers (status unconfirmed)[a]	2.9	0		
Nonresidential numbers	6.0	10.5		
Nonworking numbers	53.3	20.8	76.6	90.5
Wrong connections	4.7	1.8	6.8	7.8
No result from dial	6.3	.3	9.1	1.3
Fast busys	5.2	.1	7.5	.4
	100.0%	100.0%	100.0%	100.0%
N	5188	1252[b]		

[a] In the stratified element sample, "ring, without answer" numbers include some nonworking numbers; in the stratified cluster sample, all "ring, without answer" numbers were confirmed as working.
[b] The total number of clusters ultimately selected was 104. Each cluster had eight working household numbers generated.

the numbers generated in the second stage; they show a threefold increase in the proportion of working household numbers to 66.5%.[5] This implies that instead of every fifth number yielding a household as in the stratified sample, that for the clustered sample more often than not, the interviewer was dialing a working household number. Even combining the results from the primary and secondary selections of the clustered design produces an overall 55.8% of all numbers yielding a household. The clustered sample is clearly more efficient than the stratified element sample on this aspect of the design.

Not all unassigned numbers are connected to nonworking number recordings or operator intercepts. There are three classifications of responses that cause some problems in administering any random-digit sample. "Wrong connections" are numbers answered by people who report that their number is different from the one dialed; at least two different calls were made to these numbers before discarding them to verify that misdialings had not occurred.[6] Some numbers when dialed repeatedly yield nothing, no ringing, no busy signal, no recording; in Table A.III.1, these are labeled "no result from dial." The last category of nonworking numbers is "fast busys." The busy signal received when an assigned number is in use is a tone interrupted 60 times per minute; a "fast busy" or "reorder" signal is the same tone interrupted 120 times per minute. Sometimes this can indicate that the circuits in the area called are busy; but some nonworking numbers are also connected to these signals. The numbers in Table A.III.1 received fast busy signals at least five consecutive times throughout the month-long field period of each study. These last three categories of numbers are separated from the nonworking number group that received recordings or operator intercepts because there is a small possibility that each contains some working household numbers. "Wrong connections" could be answered by people who mislead the interviewer; "no result from dial" numbers may have been repeatedly incompletely dialed so that the system was awaiting another digit; "fast busys" could be numbers whose local system was overloaded or malfunctioning throughout the whole field period. We attempted to minimize these responses, and we believe that the vast majority of these numbers were nonworking.

We have already observed that the proportion of nonworking numbers is much lower in the clustered design than it is in the stratified element design. It is also important to note that among nonworking numbers a larger proportion are confirmed nonworking (through recordings or operator intercepts) in the clustered sample (90.5%) than in the stratified element sample (76.6%). In short, the aberrant categories of nonworking numbers are disproportionately located in hundred series that contain no working household numbers or relatively few such numbers. In addition to the gains in proportion of working household numbers, the even more dramatic decrease in "problem" numbers makes the clustered design attractive.

As we noted earlier, the epsem quality of the clustered design is sensitive to the

[5] We used the primary selections to pretest the interview schedule. In the actual field period, only the secondary selections were called. Replacement numbers were machine generated upon nightly disposition of numbers.

[6] Series of numbers within a central office code may be "bridged" together, so that those telephones can be reached by two different numbers. For example, if the 2000 and the 9000 series are bridged, the telephone with number 787-2111 can also be reached by 787-9111. This permits the company to utilize some standard test numbers in the 9000 series without opening the entire thousand series to use. Usually the customers are completely unaware of the fact that either number can be used to call their telephones. Before an interview is taken the interviewer verified that the sample number was actually reached.

existence of clusters with fewer than the desired number of working household numbers per cluster. In our use of the clustered design we selected 1 primary number and 8 secondary numbers from each of the 104 sampled clusters. Figure A.III.1 shows that the vast majority of clusters can easily support this number of selected elements. The horizontal axis of this figure has two scales: One is an estimate of the proportion of working household numbers based on the numbers required to be generated for nine working household numbers; the numbers below each of the points list how many numbers in total were generated (counting the primary number) to achieve 9 working household numbers. About 65% of the 104 clusters were estimated to have 75% or more of their numbers assigned to households; in these clusters fewer than 13 numbers needed to be generated to yield nine working household numbers. The worst experience required 43 generated sample numbers to yield 9 working household numbers. In about 10% (9.6%) of the clusters, less than half of the generated numbers were working household numbers. There are undoubtedly clusters with at least 1 but fewer than 9 working household numbers, but we found none among the 104 in the sample, and the general shape of the curve suggests that they are rare. It is likely that cluster sizes of 8–10 can be supported easily with the present densities of working household numbers within hundred series.[7]

As noted in Table A.III.1, some of the sample numbers in both designs yielded a ringing tone without response on each call. In the stratified element sample over 90% of these numbers were dialed at least ten times before the end of the field period. For that study, however, we were unable to verify how many of the "ring, no answer" numbers were working numbers. This uncertainty prevents an exact calculation of the response rate for that study, since we do not know whether to include those numbers as nonresponse or nonsample elements (the response rate ranged from 59–70%). In the administration of the clustered sample, however, we were able to verify the status of numbers which repeatedly yielded ringing without answer (and the final response rate was 71%). In all but a few of the primary numbers, this was done after more than 12 calls had been made to the primary sample number. Twenty primary numbers continually yielded ringing, 19 of those were nonworking numbers. Among the secondary selections, however, the results are somewhat different. Verification was made on 32 numbers, 30 of which had been called over 17 times. Seventeen, or 53.1% of the numbers were classified as working household numbers, and 4 of them eventually yielded interviews. These 32 numbers represent 2.6% of all secondary sample numbers generated; they fall in 28 of the 104 clusters, 4 clusters having 2 of the numbers.

In other applications of this design we will not be able to verify whether or not those numbers are working household numbers. Our attempts on national studies to obtain such information directly from the business office of the unanswered number have not been successful. For that reason, it may be instructive to simulate the effects of ignorance of the true status of these numbers. Faced with some sample numbers that constantly ring without answer, the investigators must decide whether or not to classify them as working household numbers. If they decide to treat them as working household numbers, no replacement numbers would be selected. If they decide to code them as nonworking numbers, each would be replaced by a new sample number. We can estimate the effects of both these decisions for the group of numbers that were not answered after at least 17 calls. First let us assume that all of these numbers are working

---

[7] These clusters could probably be used for another study with a desired cluster size of eight secondary numbers. Reusing the clusters in cases where they are likely to support the cluster size spreads the cost of screening primary numbers over several surveys. The danger in the scheme is the possibility of exhausting one or more clusters and departing from epsem in later uses.

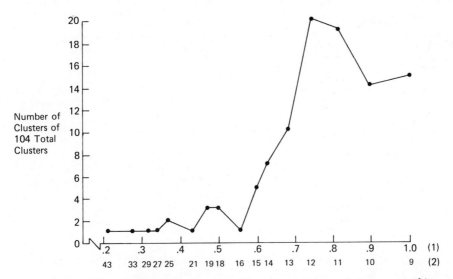

FIGURE A.III.1. Proportion of generated sample numbers that were working household numbers and total number of numbers generated per cluster for 104 clusters sampled. (1) = proportion of sample numbers from the cluster that were working household numbers; (2) = total numbers generated to produce nine working household numbers.

household numbers; we would have continued calling them and would probably have obtained as before four interviews from the 31 cases.[8] This assumption produced a correct classification for 16 of the 31 numbers. Unfortunately, there are three harmful effects of misclassifying the remaining 15. First, by including those 15 in the base of the response rate as noninterviews, the response rate is underestimated by a maximum of 18.8%.[9] The second effect is that the epsem nature of the design is destroyed; those clusters containing the "ring, no answer" numbers erroneously classified as working household numbers will have sample elements with lower probabilities of selection. The second stage probability will be 8 rather than 9, divided by the number of working household numbers. Unweighted estimates of means and proportions will be biased. Fifteen of the 104 clusters are affected in this way. Ignoring the biasing effects of the unweighted estimates it is also true that the sampling variance of a mean or proportion will be somewhat higher than that of an epsem design because of the unequal probabilities of selection. We expect that it would be about .18% higher than that estimated for the unweighted mean.[10]

[8] Thirty-one cases are used for this analysis because 1 of the 32 "ring, no answer" numbers mentioned above was a replacement sample number for one of the others.

[9] The maximum underestimation occurs with a perfect response rate among the real working household numbers. There were 104 clusters of 8 elements, or 832 elements. With perfect response the actual response rate would be 817 : 817 not 817 : 832 as implied by the assumption.

[10] This is based on an estimate of the effect of weighting: $1 - \sum p_i w_i^2 / (\sum p_i w_i)^2$ is the proportional increase in the variance if the weight w_i is applied to the proportion p_i of the sample (Kish, 1965, p. 427). Although this formula applies strictly to the effects of random weighting of a simple random sample, it provides a useful estimate of weighting effects in other samples designs also.

The other assumption that could be made about these numbers is that none of them is a working household number. In that case 16 of the 31 numbers are erroneously classified. The result is an overestimation of the response rate, a maximum error of 1.9% occurring when all 31 numbers are replaced by working household numbers yielding interviews. Once again the epsem quality of the design is destroyed, 15 of the clusters would have more than the specified nine elements selected from them; the actual variance of the mean would be about .15% higher than that calculated from the un-weighted formula.

The effects of either of these assumptions are small relative to the desired precision of much social science research, and to other sources of nonsampling error. However, two warnings should be given. First, this simulation of effects is relevant only to the case in which "ring, no answer" numbers are followed at least to the 17th call. The effects of either assumption would be greater if the decision applied to "ring, no answer" numbers called fewer times. Second, in most cases the investigator will have no knowledge of the extent of departure from epsem, because the status of these numbers cannot be obtained.

A.III.2. SAMPLING VARIANCE OF ESTIMATES FROM THE TWO DESIGNS

One way to construct variance estimates for both designs is to view each as a systematic sample, the stratified random samples as a systematic sample of elements, the clustered sample as a systematic sample of clusters. This ignores the fact that separate replicate groups are selected, collapses the selections across replicate groups, and orders the elements or clusters according to the stratification order of the population list of central office codes. The appropriate formula for this approach to the design is

$$\text{var}\left(\frac{y}{x}\right) \doteq \frac{1}{x^2}\left[\sum_{h}^{H} dy_h{}^2 + \left(\frac{y}{x}\right)^2 \sum_{h}^{H} dx_h{}^2 - 2\left(\frac{y}{x}\right)\sum_{h}^{H} dy_h\, dx_h\right]$$

where

$$\frac{y}{x} = \frac{\Sigma_h y_h}{\Sigma_h x_h} = \frac{\Sigma_h \Sigma_a \Sigma_i y_{ha_i}}{\Sigma_h \Sigma_a \Sigma_i x_{ha_i}}$$

for the hth stratum, the ath psu, and the ith individual $dy_h{}^2 = (y_{ha_1} - y_{ha_2})^2$ where a_1 is one psu in the hth stratum and a_2 is the other. In the element sample the psu's are merely elements. This is a paired difference formula that assumes two independent selections per stratum. The actual designs, systematic samples, could be viewed as having one selection per stratum. Paired differences, therefore, do ignore some of the stratification in the design and overestimate the variance but that is a negligible prob-lem in these samples.

Thirteen measures common to both surveys were used for variance calculations, and proportions based on the total sample and on various subclasses were included. The subclass variables used were age of respondent (in categories, 18–29, 30–49, 50 or more), total family income ($15,000 or less; more than $15,000), and respondent's education (0–12 years without high school diploma, high school, education beyond high school).

Table A.III.2 presents estimates concerning proportions on the total sample. We are most interested in the columns comparing the square root of the design effect, or *deft*,

TABLE A.III.2

Sampling Errors Using Paired Difference Calculations on the Total Samples by Sample Type

Estimated proportion of adults	Proportion		N		Paired differences calculations			
					Square root of design effect		Coefficient of variation[a]	
	Element	Cluster	Element	Cluster	Element	Cluster	Element	Cluster
Living in units with restricted public access	.11	.08	785	584	1.01	.98	.038	.090
Thinking family finances worse in 1 year	.15	.12	731	573	1.07	1.02	.039	.091
Feeling saving is more important now	.64	.63	800	598	1.05	1.08	.038	.091
Feeling next year good time to buy a car	.47	.40	620	539	1.08	1.12	.043	.092
Living in single family houses	.76	.69	789	596	.97	1.21	.038	.090
Feeling financially better off than last year	.38	.35	837	610	1.09	1.25	.037	.090
Feeling it's a good time to buy a house	.48	.47	753	603	1.08	1.26	.039	.091
Feeling good business conditions in next year	.60	.53	653	536	1.07	1.26	.042	.092
Living in households with unlisted phone numbers	.21	.23	795	592	1.04	1.27	.038	.090
Who are currently married	.71	.69	790	591	1.01	1.30	.038	.091
Who are nonwhite	.13	.11	782	593	1.05	1.60	.038	.090
Classifying city of residence 10,000–50,000 population.	.32	.38	720	583	1.08	1.69	.040	.092
Classifying area of residence as "rural"	.19	.20	790	608	1.10	1.91	.038	.090
Mean over 13 variables					1.05	1.30		
Mean for six attitudinal estimates					1.07	1.17		
Mean for seven demographic estimates					1.04	1.42		

[a] Coefficients of variation for cluster size in the clustered sample, for existence of an interview in the element sample. Dummy cases were inserted into the data set to represent clusters whose primary number was nonworking or in the element sample, numbers that were nonworking. This procedure attempts to reflect the lack of control of sample size on the precision of estimates, but may produce some overestimation of standard errors.

for the two sample designs. The characteristics are listed in order of their *defts,* the ratio of the actual standard error of the design to the standard error of a simple random sample of the same size.[11]

We expect that the stratified random sample has design effects equal to one on the average, since the only departure from simple random sampling is the weak stratification that we were able to introduce into the AC–CO frame. The clustered design should experience some loss of precision relative to a simple random sample because of likely homogeneity of characteristics of individuals selected from the same cluster. The mean *deft* is 1.05 for the stratified element design and 1.30 for the clustered.

Although Table A.III.2 presents estimates from paired difference calculations on the design we also used the fact that each sample was drawn in nine replicated independent subsamples. Design effects using a variance formula for a replicated design yielded average *defts* of 1.02 for the stratified random sample and 1.30 for the clustered. We prefer the paired difference calculations because of their greater stability, but note that the design effects for the stratified random design are nearly one in either method of calculation.

There are two kinds of estimates in Table A.III.2, six of them are attitudinal items about financial topics, seven others are demographic subclasses of the population that might be used as independent variables in an analysis of those attitudes. Several of the demographic variables are related to the residential location of the respondent; (e.g., size of the city, urban–rural nature of residence, race). Since exchanges are geographically based we expect higher design effects for the demographic variables in the clustered sample but not in the element sample. As the separate means below Table A.III.2 present, this is exactly what does occur. For the clustered sample, the mean demographic *deft* is 1.42 and the mean attitudinal *deft* is 1.17. For the element sample, both sets of estimates have similar average *defts*. These numbers can be interpreted as inflation factors for confidence intervals of the sample estimates; a negligible increase in the widths for the stratified element sample and a 17–42% increase for the clustered sample.

Table A.III.3 attempts to summarize design effects on the various subclasses examined. Design effects were calculated for the same 13 proportions in Table A.III.2 on the eight subclasses listed in Table A.III.3. Since some of the variance of the clustered design is due to intracluster homogeneity, we expect that the *defts* on subclasses of that design will decrease as the size of the subclass decreases.[12] There is no reason to suspect that this will be the case in the stratified element sample because subclasses will be subject to the same sources of variation as the total sample. The *defts* presented in Table A.III.3 are mean *defts* over all 13 proportions measured on the subclass question. The table shows that all of the subclass *defts* of the clustered sample are smaller than the average *deft*, 1.30, for the total sample. The subclass averages for the element sample, however, tend to vary around the mean of 1.05 for the total sample. The smaller *defts* on subclasses of the clustered sample make the design relatively more attractive for the analysis of subclass estimates than for estimates on the total sample. Much of the multivariate analysis of social science data compares subclasses of the sample and would benefit from the result. Since the clustered sample *defts* diminish

<hr/>

[11] The denominator of the *deft* is the standard error of the estimate obtained by viewing the cases of the sample as a simple random sample.

[12] The design effect can be partitioned into two components, $deff = [1 + \rho (b - 1)]$, where ρ is a measure of intracluster homogeneity and b is the average cluster size. The b of a subclass will be smaller than that of the total sample; given a ρ of similar size in the subclass, the design effect must be smaller. For an analysis of ρs on complex sample designs see Kish *et al.* (1976).

TABLE A.III.3
Average Design Effects for Age, Family Income, and Education Subclasses

| | Proportion of sample in subclass | | Mean square root of design effect over 13 variables | |
| | | | Paired difference calculations | |
	Element	Cluster	Element	Cluster
Respondent age groups				
18–29 years	.30	.33	1.04	1.19
30–49 years	.37	.33	1.02	1.14
50 and older	.30	.31	1.04	1.19
Total family income groups				
$15,000 or less	.41	.35	1.08	1.23
More than $15,000	.43	.55	1.05	1.20
Respondent education groups				
Grades 0–12	.22	.24	1.08	1.08
High school diploma	.37	.36	1.04	1.22
H. S. and additional education	.40	.34	1.04	1.17

with cluster size, we would expect the *defts* for the two samples to be roughly identical for subclasses that form only a small part of the population.

A.III.3. A VARIANCE-COST COMPARISON OF THE TWO DESIGNS

We can utilize the estimated design effects to compare the cost efficiency of the two sample designs. We utilize two cost components, c_w, the average cost of processing a working household number[13], and c_{nw}, the average cost of processing a number that is not a working household number. Let us assume that we desire a sample size from both designs that would have the same expected variance as a simple random sample of size n. Since most analysts will use the attitudinal measures as dependent variables, we use the average *defts* for that set of estimates. For the paired calculations these are approximately 1.00 for the element sample and 1.17 for the clustered sample. Using the average design effects on the total sample, we expect that $1.17^2 n = 1.37\,n$ working household numbers would be needed for the clustered sample and approximately n for the stratified element sample.

The total cost of the survey will be $n_w c_w + n_{nw} c_{nw}$ where n_w is the number of working household numbers and n_{nw} is the number of other numbers generated:

$$n_w = 1.37n \text{ for the clustered sample}$$

$$n_w = n \text{ for the stratified element sample}$$

[13] This average cost is calculated on both interview and noninterview sample numbers and includes the cost of sampling, dialing, interviewing, and later processing of the sample case.

Subtracting n_w from the total sample sizes yields the expected values for n_{nw}; we use the proportion of confirmed working household numbers from Table III.1 for these estimates:

$$n_{nw} = \frac{1.37n/b}{.217} + \frac{1.37(n - n/b)}{.665} - 1.37n$$

for the clustered sample, where b is the average number of interviews in each cluster;[14] and $n_{nw} = n/.217 - n$ for the stratified element sample.

The clustered sample will produce estimates with equal precision at lower cost if

$$(1.37n)c_w + \left[\frac{1.37n/b}{.217} + \frac{1.37(n - n/b)}{.665} - 1.37n \right] c_{nw} \tag{1}$$

$$< nc_w + \left(\frac{n}{.217} - n \right) c_{nw}$$

This expression can be generalized somewhat more by noting that a design effect can be expressed in two components, a synthetic intraclass correlation, ρ, and the number of interviews in each cluster, b, so that $deff = [1 + \rho(b - 1)]$. Using this expression, Eq. (1), and solving for the cluster size, we find that the clustered sample will produce estimates with equal precision at lower cost if

$$b < \frac{\rho c_w + c_{nw}(3.104 - 2.601\rho)}{\rho c_w + .504\rho c_{nw} + [c_{nw}(3.105 - 3.105\rho)/b^2]}. \tag{2}$$

In this use of the sample, the average synthetic intraclass correlation is approximately .08 for attitudinal variables.[15] Table A.III.4 presents maximum values of b from Eq. A.III.2 for designs where $\rho = .08$ and for various combinations of processing costs for household numbers and other numbers. When the costs are equal for the two kinds of numbers, a situation approximated with single question interviews, the average number of interviews per cluster could be 23.7 or less. As the cost of processing a working household number increases relative to others, a result of increasing the length of the interview, the desired cluster size becomes smaller. For example, when the costs of processing eligible numbers is five times that of ineligible numbers the maximum cluster size for cost savings is 6.5 interviews. If the cost of processing an eligible number is greater than 33 times the cost of processing an ineligible number, it is not possible to achieve equal precision at lower cost from the clustered design.

We should note that this analysis is a simplified one, utilizing total sample estimates for attitudinal variables and examining cost and variance components only, while ignoring nonsampling errors. The results are sensitive to choice of sample estimates; if we had included demographic variables the maximum cluster sizes would have been smaller. Thus in surveys studying phenomena that are spatially clustered, the clustered sample becomes less cost efficient. In addition, we note that the cluster sizes calculated

---

[14] The proportion of working household numbers generated in the first stage of the clustered sample should be equal to the proportion for the stratified sample. In the stratified sample, 21.6% were confirmed working household numbers. We estimate that another .1% were working among the unanswered numbers.

[15]
$$\rho = \frac{deff - 1}{b - 1} = \frac{.37}{(585/104)_i - 1} = .08,$$

where b = (number of interviews)/(number of sample clusters).

TABLE A.III.4
Maximum Number of Interviews per Cluster Yielding Equal Precision at Lower Cost for Clustered Design Relative to Stratified Element Design for Different Values of C_w and C_{nw}

Processing costs		Maximum number of interviews per cluster
Working household numbers C_w	Other numbers C_{nw}	
1	1	23.7
1.25	1	20.4
1.5	1	17.8
1.75	1	15.8
2	1	14.3
2.5	1	11.9
3	1	10.2
4	1	7.9
5	1	6.5
10	1	3.4
25	1	1.4
33	1	1.0

are those for the total sample; if only subclass statistics are to be presented, the total cluster size could be somewhat larger. Finally, we should be sensitive to sources of nonsampling errors in each design. For example, a larger number of working household numbers may create higher morale among interviewers and yield benefits for data quality not reflected in the calculations above.

A.III.4 SUMMARY AND CONCLUSIONS

The two epsem random-digit telephone sample designs produced very different proportions of working household numbers. Nearly a threefold increase in the proportion of working household numbers (to 55.8%) can be obtained by choosing nine numbers from each sample cluster defined by hundred series within central office codes. Larger gains could be achieved by increasing the cluster size beyond nine. An added benefit of the clustered design is the reduction in "problem" numbers whose status is difficult to confirm. The standard errors among attitudinal variables considered for the clustered sample were 9–17% higher than those of the stratified element sample. For demographic variables the analogous figures are 37–42%. It was shown, however, that the clustered sample can offer equal expected variance for attitudinal estimates at a lower cost if the cost of processing a working household number is less than about 33 times the cost of processing other numbers. For much social science research it is likely that the loss of precision in the clustered design is more than balanced by the advantages of relatively more working household numbers in the sample.

Appendix IV

Calculation of Sampling Errors

In all three of the designs used in this project, sampling variance arises from two different sources, differences among persons that happen to be selected on different draws of the sample and differences of sample size achieved in different draws. The characteristics of the selected persons over different draws vary in any design, both simple element samples and clustered samples; the difference in the size of the samples is a larger problem in clustered designs than in element samples. In clustered designs, estimates of the size of sample areas are used to determine their probabilities of selection, and those same estimates are used to set within-area sampling fractions. Since the most recent census data are generally employed to construct these size measures, they are subject to some errors because of movement of population, new housing construction, or demolition of old residential neighborhoods. Because of these changes in the sizes of areas sampled, the number of households actually selected departs from the expected number. This variation creates different total sample sizes across applications of the same design. Both the personal interview sample and the clustered telephone sample are subject to this source of variation in sample size.

In addition, random-digit dialed samples experience sample size variation because they sample a subset of the entire population of 10-digit telephone numbers. There is no control on what proportion of sample telephone numbers will be working household numbers. In this project about 22% of all sample numbers were household subscriptions, but other samples by chance could have experienced a higher or lower proportion of eligible numbers. This source of sample size variation is present in both telephone samples. Finally, sample size of the clustered telephone design varies for one additional reason. Some telephone exchanges serve both households within and outside a primary area of the SRC national sample. Telephone numbers selected from these

345

exchanges were screened, and in total we found that about 70% of them serve house-holds within the primary area. Unfortunately, there is no control on this proportion and it could vary over different sample draws creating different totals of eligible household numbers generated.

The variation in sample size for all three samples implies a different kind of sample mean than that derived from a simple random sample. Instead of the mean being a sample total divided by a constant sample size $(\sum y_i/n) = (y/n)$, the mean is a ratio of two random variables (y/x) where x is the variable sample size. Means calculated from designs with variable sample sizes are called ratio means and their sampling variance is the sum of three different components:

$$\text{var}\left(\frac{y}{x}\right) \doteq \frac{1}{x^2}\left[\text{var}(y) + \left(\frac{y}{x}\right)^2 \text{var}(x) - 2\left(\frac{y}{x}\right)\text{cov}(y, x)\right], \tag{1}$$

where $y/x = (\sum_{y_i}/\sum_{x_i})$ over i individuals in the sample and $\text{cov}(y,x)$ is the covariance between the sample total and the number of elements in the sample.

Two different methods could be employed to estimate the sampling variance for means and proportions on the two telephone samples. The first views each design as consisting of nine replicate groups, nine samples of identical design. Each of these replicate groups is subject to some variation in size because of variation in the propor-tion of working household numbers and in the proportion of nonrespondents. The variance can be estimated through comparison of the nine replicate groups, nine samples of identical design. Each of these replicate groups is subject to some variation in size because of variation in the proportion of working household numbers and in proportion of nonrespondents. The variance can be estimated through comparison of the nine replicate groups:

$$\text{var}\left(\frac{y}{x}\right) \doteq \frac{9}{x^2 \cdot 8}\left[\sum_{r=1}^{9} y_r^2 + \left(\frac{y}{x}\right)^2 \sum_{r=1}^{9} x_r^2 - 2\left(\frac{y}{x}\right)\sum_{r=1}^{9} y_r x_r\right], \tag{2}$$

where

$$\frac{y}{x} = \frac{\sum_{r=1}^{9}\sum_i y_{ri}}{\sum_{r=1}^{9}\sum_i x_{ri}};$$

i is an index for individuals in the sample and r for replicate group; y_{ri} is a 0–1 indicator variable, x_{ri} a count variable. The advantage of this view of the design is its simplicity; all the effects of stratification, clustering, and variation in size are taken into account through the comparison of replicates. The disadvantage of the approach is that the degree of freedom of the variance estimate itself (about eight) is constrained by the small number of replicate groups.

One way to increase the precision of the variance estimate is to view the stratified element design as a systematic sample and the clustered telephone sample as we normally view the SRC national sample of dwellings. For the stratified element sample, this ignores the fact that separate replicate groups were selected, orders the elements according to the stratification order of the population list of central office codes, and calculates:

$$\text{var}\left(\frac{y}{x}\right) \doteq \frac{1}{x^2}\left[\sum^{H} dy_h^2 + \left(\frac{y}{x}\right)^2 \sum^{H} dx_h^2 - 2\left(\frac{y}{x}\right)\sum^{H} dy_h\, dx_h\right], \tag{3}$$

where

$$\frac{y}{x} = \frac{\Sigma\Sigma\Sigma y_{ha_i}}{\Sigma\Sigma\Sigma x_{ha_i}}$$

for the ith individual in the ath psu of the hth stratum.

$$dy_h{}^2 = (y_{ha_1} - y_{ha_2})^2$$

where a_1 is one psu in the hth stratum and a_2 is another. This is a paired difference formula that assumes two independent selections per stratum. The actual design is more properly viewed as having one selection per stratum. Paired differences, therefore, ignore some of the stratification in the design and overestimate the variance, but this is probably a negligible problem in the stratified element sample because the only stratification implemented was on the central office code level, and we expect its effects to be small.

Once we ignore the replicated nature of the telephone designs, the clustered telephone and the personal interview sample calculations can be made using a similar formula. The variance computations in clustered designs do not compare individual sample elements but rather are functions of cluster totals. Specifically, the non-self-representing areas in the SRC national sample were each single selections from 1 of 62 strata. We can employ a "collapsed stratum" method, treating the sample as if it had two selections from 31 different strata. As with the calculation form for the stratified element telephone sample above, this ignores a small part of the stratification and slightly overestimates the actual variance. The pairing is performed using the modes of stratification, geography and urbanization (see Kish & Hess, 1965).

Within the self-representing areas, the design of the clustered telephone sample differs from that of the personal interview sample. For the personal interview sample, clusters of households were drawn; in the clustered telephone sample, stratified random samples of telephone numbers were selected. For the personal interview sample, over 100 primary selections were made within the 12 self-representing areas. These are city blocks, census tracts, suburbs, and groups of households called "segments." For estimation of sampling variance arising from the selections within the self-representing areas these 100 or so selections can be sorted into 20 pairs of computational units which have roughly equal sizes, and compared in a paired difference formula.[1] For the personal interview sample, therefore, calculations are made for 20 self-representing strata and 31 non-self-representing strata using paired differences:

$$\operatorname{var}\!\left(\frac{y}{x}\right) \doteq \frac{1}{x^2}\left[\sum_{h=1}^{51} dy_h{}^2 + \left(\frac{y}{x}\right)^2 \sum_{h=1}^{51} dy_h{}^2 - 2\!\left(\frac{y}{x}\right)\sum_{h=1}^{51} dy_h\, dx_h\right]. \tag{4}$$

For the clustered telephone sample, no clustering was introduced into the design within the self-representing areas. Instead, we stratified exchanges within the areas by size and geography and selected directly telephone numbers within them. With such a design we can use the elements themselves to calculate sampling variances; we can view the 12 self-representing areas as 12 different populations sampled using stratified element techniques. In most cases the within-area stratification has little or no effect because with the required sample size, sample numbers were generated from all central

---

[1] See Kish and Hess (1965) for a description of this procedure.

office codes. With that reasoning we can compute sampling errors with simple random sample formulas for 12 strata for the self-representing areas and with paired differences for 31 strata for the 62 non-self-representing areas:

$$
\begin{aligned}
\operatorname{var}\left(\frac{y}{x}\right) \doteq \frac{1}{x^{2}} \Bigg\{ & \left[\sum_{h=1}^{12} \frac{1}{x_{h}-1}\left(x_{h} \sum_{i=1}^{x_{h}} y_{h_{i}}^{2}-\left(\sum_{i=1}^{x_{h}} y_{h_{i}}\right)^{2}\right)+\sum_{h=13}^{43} d y_{h}{ }^{2}\right] \\
& +\left(\frac{y}{x}\right)^{2}\left[\sum_{h=1}^{12} \frac{1}{x_{h}-1}\left(x_{h} \sum_{i=1}^{x_{h}} x_{h_{i}}{ }^{2}-\left(\sum_{i=1}^{x_{h}} x_{h_{i}}\right)^{2}\right)+\sum_{h=13}^{43} d x_{h}{ }^{2}\right] \\
& -2\left(\frac{y}{x}\right)\left[\sum_{h=1}^{12} \frac{1}{x_{h}-1}\left(x_{h} \sum_{i=1}^{x_{h}} y_{h_{i}} x_{h_{i}}-\left(\sum_{i=1}^{x_{h}} y_{h_{i}}\right)\left(\sum_{i=1}^{x_{h}} x_{h_{i}}\right)\right)\right. \\
& \left.+\sum_{h=13}^{43} d y_{h} d x_{h}\right] \Bigg\}
\end{aligned}
\tag{5}
$$

where x_{h} is a count of the number of sample elements in the hth stratum, i is an index for sample element, Strata 1–12 are associated with the 12 self-representing areas and Strata 13–43 are associated with the 62 non-self-representing areas.

An earlier comparison of replicated and paired differences approaches to calculating the variances for the telephone samples, found that the increased stability of the paired difference calculations was considerable and we decided to use the paired difference formula Eq. (3).

References

Brunner, J. A., & Brunner, G. A. Are voluntarily unlisted telephone subscribers really different? *Journal of Marketing Research,* 1977, *8*:121–124.

Bryant, B. E. Respondent Selection in a Time of Changing Household Composition. *Journal of Marketing Research,* 1975, *12*:129–135.

Cannell, C. F., Lawson, S. A., & Hausser, D. L. *A Technique for evaluating interviewer performance: A manual for coding and analyzing interviewer behavior from tape recordings of household interviews.* Ann Arbor: Survey Research Center, Institute for Social Research, The University of Michigan, 1975.

Cannell, C. F., Oksenberg, L., & Converse, J. M. Striving for response accuracy: Experiments in new interviewing techniques. *Journal of Marketing Research,* 1977, *14*:306–315.

Chilton Research Services, *A national probability sample of telephone households using computerized sampling techniques,* no date.

Clausen, A. R. Response validity: Vote report. *Public Opinion Quarterly,* 1968–1969, *32*:588–606.

Colombotos, J. The effects of personal vs. telephone interviews on socially acceptable responses. *Public Opinion Quarterly,* 1965, *29*:457–458.

Coombs, L., & Freedman, R. Use of telephone interviews in a longitudinal fertility study. *Public Opinion Quarterly,* 1964, *28*:112–117.

Cooper, S. L. Random sampling by telephone: A new and inproved method. *Journal of Marketing Research,* 1964, *1*:45–48.

Dillman, D. A., Gallegos, J. G., & Frey, J. H. Reducing refusal rates for telephone interviews. *Public Opinion Quarterly,* XL (Spring, 1976), 66–78.

Dohrenwend, B. S., Colombotos, J., & Dohrenwend, B. P. Social distance and interviewer effects. *Public Opinion Quarterly,* 1968, *32*:410–422.

349

Freeman, J., & Butler, E. W. Some sources of interviewer variance in surveys. *Public Opinion Quarterly*, 1976, *40*:79–91.

Glasser, G. J., & Metzger, G. D. Random-digit dialing as a method of telephone sampling. *Journal of Marketing Research*, 1972, 9:59–64.

Glasser, G. J., & Metzger, G. D. National estimates of nonlisted telephone households and their characteristics. *Journal of Marketing Research*, 1975, *12*:359–361.

Goodman, L. A. The multivariate analysis of qualitative data: Interactions among multiple classification. *Journal of the American Statistical Association*, 1970, 65:226–256.

Hansen, M. H., Hurwitz, W. N., & Madow, W. G. *Sample survey methods and theory* (Vol. II). New York: John Wiley & Sons, 1953.

Hanson, R. H., & Marks, E. S. Influence of the interviewer on the accuracy of survey results. *Journal of the American Statistical Association*, 1958, 53:635–655.

Henson, R., Roth, A., & Cannell, C. F. Personal vs. telephone interviews and the effects of telephone reinterviews on reporting of psychiatric symptomatology. (Research Report.) Survey Research Center, Institute for Social Research, The University of Michigan, 1974.

Hochstim, J. R. A critical comparison of three strategies of collecting data from households. *Journal of the American Statistical Association*, 1967, 62:976–989.

Ibsen, C. A., & Ballweg, J. Telephone interviews in social research: Some methodological considerations. *Quality and Quantity*, 1974, 7:181–192.

Kegeles, S. S., Fink, C., & Kirscht, J. P. Interviewing a national sample by long distance telephone. *Public Opinion Quarterly*, 1969, 33:412–419.

Kish, L. A procedure for objective respondent selection within the household. *Journal of the American Statistical Association*, 1949, 44:380–387.

Kish, L. Studies of interviewer variance for attitudinal variables. *Journal of the American Statistical Association*, 1962, 57:92–115.

Kish, L. *Survey sampling*, New York: John Wiley & Sons, 1965.

Kish, L., Groves, R. M., & Krotki, K. P. Sampling errors for fertility studies. *World Fertility Survey Occasional Papers*, 1976, *17*:1–61.

Kish, L., & Hess, I. On noncoverage of sample dwellings. *Journal of the American Statistical Association*, 1958, 53:509–524.

Kish, L., & Hess, I. A 'replacement' procedure for reducing the bias on nonresponse. *The American Statistician*, 1959, *13*:17–19.

Kish, L., & Hess, I. The Survey Research Center's national sample of dwellings. Ann Arbor: Survey Research Center, Institute for Social Research, The University of Michigan, 1965.

Klecka, W. R. Potential coverage problems on telephone surveys. Unpublished, 1976.

Lahiri, D. B. A method of sample selection providing unbiased ratio estimates. *Bulletin of the International Statistical Institute*, 1951, 33:144–152.

Larson, O. N. The comparative validity of telephone and face-to-face interviews in the measurement of message diffusion from leaflets. *American Sociological Review*, 1952, *17*:471–476.

Locander, W. B., Sudman, S., & Bradburn, N. M. An investigation of interviewing method, threat, and response distortion. *Proceedings of the American Statistical Association* , Social Statistics Section, 1974. Pp. 21–27.

Locander, W. B., & Burton, J. P. The effect of question form on gathering income data by telephone. *Journal of Marketing Research*, 1976, 33:189–192.

Lucas, W. A., & Adams, W. C. *An assessment of telephone survey methods.* Santa Monica, California: The Rand Corporation, 1977.

Reingen, P. H., & Kernan, J. B. Compliance with an interview request: A foot-in-the-door, self-perception interpretation. *Journal of Marketing Research,* 1977, *14*:365–369.

Rogers, T. F. Interviews by telephone and in person: Quality of responses and field performance. *Public Opinion Quarterly,* 1976, *40*:51–65.

Schmiedeskamp, J. Reinterviews by telephone. *Journal of Marketing,* 1962, *26*:28–34.

Spaeth, M. A. Recent publications on survey research techniques. *Journal of Marketing Research,* 1977, *14*:403–409.

Sudman, S. The uses of telephone directories for survey sampling. *Journal of Marketing Research,* 1973, *10*:204–207.

Trodahl, V. C., & Carter, R. E., Jr. Random selecting of respondents within households in telephone surveys. *Journal of Marketing Research,* 1964, *1*:71–76.

Tuchfarber, A. J., & Klecka, W. R. *Random-digit dialing: Lowering the cost of victimization surveys,* Police Foundation, 1976.

U. S. Department of Commerce, Bureau of the Census, *Current population reports, population characteristics, Series P-20.* Washington: U. S. Government Printing Office, 1973.

U. S. Department of Commerce, Bureau of the Census, *Statistical abstract of the United States: 1974.* Washington, D.C.:U. S. Government Printing Office, 1974.

Waksberg, J. Sampling methods for random-digit dialing. *Journal of the American Statistical Association,* 1978, *73*:40–46.

Wiseman, F. Methodological bias in public opinion surveys. *Public Opinion Quarterly,* 1972, *34*:105–108.

Index

QUANTITATIVE STUDIES IN SOCIAL RELATIONS

Consulting Editor: Peter H. Rossi

UNIVERSITY OF MASSACHUSETTS
AMHERST, MASSACHUSETTS

Peter H. Rossi and Walter Williams (Eds.), EVALUATING SOCIAL PRO-GRAMS: *Theory, Practice, and Politics*

Roger N. Shepard, A. Kimball Romney, and Sara Beth Nerlove (Eds.), MULTIDIMENSIONAL SCALING: *Theory and Applications in the Behavioral Sciences,* Volume I – Theory; Volume II – Applications

Robert L. Crain and Carol S. Weisman, DISCRIMINATION, PERSON-ALITY, AND ACHIEVEMENT: *A Survey of Northern Blacks*

Douglas T. Hall and Benjamin Schneider, ORGANIZATIONAL CLIMATES AND CAREERS: *The Work Lives of Priests*

Kent S. Miller and Ralph Mason Dreger (Eds.), COMPARATIVE STUDIES OF BLACKS AND WHITES IN THE UNITED STATES

Robert B. Tapp, RELIGION AMONG THE UNITARIAN UNIVERSAL-ISTS: *Converts in the Stepfathers' House*

Arthur S. Goldberger and Otis Dudley Duncan (Eds.), STRUCTURAL EQUATION MODELS IN THE SOCIAL SCIENCES

Henry W. Riecken and Robert F. Boruch (Eds.), SOCIAL EXPERIMENTA-TION: *A Method for Planning and Evaluating Social Intervention*

N. J. Demerath, III, Otto Larsen, and Karl F. Schuessler (Eds.), SOCIAL POLICY AND SOCIOLOGY

H. M. Blalock, A. Aganbegian, F. M. Borodkin, Raymond Boudon, and Vittorio Capecchi (Eds.), QUANTITATIVE SOCIOLOGY: *International Perspectives on Mathematical and Statistical Modeling*

Carl A. Bennett and Arthur A. Lumsdaine (Eds.), EVALUATION AND EX-PERIMENT: *Some Critical Issues in Assessing Social Programs*

Michael D. Ornstein, ENTRY INTO THE AMERICAN LABOR FORCE